a
manual
of
worship

a manual of worship

JOHN E. SKOGLUND

THE JUDSON PRESS
Valley Forge

A MANUAL OF WORSHIP

ACKNOWLEDGMENTS

A large measure of credit for this book must go to the members of my classes and seminars in worship at Colgate Rochester Divinity School. For a number of years a recurring seminar has concerned itself with materials and orders for worship. Worship structures have been written and discussed. *The Service for the Lord's Day*, the special services and many of the materials for worship included in this manual came out of these seminars. The book itself in its initial form was put together in a seminar made up of the following men: Archibald Allen, Alan Doksansky, Donald Fonda, William Jacob, David Malone, Paul Olcott, C. Jack Richards, Richard Wereley, and Edward Wright.

In addition, substantial help and encouragement in the task of developing the book came from my colleague, Professor Winthrop S. Hudson; also from Rev. Stephen

S. Winward of the Sutton Coldfield Baptist Church, England; Rev. Hugh Q. Morton, First Baptist Church, Keene, New Hampshire; and three of my former students, Rev. Orrin Judd, Rev. Richard Bowser, and Mr. John U. Miller. *The Service of Licensing* is based upon one used at the Judson Baptist Church, Kalamazoo, Michigan, Rev. Jerold Savory, pastor.

Many suggestions for improvement of the book were incorporated into the text as a result of the comments of the readers of the manuscript. To them and to Ellwood S. Wolf and Judith Brown of the Judson Press, who shepherded the book through a long process of development, deep gratitude is owed. Thanks too to Katherine Bishop, Ruth LeBeouf, Henrietta Levine, and Joanne Oliver for their invaluable help in typing and duplicating the manuscript.

The Scripture quotations are, except in rare instances, from the Revised Standard Version of the Bible, copyright 1946 and 1952 by the Division of Christian Education of the National Council of the Churches of Christ in the United States of America, and are used by permission.

The author and publisher acknowledge with thanks the generosity of the many copyright owners who have granted permission to reprint materials under their control, including the following:

The Baptist Union of Great Britain and Ireland for *Orders and Prayers for Church Worship*, compiled by Ernest A. Payne and Stephen F. Winward from pages 5, 6, 30, 105, 133, 134, 154, 159, 258.

The Committee on Public Worship and Aids to Devotion of the Church of Scotland for the *Book of Common Order*, pages 11, 32, 57, 67, 175, 259, 308.

Eden Publishing House for *Book of Worship*, page 354.

Hope Publishing Company for *Inter-Church Hymnal*, Selection Number 537.

John Knox Press for *An Experimental Liturgy* by Davies, Cope, and Tytler, page 32.

McGraw-Hill Book Company for Roy Pearson's *Hear Our Prayer*, page 38.

The Methodist Publishing House for *Proposed Revisions for the Book of Worship*, page 201.

Stephen F. Winward for *Responsive Praises and Prayers* published by Hodder and Stoughton, pages 57, 59, 80, 113, 141.

United Church Press for *The Lord's Day Service*, pages 10-11, 16; and a selection from Martin Luther in *Book of Prayers for Church and Home*, page 171.

The Westminster Press for *Service for the Lord's Day and Lectionary for the Christian Year*, page 19. Copyright © 1964, W. L. Jenkins.

Excerpts from *A Diary of Private Prayer*, by John Baillie, pages 23, 28, 65, 71, are used by permission of Charles Scribner's Sons. Copyright 1949 Charles Scribner's Sons. British edition by Oxford University Press.

The Book of Common Prayer is Crown copyright and extracts from it are used by permission.

Many hands had a part in the making of this book. It has not always been possible to trace the source of some of the material used. If any has been included without suitable acknowledgment, such acts have been unintentional and will, it is hoped, be pardoned.

CONTENTS

INTRODUCTION

WORSHIP[1] CANNOT BE UNDERSTOOD apart from what the Church is and does. In order to answer the question "Why worship?" we need to look at the question "Why the Church?" Christian history has given many answers. Some have seen the Church as an end in itself, concerned primarily with its own inner life. The attitude has caused the Church to center its thought and action in worship. On the other hand, many contemporary writers see the Church not as an end in itself but as a means or instrument which functions in relation to an end. Such writers say "The Church is mission" or "The Church exists for mission."

[1] Fuller treatment of Christian worship, particularly in the free-church tradition, can be found in John E. Skoglund, *Worship in the Free Churches* (Valley Forge: Judson Press, 1965) and Stephen F. Winward, *The Reformation of Our Worship* (Richmond: John Knox Press, 1965).

They declare that the mission of God in history is to reconcile all things to himself or to bring about his *shalom*, or "peace," in the orders of being. Thus the Church takes its place "outside the camp" (see Hebrews 13:12-13). It lives in the world where God is at work, and there, in the midst of the structures of society and the world of men, gives witness to "the acts of God." As Professor J. C. Hoekendijk has said, "The church exists only *in actu*, in the execution of the apostolate, i.e., in the proclamation of the gospel of the kingdom to the world."[2]

Certainly the Church exists by and for mission, but it is not itself the mission. The mission is God's. The Church is not called to make churches in the world, or even to make Christians, but to be caught up in God's mission. That mission centers in Christ, the Reconciler, under whom God has put all things and has made the head over all things (cf. Ephesians 1:22), "for he has made known to us in all wisdom and insight the mystery of his will, according to his purpose which he set forth in Christ as a plan for the fullness of time, to unite all things in him, things in heaven and things on earth" (Ephesians 1:9-10).

To put it plainly, God is at work in the world. The role of the Church is to witness to the divine activity and to help men to come to a clear acknowledgment that "God was in Christ reconciling the world to himself" (2 Corinthians 5:19). What then does this understanding of the Church's mission in relation to God's mission indicate concerning worship? It might seem that worship has no place in such a view of the Church, for it might well be asked, "If God is out in the world and not in the Church, why does the Church gather?" Such a question arises from a failure to understand not only the nature and function of the Church but the nature and function of worship.

[2] J. C. Hoekendijk, *The Church Inside Out* (Philadelphia: The Westminster Press, 1966), p. 43.

What are the principles of worship as they arise from an understanding of the Church's participation in God's mission? Eight are suggested:

1. *Worship cannot be separated from the Church's involvement in God's mission in the world. Worship and witness stand together.*

Liturgy (congregational worship) basically means a "work of the people." This work is performed not only in terms of ritual acts but also in the world. To be involved in God's activity in the world is as much a service of worship as the faithful performance of a high ritual within the confines of a sanctuary. Among those who walked from Selma to Montgomery in the now-famous civil rights march was Dom Orisini, an Episcopalian priest. A Negro saw him cleaning one of the wooden portable latrines and said, "I never thought I'd see ministers getting dirty doing our menial jobs." Father Orisini, in reflecting on the experience—latrines and all—said that the whole march was "one great act of worship."[3]

What Father Orisini and the thousands who marched along that rain-soaked highway from Selma to Montgomery came to know was this: Worship cannot be identified solely with one Sunday hour of quiet meditation, separated from the world, but must instead be seen as the whole work of the people of God, both as they pray and as they engage themselves in the hard struggles of the world. Even as Jesus "suffered outside the gate," so the Church must take its place beside him, "bearing abuse for him."

2. *Congregational worship is essentially celebration.*

The worship of a Christian congregation is essentially

[3] See Robert W. Spike, *The Freedom Revolution and the Churches* (New York: Association Press, 1965).

the coming together into a common fellowship of those who find God's place for them in the world. They come for the joyful celebration of God's acts in the contemporary world and joyful remembrance of his mighty acts in the past. Worship does not stand apart from the participation of the Church in God's mission in the world. It is not a flight from the world or an effort to get away from it all. Rather it is a coming together to celebrate what God has done and is doing and will do in the world to bring about the fulfillment of his glorious kingdom.

The story of God's dealing with men, as recorded in the Holy Scriptures, stands at the center of worship. The Scriptures inform worship. They show how God acted in the people Israel to draw them out from the children of men in order that Israel might minister to the children of men. They tell the story of Jesus Christ and his ministry of reconciling love. They show how the Church came into being to become an ambassador and a minister of reconciliation (see 2 Corinthians 5:17-21). These acts the worshiping congregation remembers with thanksgiving.

The Church celebrates with joy not only the acts of God in the past but also his present acts. By being in the world it discovers those places within the structures of human society where God is at work to bring about his *shalom* among men.

Worship also is celebration of the anticipated victory of God over all those who oppose him and the ultimate establishment of his kingdom. With great joy and fervent hope the Christian prays, "Thy kingdom come . . . on earth as it is in heaven."

It is because God acts in history, in the contemporary world, and in the world to come, that Christian worship is possible. Christian worship is essentially response to the action of God. In sermon and in communion the gospel is remembered and reenacted. The reenactment is

16

not only of the good news once proclaimed in Jerusalem, Corinth, and Rome, but also the good news proclaimed now and the good news of what is to come.

Thus the hymns, Bible readings, and sermon must be faithful to the story. We need to ask ourselves, as we come to worship: "Is the music, as expressed by hymn, anthem, or organ, a proclamation of God's decisive acts among men, or is it something that is designed to create subjective moods or feelings among those who have gathered? What of the sermon? Does it faithfully retell the story and seek to relate that story to contemporary events? Are the prayers truly the glad and joyous praise, thanksgiving, and intercession of the people of God? Are they the grateful recognition of what God has done, is doing, and will do, as told in the story? Is the communion a church ritual designed primarily to make the people feel inwardly good, or is it the retelling of God's mightiest act in Christ, in which the Lord comes before them once again as the one who, in his ultimate love, gave himself to the world?"

3. *The structure of worship is determined (a) by objective factors, primarily the reading and preaching of the Word and the observance of the Lord's Supper; and (b) by the response which the congregation makes to word and sacrament: in adoration to God for his faithfulness, in humble repentance for man's unfaithfulness, in thanksgiving for God's continued mercies (especially for his gift of Jesus Christ), in petition for his never-failing grace, in dedication to obedient discipleship, and in intercession for all who stand in need of God's mercy within the fellowship and in the world.*

Word and Table provide the basic means of proclaiming the gospel within the worshiping congregation. Through these objective signs the congregation is brought into the living stream of God's action in history. The congregation is caught up once again in the story of redemption and it becomes a part of the contemporary telling of the story. The congregational celebration of his words and deeds offers a new occasion for new encounter. God's Word spoken long ago can be heard afresh calling men to obedience in their life situations.

The reading and preaching of the Scriptures and the observance of the Lord's Supper are central in Christian worship. All other elements of worship must be governed by these two fundamental acts. One can have corporate worship pared down to the reading of the Word, preaching, and the communion, but one cannot have worship in the Christian sense without them. They serve as the foundation stone upon which the whole structure of Christian worship is built, for they are the chief verbal and visible means of making known the gospel. Even if a service of worship could be designed in which the reading and preaching of the Word and the Communion were not present, that service, to be Christian, could not fail to have them there as silent symbols bringing to the congregation's remembrance the fundamental facts of the gospel.

In Christian worship man responds from the depth of his being to God's mighty acts, particularly his act of love, forgiveness, and reconciliation in Jesus Christ. Thus, worship is dialogue between God and his people. God who has made himself known to man in Jesus Christ and whose acts are brought to remembrance with the reading of the Scriptures, the preaching of the Word, and the administration of the sacraments comes in worship as a living presence by the power of the Holy Spirit. Man in turn responds to God's gracious self-giving by offering adoration, praise, and thanksgiving; he confesses his sin and petitions God's presence, dedicates himself and his gifts (which are the symbol of his work), and prays for

18

an employs at least two outward signs of offer-
[ ]self in response to the divine initiative: the giving
[ ]substance and baptism. Each of these acts is a
[ ]which proclaims the individual's gratitude and
[ ]ion as he responds to God's Word and Table.

[ ]an worship expresses this encounter between God
and man. Like the angels ascending and descending the
heavenly ladder in the patriarch's dream, God's giving of
himself comes to meet our self-offering and we worship.
Orders of Christian worship must reflect this rhythm of
revelation and response. Worship orders become the sys-
tematic structures to help man in the light of God's revelation to most worthily "ascribe to the Lord the glory of
his name."

These responsive elements of worship can readily be
recognized as the elements of prayer. In the service of
worship they need not be grouped together in one long
pastoral prayer but can become the various parts of the
total worship service. The worship service then becomes
common prayer, and can be outlined as follows:

Preparation	*Adoration*
	Confession
The Word	*Reading* and *Preaching* of God's Word
The Table	*Offertory* (gifts, elements, and self)
	Petition
	Dedication
	Remembrance and *Thanksgiving*
	Lord's Supper
	Intercession
Into the World	*Dismissal* and *Blessing*

This structure is the basis for *The Service for the Lord's
Day* (see page 43 ff.).

*4. Careless and undisciplined worship is an o̶ ̶
God and can be the means of destroying, rathe̶
building up, the faith of his people.*

Look carefully at the chaotic disorder which the
church in Corinth created for itself (1 Corinthians 12–14).
Paul urged the Christians of Corinth that "all things should
be done decently and in order" (1 Corinthians 14:40),
and "When you come together, each one has a hymn, a
lesson, a revelation, a tongue, or an interpretation. Let all
things be done for edification. . . . For you can all prophesy
one by one, so that all may learn and all be encouraged.
. . . For God is not a God of confusion but of peace" (1
Corinthians 14:26,31,33). In these words Paul encouraged
the Christians of his day to express their joyful thanks to
God by means of ordered worship.

Careful ordering of worship does not mean that all
services of worship will be identical or that the same set
prayers and responses will be used. Rather, such ordering
opens the way to use rightly the great treasure house of
worship material and to bring into worship almost endless
variations upon the basic themes, for within the common
framework of a responsible order there is room for great
variety. Careful attention to the valid ordering of worship
means that the variable elements will be selected not
haphazardly but with purpose. God will honor such worship as a fitting means of his continuing self-revelation to
his people and as man's worthy thanks for his grace.

*5. The responsibility for ordering public worship be-
longs to the congregation.*

Congregational worship expresses itself in liturgy. But
what does liturgy have to do with worship in a so-called
free church? Does not liturgy belong to what are known as
the liturgical churches? Did not the free churches come

into being as a protest against liturgical forms and ceremonies?

The word liturgy comes directly from the French word *liturgie*. This in turn can be traced through the Middle Latin to the Greek *leitourgia* which in turn comes from *laos* (people) and *ergon* (work). Thus liturgy is a "work of the people." Christian worship is fundamentally a work of the people both as the congregation gathers for common prayer and praise in the meeting house and as it scatters in the world.

Obviously the liturgy practiced in most churches is *not* a work of the people. Except for the hymns (and they are often not too unanimously or wholeheartedly sung by the congregation) and a possible responsive reading, congregational participation is almost *nil*. Free-church worship has become in large measure a modern variation of the medieval "dance of the clergy." It is a one-man show. The minister prepares the service, gives the opening sentences and the calls to prayer, reads the Scriptures, preaches the sermon, gives the benediction, and if there is a celebration of the Lord's Supper, conducts that service from beginning to end. If he is assisted, it is generally by a choir composed of a relatively small part of the congregation or, in some instances, professional singers who are hired to do the music. The congregation, for the most part, sits, listens, and watches.

In the beginning days of Christianity, congregations participated in an active, lively fashion in the worship of the Church. Sometimes participation became unrestrained and undignified. Paul's Corinthian letters deal in part with this, but the apostle did not try to shut down on congregational participation; he rather indicated that it should be done in an orderly fashion.

When the cult of the clergy began, worship moved further from the people. The development of church

21

buildings reflects this removal. The earliest church buildings provided a simple space for a company of people to gather about a Table, but in time the Table was moved to one side of the room. Later it was moved to an end of the room and finally it was enclosed behind a chancel screen. The chancel became the sacred precinct of the clergy and there they gathered to conduct the worship. The people stood in the nave as observers, but not as active participants.

Did not the Reformation change all that? True, it brought back the priesthood of all believers, but the Reformation went only part of the way in restoring worship to the whole congregation. Now psalms and hymns were composed in the vernacular and were sung not by choirs of monks, or clergy "in choir," but rather by the congregation. Books of common order were written in which the people, in their own language, participated at various points in the act of worship. But the Reformation only partially restored congregational worship. Clericalism survived and tended to dominate the service. It has been said that the new presbyter was but old priest writ large. Ulrich Zwingli, the Zürich reformer to whom many free churchmen look as their patron in the Reformation, abolished singing, took away common prayer, and caused the congregation to sit in silence during the whole of the Sunday service. This making of the Sunday service into a ministerial monologue has persisted, especially in free-church tradition.

Great suspicion was cast by many of the reformers upon the use of art and action in worship. Worship became almost entirely verbal. The unlettered man found it difficult to verbalize his faith, so he tended to remain quiet and let the educated clergymen do it for him. Set prayers, while used in some of the Reformation churches, were thrown out in others. Prayer became extemporary, and the so-called "long" prayer or "pastoral" prayer was substituted for congregational and responsive prayer.

Obviously such worship cannot be described as liturgy, that is, a "work of the people." How then should we look at worship? Christian worship is the act of a congregation, rather than that of a minister. The minister is a leader of the congregation of which he is a member. The members of the congregation are active participants and not spectators.

Christian worshipers are not an audience viewing a religious show. They are the participants in an act of worship. Christian worship has no place for such theatricals as elocutionary Scripture reading, pulpiteering, or virtuoso singing—in short, for any kind of "performance." The true choir is the whole people of God, the congregation, singing the hymns, introits, psalms, doxologies, glorias, and prayer responses. When a special choir is used, it is best to have it seated in the back of the congregation where it easily merges with the congregation and can serve as reinforcement in singing the hymns as well as other musical parts of the service. Such location and use of the choir removes it from the temptation to make of it a performance company which puts on a brief religious concert in each worship service. Stephen Winward, who did so much in the church in Higham's Park, a London suburb, to bring about renewal in worship, has written:

The primary function of a choir is to help and lead the whole congregation in praising God. Unless it does this, it is the enemy of congregational participation. So often choirs want to sing *to* the people or *for* the people, instead of singing *with* the people to God. But if this primary purpose is understood and accepted, a choir can contribute in several ways to corporate worship. By singing the appropriate parts of the liturgy, psalms, hymns, canticles, creed, sanctus, gloria in excelsis, to simple settings, a choir can lead and inspire all the people to praise God. A good solo voice, heard in the introit, in the antiphonal singing of the psalms, in sacred song, in gospel hymn, in the solo parts of the anthem, can uplift all hearts to God. And could we not make more use of gifted instrumentalists? The author of Psalm 150 obviously did not assume that one instrument only could be used in the worship of God.[4]

All the hymns used in congregational singing ought to be rehearsed by the choir, and the choir should actually lead in the singing of the hymns. One important function of the choir is to teach new hymns.

Apart from singing, how do laymen enter into active participation in the worship of the church?

A. Laymen can participate in the preparation for worship. Many people do not know how to worship, because they lack training in the meaning and purpose of worship. Lay groups such as the board of deacons, church school classes, and discussion groups can make worship an object of study. In such a study a board of deacons has primary responsibility, for the deacons are commonly responsible for the public worship of the congregation. Too often they, like the congregation, pass this duty to the pastor.

The congregation has more than just a need to become involved in a study of the meaning and purpose of worship. Through its designated boards or committees it should actually enter into the planning of worship. A board of deacons might well undertake responsibility for determining a proper order of worship to be used by the congregation in its regular worship services. Suggested orders can be found in the books referred to above, in

[4] Stephen F. Winward, *The Reformation of Our Worship* (Richmond: John Knox Press, 1965), p. 111-112.

Sections 2 and 6 of this manual, and in the many worship manuals prepared by denominations and individuals. Any order should be built on the basis of clearly thought-through principles for free-church worship. When the deacons or another designated committee have developed a structure for worship, it should then be presented to the congregation at a church meeting with careful explanations concerning the various points in the order, as well as concerning its structure as a whole. Nothing can be more fatal to a new order of worship than to spring it suddenly upon a congregation.

B. Laymen can be trained for participation in the leadership of worship. Here we need to remember what the Apostle says about the gifts bestowed upon people. Not all laymen are able or ever will become able to stand up before the congregation and lead worship; but some, when they are trained, have special gifts which can make a vital contribution to the worship of the whole congregation. It is the task of the minister to see that those who have such gifts receive appropriate training. For what should they be trained?

Laymen can be used in the reading of the Scripture lessons. This practice has become common in the Roman Catholic Church; why not in the free churches? Such reading needs careful preparation and practice. Prayers also can be led by laymen. If the so-called long or pastoral prayer is broken up into separate prayers of confession, dedication, thanksgiving, petition, and intercession, laymen can lead in offering them in their proper places in the service. A layman will often do well in expressing a short prayer when he would be frightened by the idea of wording the long pastoral prayer. At the Higham's Park Church, the ancient threefold way of intercessory prayer has been brought back into usage. A deacon, the congregation, and the minister each have a special function in this threefold process. The deacon comes to the front of the congregation and bids, "Let us pray for. . . ." Then in silence the congregation prays as the deacon has invited. After each period of silence the minister collects (the original meaning of the prayer known as the "collect") the unspoken prayers of the congregation into a few brief, direct, audible sentences of prayer. Then the deacon presents another bidding, there is silence, and another collect. This procedure is carried forward until the intercessions have been completed. Laymen can also participate in the offertory prayer. As they bring the offering to the Table, one of the laymen can, with the utmost of suitability, offer the gifts and the lives of those who gave them to God.

In times past, spontaneous free prayers were often offered by members of the congregation. Such prayers generally arose from the experiences of the members of the congregation in the world. Cannot such a practice be renewed, particularly through small group fellowships? Conceivably, out of such groups will come concerns and thanksgivings which can suitably be brought before the entire congregation. It is not outside the realm of possibility that even in somewhat formal worship, times of spontaneity can become effective and can bring to the congregation a sense of freedom in the spirit. The prayers in this manual are not intended to do away with extemporary prayer or eliminate spontaneity; they can well be used as guiding material in the preparation for spontaneous prayer.

C. Congregational participation can be increased by the use of dialogue in worship. Responsive readings provide one such means, but it is also practical for prayers, introductory sentences, and other parts of worship to be conducted in dialogue fashion. A common form of such dialogue is:

The Lord be with you.
And with thy spirit.
Lift up your hearts.
We lift them up unto the Lord.

Common introductions to prayer can, after some usage, be readily memorized by the members of the congregation and when the minister begins, members of the congregation naturally follow. A collection of such introductions, or versicles, can be found in Part 3, selections 112-128 of this manual. Other types of dialogical material have been included in other parts of the manual.

D. Another important means of congregational participation is the reintroduction of the people's audible *Amen*. The use of the spoken *Amen* involves the congregation in every prayer. Too often such *Amens* are sung only by the choir, but why can they not be either said or sung by the congregation as a whole? Most hymnals include a collection of *Amens*, numbering from one to sevenfold, which the people can learn with but little teaching. However, the spoken *Amen* does have the advantage that even the most tone-deaf can say to a prayer: "So be it."

E. It is most important that the congregation must learn to listen as well as to speak. Too often men come to worship with minds that are filled with a thousand matters which are anything but praise and thanksgiving to Almighty God. How, then, can a congregation prepare for worship? As with prayer, training opens the way. If a congregation understands the purpose and meaning of worship, as well as the part that each aspect of a liturgy plays in the total service of worship, there is apt to be more careful listening. Occasional explanation of some part of the service of worship by the minister or an informed layman immediately before that part is entered aids the congregation. How often the word "offertory" is associated with music especially played to cover up the jangle of coins during the receipt of the collection! Historically, the offertory is the offering of self and substance in thanksgiving as response to the good news which has been proclaimed in the reading and preaching of the Word. Furthermore, it is the bringing of the elements which are to be used in the Lord's Supper. Thus self, substance, and the bread and wine become the "materials" of offertory. When music is used, it should express man's act of giving himself and his substance gladly to God in praise and thanksgiving.

The church paper or bulletin can be used effectively in training the congregation to participate in worship, and particularly to listen to the elements of the liturgy. For example, why a gloria? A doxology? The psalter? The various ascriptions? And what is the nature of confession?

A studied and careful program of training, through whatever means, will bring a congregation more meaningfully into an experience of that event which is central to the church as a gathered people. Then the congregation will be able to "worship God in the beauty of holiness."

6. *A primary role of the congregation is the relating of the issues of the world to worship. Worship is essentially the celebration of God's work in the world. It is the congregation gathering to remember his mighty acts (in the world) in the past, especially the act in which he "so loved the world that he gave his only Son"; but it is also celebration of his acts in the world in our day, and the looking forward to that final act when all things shall be gathered up in him.*

Out of the world the members of the congregation bring these issues, wherein God's worldly Word is spoken. Who is better able to know the world than the layman who is in the world? Given the opportunity, he can bring to the congregation (the household of faith) those concerns and issues that need to be seen and celebrated in the light of God's word. These concerns and issues become, in part, the agenda for worship. Then into the world the congregation goes with new insights and understanding to witness to God's acts in the lives of men and structures of society.

7. *Christian worship centers in God and in his self-revelation in Jesus Christ. This direction of worship is objective rather than subjective. In worship we praise God, not man. We pray to be heard by God, not man. We proclaim God's Word, not man's. We sit at God's Table, not man's.*

Too often in worship we try to do what "sounds nice," "looks nice," or "creates a nice feeling." Subjectivism is the demon that constantly attacks worship. How sentimental the hymns, solos, and anthems can become! They are filled with personal pronouns which express man's pious feelings, rather than what God has done and is doing. Many of the so-called "gospel songs" have very little to do with the gospel—the story of God's mighty acts among men—but are maudlin expressions of man's religious feelings and, as such, are an affront to the very gospel which they seek to express. Sermons and prayers can become egocentric ramblings, filled with "I . . . I . . . I" rather than testimony and response to God and his acts in Christ and the world.

To stress so strongly that worship must be objective does not mean that the subjective has no place. Man's feelings are powerful factors in his life and must express themselves as he gives glory to God. But strong feeling must come in response to God's acts, not as sentimentalized versions of man's own inadequacies. It was written even of John Calvin, regarding his worship in Geneva

29

which seemed so barren when compared with the liturgy of Rome: "Shall it be said . . . the true Calvinian cultus was by nature cold and impoverished? Those who were present at the service have told us that often they could not keep back the tears of their emotion and joy."[5]

8. *Christian worship must offer opportunity for a true freedom in the Spirit.*

Christian worship finds its rootage not only in the acts of God as recorded in Scripture and in the Upper Room, but also in Pentecost; thus worship is scriptural, sacramental, and pentecostal. The deadly enemy of the pentecostal experience is formalism. To have the right words and the right forms is not enough, for words and forms are but channels for the living Spirit of God. Paul speaks of worship not only as "glorying in Christ," but as "worship by the Spirit of God." Thus the materials of a manual such as this one are not intended to bind, but to free. They offer themselves as channels. But merely to repeat words does not guarantee the Spirit's presence. That depends far more upon the faithfulness of the congregation in its pursuit of its vocation of witness, its sense of togetherness, and its openness to the Holy Spirit.

The goal of pentecostal worship is not undisciplined spontaneity. Disciplined devotion to "the apostles' teaching and fellowship, to the breaking of bread and the prayers" brought into the early Church the continuing pentecostal experience. Is not such disciplined spontaneity the way of the Church's worship in the present time as well?

This manual is intended to help a congregation to discipline itself in its worship life. The orders, prayers, and

[5] From E. Domergue, *Essai sur l'Histoire du Culte Reformé* (Lausanne, 1890), vol. 5, p. 504.

other materials offer helps, but they are not intended to be slavishly used or binding upon any congregation as its necessary and only correct way to worship. Rather these materials can be the means to free a congregation for meaningful worship. It is in this spirit and for this use that they are presented so that, as "the fellowship of the Holy Spirit," the local Church should seek to develop a truly congregational worship, using the gifts of all of its members, "that together you may with one voice glorify the God and Father of our Lord Jesus Christ."

PART 1

PREPARATION FOR WORSHIP

(Here, and at the beginning of each succeeding part of this book, suggestions are made for the use of the materials included. These explanatory paragraphs have at least two purposes—to help in the understanding of the meaning and use of the included materials and to provide instruction in worship.)

This section is intended to help those responsible for worship to fulfill their roles more meaningfully. Prayers of preparation are given for congregation, minister, choir, and deacons. If this manual is not available to every member of the congregation, prayers for the congregation may be printed in the bulletin preceding the order of worship. Through quiet recollection and purposeful meditation, these are intended to prepare the minds and hearts of those who are to engage in worship. The prayers of the minister are especially designed to make him ready for his role of leadership. They are to enable him to participate actively in worship as well as to lead it. As the minister meets with the choir he may use the suggested prayers or other forms. These are intended to prepare the choir for its important function of leading the congregation in the musical aspects of worship and to help the choir members to enter fully into the congregation's worship. The deacons are vested with the responsibility for leadership in the spiritual and physical ministries of the church. The prayers of the deacons bring them to discover their full responsibilities in a meaningful way.

PRAYERS FOR USE BY
MEMBERS OF THE CONGREGATION

1. Eternal Father, help us in this hour of worship to so contemplate the image of the crucified and glorified Christ that we shall be conformed to him in his death and in his glory. Help us to take up the cross and so share in his agony that like him we may be lifted up and transformed from glory to glory. Amen.

2. Eternal Father, help us to know the joy of our salvation. Enable us to discover the happiness of a simple follower of Jesus Christ and be so overcome by his grace that we sing praise to him with humble hearts. Give to us the assurance that our lives are so embedded in thee that we can truly live in the world. Overrule our pride with thy grace, that we may be as ready to receive as thou art to give. Amen.

3. Help us, O God, to know that to live is Christ. Give to us in this hour of worship renewed commitment to that single-minded discipleship in which we seek to conform ourselves to the image of Christ and to give ourselves to him in unquestioning obedience. Amen.

Gracious Father, give to us the grace to be honest in our 4.
worship. Cause us to get beneath the little sins, which we
can so readily confess, to our greater sinfulness which
stands in such solid rebellion against thee. Cleanse our
thanksgiving, that it may be more than the callous recital
of thanks for those things which have come because we
have selfishly pursued our own desires. May our thanks
be for thy great love as manifested in Jesus Christ. Open
our hearts that we may pray not only for ourselves but
for others according to their particular needs, and, having
prayed, that we may go out and seek in thy name to serve.
Amen.

O God, who through the grace of thy Holy Spirit pourest 5.
out the gift of love into the hearts of thy faithful people,
grant unto us health of mind and body, that we may love
thee with our whole strength and may perform those
things in our worship and service which are pleasing unto
thee this day; through Christ our Lord. Amen.

Lord of life and love and beauty, help us to worship thee 6.
in the beauty of thy holiness with such sincerity that thy
holiness may appear before us. Quiet us in thy presence
with the stillness of a wise trust and a sense of being not
in our hands but in thine. Lift us above the narrowness of
self-interest and the smallness of status seeking, that we
may begin today, from the height of prayer, to live as
sons and daughters of an eternal inheritance. Amen.

O God, source of all pure desires and holy affections, give 7.
to us reverent and devout minds that we may worship thee
in fullness and truth. Cause us to come to know again him
who is the Way, the Truth and the Life, even Jesus
Christ our Lord and Savior. Amen.

8. O Lord, be with us in this thy house and let thy Spirit guide our worship. May hearts be turned to thee, here and everywhere, through the reading and the preaching of thy Word and in thanksgivings and supplications. Keep us from being proud that we are here rather than in the world. Help us to know that this worship is for us a sacred trust and a calling to discipleship among men. Amen.

PRAYERS OF THE MINISTER

9. O Lord, thou hast searched me and known me!
Thou knowest when I sit down and when I rise up;
    thou discernest my thoughts from afar.
Thou searchest out my path and my lying down,
    and art acquainted with all my ways.
Even before a word is on my tongue,
    lo, O Lord, thou knowest it altogether.
Thou dost beset me behind and before,
    and layest thy hand upon me.
Such knowledge is too wonderful for me;
    it is high, I cannot attain it.
How precious to me are thy thoughts, O God!
    How vast is the sum of them!
If I would count them, they are more than the sand.

Help me to lead thy people in worship this day in the assurance of thy abiding presence. Amen.

10. O God, it is so easy for me to talk glibly about thy love and never to understand its depth. Help me to be so truly sensitive to the working of thy love in myself and in others that when I speak of love they shall know that I speak of thee. Amen.

O send out thy light and thy truth; let them lead me,   11.
let them bring me to thy holy hill and to thy dwelling!
Have mercy on me, O God, according to thy steadfast
love; according to thy abundant mercy blot out my
transgressions.
Create in me a clean heart, O God,
    and put a new and right spirit within me.
O Lord, open thou my lips,
    and my mouth shall show forth thy praise.
    I will give thanks to the Lord with my whole heart;
    I will tell of all thy wonderful deeds.
Open my eyes, that I may behold wondrous things out of
    thy law.
Let the words of my mouth and the meditation of my
    heart be acceptable in thy sight,
    O Lord, my rock and my redeemer. Amen.

Lord, make me an instrument of thy peace!   12.
    Where there is hatred, let me sow love;
    Where there is injury, pardon;
    Where there is doubt, faith;
    Where there is despair, hope;
    Where there is darkness, light;
    Where there is sadness, joy.
O Divine Master,
Grant that I may not so much seek
    To be consoled as to console;
    To be understood as to understand;
    To be loved as to love:
For . . .
    It is in giving that we receive;
    It is in pardoning that we are pardoned;
    It is in dying that we are born to eternal life. Amen.

O Lord God, keep my ministry this day from being merely   13.

a performance. Too often have I sought to lead others in worship and have not worshiped myself. Make this day different from those other days. Let me rejoice and find gladness in praise and prayer. Bring together the scattered fragments of my spirit. Enable me to remove myself from the small business of each day. Cause Jesus Christ to walk the ways of my mind and fill me with his Spirit. May he be with me and in me, and may I find my strength in him. Amen.

Before the Lord's Supper

14. Holy Father, grant to me thy help as I now prepare myself for coming to thy holy Table. Have mercy upon me, cleanse me, and forgive all my sins as I now freely forgive all who have sinned against me. Assist me with thy grace, that I may set forth this memorial of my Savior's death with adoration and thanksgiving. Open my eyes to behold the vision of his love. Grant that, feeding on Christ by faith, I may be strengthened with might by thy Holy Spirit. Help me to speak the words and perform the actions of the Lord's Supper with a holy intention, a sincere purpose, and a kindled devotion. Grant that our worship and my ministry therein may be acceptable in thy sight; through Jesus Christ, our Lord. Amen.

15. O thou whose eternal love for our weak and struggling race was most perfectly shown forth in the blessed life and death of Jesus Christ our Lord, enable me now to so meditate upon my Lord's passion that, having fellowship with him in his sorrow, I may also learn the secret of his strength and peace.

I remember Gethsemane;
I remember how Judas betrayed him;
I remember how Peter denied him;
I remember how they all forsook him and fled;

I remember the scourging;
I remember the crown of thorns;
I remember how they spat upon him;
I remember how they cursed him;
I remember how they smote him on the head with a
     reed;
I remember his piercéd hands and feet;
I remember his agony on the cross;
I remember his thirst;
I remember how he cried, *My God, my God, why hast
     thou forsaken me?*

Grant, O most gracious God, that I who now kneel before
thee may be embraced in that great company of those to
whom life and salvation have come in the cross of Christ.
Let the redeeming power that has flowed from his sufferings through so many generations flow now into my spirit.
Here let me find forgiveness of sin. Here let me learn to
share with Christ the burden of the suffering of the world.
Of thy marvelous love make me a faithful minister. Amen.

Give me the spirit of a true pastor. Grant that in the   16.
reading and preaching, the breaking of bread and the
pouring of the cup I am not mechanically performing a
ritual but rather ministering in thy name to thy people;
and that their concerns which are thy concerns will become my concerns; through Jesus Christ. Amen.

PRAYERS OF THE CHOIR

MINISTER: Praise ye the Lord.   17.

   RESPONSE: **The Lord's name be praised.**

PRAYER: O Lord our God, who art worthy to be praised
and be held in reverence by all who art about thee: grant
unto us, as we lead the worship in thy house, the gift of

39

thy Holy Spirit that, being cleansed and sanctified, we may serve thee with gladness and find our joy in singing to thy glory; through Jesus Christ our Lord. Amen.

18. MINISTER: Serve the Lord with gladness.

RESPONSE: **Let us come before his presence with singing.**

PRAYER: O God whose glory the countless hosts of heaven do ceaselessly proclaim, graciously aid us, we beseech thee, as we seek worthily to fulfill our ministry and service in thy house. Help us in psalms and hymns and spiritual songs to make melody with our whole hearts; through Jesus Christ our Lord. Amen.

19. O God who art spirit, help us now to worship thee in spirit and in truth; to praise thee not only with our lips but also with our minds and hearts; and grant that when our worship is ended we may continue to glorify thee in our lives; through Jesus Christ our Lord. Amen.

20. O God who hast taught us in thy holy Word to serve thee with gladness, and to come into thy presence with singing, fill us now with thy Holy Spirit that we may make melody to thee with all our heart, and always and for everything give thanks in the name of our Lord Jesus Christ. Amen.

21. O eternal God, deliver us as we now draw near to thee from irreverence and formality, from wanderings of mind and coldness of heart, from praising thee with our lips while our hearts are far from thee. Kindle our emotions and enlighten our minds, that we may sing with the spirit and with the understanding also. Above all, grant to us now and at all times the pure intention to do all things for thy glory; through Jesus Christ our Lord. Amen.

We thank thee, our Father, for the gift of music. We 22.
praise thee for those poets and composers who have combined words and notes to thy glory. Cause us to be faithful to their inspiration, that we as they may worthily
magnify thy holy name; through Jesus Christ our Lord.
Amen.

PRAYERS OF THE DEACONS

Holy Father, thou hast called us to be thy servants in 23.
thy house and in the world. Help us in worship to learn
of him who in service girded himself with the towel and
washed the feet of the disciples. Help us in that same
spirit to serve those to whom we are called; through Jesus
Christ our Lord. Amen.

Holy Father, go before us in all our doing with thy most 24.
gracious favor and further our work with thy continued
help, that all of our acts may be begun, continued, and
ended in thee and· that our service may glorify thy holy
name and secure thy blessings to those to whom it is
offered; through Jesus Christ our Lord. Amen.

Eternal Father, we are folk who come from the ordinary 25.
walks of life, yet thou hast seen fit through thy Church
to set us apart for special service. Cause us to see beyond
the business of the things that we do in thy name to their
true meaning, that, in what we do, we may rightly interpret thy Word and thy Will to those whom we serve;
through Jesus Christ our Lord. Amen.

Merciful Father, we pray for all who come into thy house 26.
this day. We commend to thy holy keeping all who are
faced with great temptations, all who are anxious and
whose minds are filled with doubt concerning thee or their
neighbors, those whose family circles have been broken

by death, those who are oppressed by injustice, those who may be lonely strangers within our gates, those into whose lives have come some new-found joy. For these and for ourselves we pray that this day may be full of thy goodness and thy grace and that we may be ready for thy blessings; through Jesus Christ our Lord. Amen.

Before the Lord's Supper

27. Our Father, through thy Church we have been set apart to serve at thy Table. Help us to remember him who loved us and gave himself for us that we may worthily serve in his name. Cause the light of thy countenance to shine upon our pastor as he leads us in worship, and upon thy people that thy Word may be spoken and heard and that the symbols of bread and wine may truly become for us the signs of the living presence of Jesus Christ our crucified and risen Savior. In his name we pray. Amen.

PART 2

THE SERVICE
FOR THE LORD'S DAY

Two orders of *The Service for the Lord's Day* are described here. The first of these includes the observance of the Lord's Supper. The second service does not include the visible observance of the Lord's Supper, but nevertheless its second half is governed by the Lord's Table. The first service is that of Word and of Table; the second, Word and Prayers.

At the beginning of either service there is an affirmation of purpose by the minister and congregation. Immediately after this comes the "processional," which, in free-church worship, is the bringing in of the Bible. Likewise, the proper "recessional" is the closing of the Bible and the taking of it by a deacon from the pulpit to its place by the door, and symbolically by the congregation into the world. When there is an observance of the Lord's Supper, a second processional takes place as the offerings of bread and wine and the gifts of the people are brought by the deacons to the Table. The bread and wine are then removed when the Bible is taken from the pulpit, and all are taken to a place by the door, and symbolically by the congregation into the world.

Adoration follows the affirmation and processional. This section may include Scripture sentences, introit, hymn, prayer of adoration, and ascription. It is to be noted that neither of the orders of service contains a so-called pastoral or long prayer, but rather numerous specific prayers of adoration, petition, dedication, thanksgiving, intercession, and dismissal. This means that the prayers will be generally in the form of collects, and relatively short. Some are in the form of responsive prayers; all can be used as unison congregational prayers. Each one may be followed by the people's Amen.

Adoration naturally leads to the next section of the service, confession. This section embraces a call, prayer, *Kyrie* or *Agnus Dei*, affirmation of forgiveness, and some form of praise such as the *Gloria Patri, Gloria in Excelsis,* or a hymn.

The congregation is now ready for the Ministry of the Word, the important section for which the first half of both services is named. Components of this section are Scripture lessons, prayer for illumination, sermon, and affirmation of faith.

In both services, the first part, controlled by the Word, concludes after the affirmation of faith. In the first service, the second half includes the Table; and in the second service, the second half includes Prayer. Each of the orders of service, however, contains the offertory as the transition between its two main parts.

The offertory follows the Ministry of the Word. In the full service this includes the offering of not only the money gifts of the people but also the bread and wine for the communion and the self-offering of the members of the congregation. In Christian worship this is the only right and proper place for the offertory. The offering of gifts, the offering of self, and the offering of the elements of the Supper come as a response to the Word which has been read and proclaimed. If a hymn of invitation is desired, it can most properly be included as a part of the offertory. It is at this point in the service that commitment to Christian discipleship in response to the message of the Word can most appropriately take place.

The second half of the service which includes the Lord's Supper begins with the Ministry of the Table. This embraces the offertory (already mentioned), prayer of dedication, invitation to communion and response, affirmation of unity and peace with Scripture sentences and the right hand of fellowship, institution of the Lord's Supper, prayer of thanksgiving, prayer for the presence of the Holy Spirit, the Lord's Prayer, breaking and distribution of the bread, eating the bread, pouring and distribution of the wine, drinking the wine, *Sanctus*, prayer of petition, and prayer of intercession.

The right hand of fellowship or, as it was called in the ancient church, "the kiss of peace," is included in the Ministry of the Table. This procedure is a symbolic portrayal of the unity of the congregation and the common gathering as one family under God.

Two prayers follow the institution of the Lord's Supper. There are two prayers here, rather than one, because they have to do with widely different subjects and distinctly different attitudes of the people. The first of these prayers is the prayer of thanksgiving. Its basic expression is that of joy for God's great gift in Jesus Christ. In the ancient church this prayer was known as the *eucharistia*, a word from which the whole service drew its name. The second of the two prayers is the invocation of the presence of the

Holy Spirit, or the *epiclesis*. This prayer is a special request that the Holy Spirit may be in the recipients of the bread and wine as they express their remembrance of and thanksgiving for Jesus Christ.

Prayers of intercession come after the communion. In these, the congregation turns its attention from the subjective worship of Almighty God to the objective attention to the world. The Church now prays to God on behalf of the world and of those who have special needs.

The dismissal further stresses the true role of the Church, which is to witness to the world. Worship ought never to give the impression that God is confined within the walls of the meeting house, but rather that his primary locus is in the world. The role of the worshiping congregation is to gather to acknowledge and give thanks to the God who is in the world. The Church gathers to seek wisdom for worldly encounter and witness.

The second service described in Part 2 is like the first service, excepting that it does not include the visible observance of the Lord's Supper. Nevertheless, even in this alternate service the Supper governs the second half. Although the elements are not present, they are symbolized through the offertory and the acts of remembrance and thanksgiving. The offertory and the prayers are the responses to the Word which has been read and preached.

Such special observances as baptism, the ordination or installation of a minister, the installation of deacons, the dedication of church officers, or a Christian marriage service may take place within *The Service for the Lord's Day* at the time of the offertory. In each of these instances those involved are offering themselves for special service and are dedicating their lives to their calling.

Music can be used at many points to enrich the service of worship, but music should always serve as the handmaiden of worship and should be suitable to the various parts of the service in which it is included. Ideally, the musical parts of the service should be sung by the whole congregation. The chief function of the choir is to strengthen congregational participation in worship, both as teacher and leader. Prelude, postlude, anthem, and responses, as well as introits, glorias, and doxologies, all have their appropriate place. When they are done well they can serve to enrich worship and give glory to God.

If an anthem or solo is used, it should be movable. For example, if its theme is adoration, it should come at the beginning of the service. If it is a psalm from the Old Testament, it can be included in the liturgy of the Word. If it has to do with offertory, it can be used to enrich that part of the service. If it is related to the various prayers at the end of the service, it might be utilized at those points. Never should the anthem or solo be a "performance number."

Hymns play a primary part in worship. As with other musical selections, these can come at any appropriate place in the service to give strength where they occur. Most hymns are prayers and ought to be thought of in that light. They offer the opportunity for the congregation to adore, confess, give thanks, dedicate, or intercede.

In the pages which follow, each service is first outlined, then delineated in full.

OUTLINE OF
THE SERVICE FOR THE LORD'S DAY
(with the Lord's Supper)

AFFIRMATION OF PURPOSE AND ENTRY OF SCRIPTURES
ADORATION
    Scripture sentences
    Hymn

Prayer
Ascription
CONFESSION
Call
Prayer
Kyrie or *Agnus Dei*
Assurance of forgiveness
Praise: *Gloria Patri, Gloria in Excelsis,* or hymn
MINISTRY OF THE WORD
Scripture lessons
Prayer for illumination
Sermon
Affirmation of faith
MINISTRY OF THE TABLE
Offertory: gifts, bread and wine, and self
Prayer of dedication
Invitation to communion and response
Affirmation of unity and peace
Scripture sentences
Right hand of fellowship (peace)
Institution of the Lord's Supper
Prayer of thanksgiving
Prayer for the presence of the Holy Spirit
Lord's Prayer
Breaking and distribution of the bread
Eating the bread
Pouring and distribution of the wine
Drinking the wine
Sanctus or *Agnus Dei*
Prayer of petition
Prayer of intercession
INTO THE WORLD
Hymn or *Nunc Dimittis* and Recessional of Scriptures
and bread and wine
Dismissal

(with the Lord's Supper)

AFFIRMATION OF PURPOSE AND ENTRY OF SCRIPTURES

On a table near the door of the church shall be placed the Bible, the bread and wine for the Lord's Supper, and a receptacle where the people may leave their gifts as they enter.

Let there be silence as the people gather for worship. At the appointed hour, the people stand and the minister says:

Why are we gathered in this place at this hour?

We are gathered as the people of God to acknowledge him as Lord, to confess before him our sin, to offer him our sacrifice of praise and thanksgiving, to pray for the world, and to reconsecrate ourselves as his servants in the world.

Then let us worship the God before whom we stand.

The people are seated, and as a prelude is played the deacon brings the Bible to the Table or pulpit.

ADORATION

The minister or deacon from the Table or pulpit says one of the following (or the choir may sing an introit):

Our help is in the name of the Lord, who made heaven and earth.

Enter his gates with thanksgiving, and his courts with praise! Give thanks to him, bless his name! For the Lord is good; his steadfast love endures for ever, and his faithfulness to all generations.

Then shall a hymn of adoration be sung, followed by a prayer of adoration. The minister then says:

Worthy of praise from every mouth, of confession from every tongue, of worship from every creature, is thy glorious name, O Father, Son, and Holy Spirit

Who didst create the world in thy grace and by thy compassion didst save the world.

To thy majesty, O God, ten thousand times ten thousand bow down and adore, singing and praising without ceasing and saying:

Holy, holy, holy, Lord God of hosts: heaven and earth are full of thy praises: Hosanna in the highest. Amen.

CONFESSION

The minister says:

If we say we have no sin, we deceive ourselves, and the truth is not in us. Let us, therefore, humbly confess our sin to God and seek his forgiveness through Jesus Christ our Savior.

Then shall be offered the prayer of confession extempore, or by the congregation as follows:

Almighty and most merciful Father, we have erred, and strayed from thy ways like lost sheep. We have followed too much the devices and desires of our own hearts. We have offended against thy holy laws. We have left undone things which we ought to have done; and we have done those things which we ought not to have done; and there is no health in us. But thou, O Lord, have mercy upon us, miserable offenders. Spare thou those, O God, who confess their faults. Restore thou those who are penitent, according to thy promises declared unto mankind in Christ Jesus our Lord. And grant, O most merciful Father, for his sake, that we may hereafter live a godly, righteous, and sober life, to the glory of thy holy name. Amen.

Almighty and most merciful God, we acknowledge and
confess that we have sinned against thee in thought and
word and deed; that we have not loved thee with our
heart and soul, with all our mind and strength; and that
we have not loved our neighbors as ourselves. Forgive
us, O God, for what we have been, and help us to become
what we ought. Let love fill our lives that we give of
ourselves even as Christ has given of himself for us.
Amen.

*After the prayer of confession there shall be silence in
which each person confesses his own sin; then the following may be said or sung:*

Lord, have mercy upon us.
Christ, have mercy upon us.
Lord, have mercy upon us.

or

O Lamb of God, who takest away the sins of the world,
Have mercy upon us.
O Lamb of God, who takest away the sins of the world,
Grant us thy peace.
The minister shall then say one of the following:

The saying is sure and worthy of full acceptance, that
Christ Jesus came into the world to save sinners. Therefore, if any one is in Christ, he is a new creation; the old
has passed away, behold, the new has come.

or

God shows his love for us in that while we were yet

sinners Christ died for us. There is therefore now no condemnation for those who are in Christ Jesus.

O Lord, open thou our lips,
And our mouths shall show forth thy praise.

The Gloria Patri, the Gloria in Excelsis, or a hymn of praise is sung.

Here a welcome to the congregation and any necessary notices may be given and the gifts of the people gathered (if they have not previously been left at the door).

MINISTRY OF THE WORD

The minister or deacon opens the Bible to the first lesson and says:

Hear the Word of God in the . . . .

An Old Testament and/or an Epistle lesson may be read followed by the singing or responsive reading of a Psalm.

After each lesson the reader says:

Here ends the reading of the lesson (Old Testament, Epistle, or Psalm).

The minister or deacon then opens the Bible to the Gospel lesson and says:

Hear the Word of God in the . . . .

Here the Gospel lesson is read.

After the reading of the Scriptures prayer is offered asking that the Holy Spirit bring to understanding the words which have been read.

The minister says, Let us pray:

Gracious Father, by thy Holy Spirit cause these words which have been read to become for us the very Word of life. Amen.

A sermon based upon one or more of the Scriptures read shall be preached.

After the sermon an invitation may be given to any who feel called to confess their faith in Christ or renew their obedience to him publicly. A hymn of invitation may be sung at this time.

The people may then stand and together affirm their faith, using the Apostles' or Nicene Creed, or an affirmation of faith of the congregation.

MINISTRY OF THE TABLE

The minister shall say an offertory sentence. The gifts and the bread and wine are then brought by the deacons to the Table as the Doxology or a suitable hymn is sung. The deacons shall take their places about the Table for the serving of the Lord's Supper. After receiving the gifts the minister shall pray:

Our Father, we offer to thee this bread and wine, to be set apart for the remembrance of the passion of thy Son, our Lord; we present to thee these gifts, thanking thee for the strength and skill to do our daily work; and together with them we offer ourselves, asking that thou strengthen us that all our work may be thy service, all our meals a thankful remembrance of thy bounty to us, and that we ourselves might be a living sacrifice, holy and acceptable to thee; through our Lord Jesus Christ. Amen.

The minister, standing at the Table, shall say:

We read that he was made known to them in the breaking of bread. All who believe in him and who are in love and fellowship with the brethren are invited to partake of the Supper of the Lord.

Our Father, we come to this Table in faithful trust that through these elements of bread and wine we shall come to thankful remembrance of Jesus Christ and he will be made known to us as living Lord. Amen.

The minister shall then say:

Our Lord said, A new commandment I give to you, that you love one another; even as I have loved you.

We know that we have passed out of death into life, because we love the brethren.

Behold, how good and pleasant it is when brothers dwell in unity!

Because there is one loaf, we who are many are one body, for we all partake of the same loaf.

The peace of God be with you.

Here each worshiper may extend the Right Hand of Fellowship to those sitting on either side, saying to each, "The peace of God be with you," or the Right Hand of Fellowship may be passed from the minister to the deacons and then by them to the congregation, each saying upon giving it, "The peace of God be with you."

The minister, taking the bread and then the cup, shall say:

Hear the words of the Institution of the Lord's Supper as written by Paul the apostle: The Lord Jesus on the night when he was betrayed took bread, and when he had given thanks, he broke it, and said, "This is my body which is for you. Do this in remembrance of me." In the same way also the cup, after supper, saying, "This cup is the new covenant in my blood. Do this, as often as you drink it, in remembrance of me." For as often as you eat this bread and drink the cup, you proclaim the Lord's death until he comes.

Beloved, this is the joyful feast of the people of God.

Men will come from east and west, and from north and south, and sit at table in the kingdom of God.

The Lord be with you.
And with thy spirit.
Lift up your hearts.
We lift them up unto the Lord.
Let us give thanks unto the Lord our God.
O thou great God, thou in whom we live and move and have our being, we lift our hearts and offer thanks to thee for the wonders of the world about us, for human kind with its richness of love, and for each new day with its forgiveness and grace.

Here may be added such special thanksgivings as are appropriate for the occasion.

Great and wonderful are thy deeds, O Lord. Just and true are thy ways. Glory be to thee, for thou alone art holy.
Holy, holy, holy, Lord God of hosts, heaven and earth are full of thy glory. Glory be to thee, O Lord most high. Blessed be he who comes in the name of the Lord. Hosanna in the highest.

With thanksgiving we remember our Lord Jesus Christ who was with thee in the beginning, through whom all things were made, whose life is the light of men.

For his life and ministry, for his teaching and example, and for his love

We thank thee, O God.

For his sufferings and his death upon the cross

We thank thee, O God.

For the hope that comes through his resurrection

We thank thee, O God.

For the promise that in him all things shall be made new

We thank thee, O God.

Grant, our Father, that thy Holy Spirit may be with us, and that through the bread and wine set apart for this remembrance and thanksgiving Christ may come to dwell among us, and through him we may know thee whom to know is life eternal.

Here silence may be observed, in which each member of the congregation offers his own petition for Christ's presence. The silent prayer is followed by the Lord's Prayer.

Our Father who art in heaven, hallowed be thy name. Thy kingdom come, thy will be done, on earth as it is in heaven. Give us this day our daily bread; and forgive us our debts, as we also have forgiven our debtors; and lead us not into temptation, but deliver us from evil. For thine is the kingdom and the power and the glory, forever. Amen.

The minister shall break the bread* and give it to the deacons, who in turn shall give it to the people. After all have been served, the minister shall say:

Jesus said, "Take, eat; this is my body which is broken for you. Do this in remembrance of me."

The minister shall pour the wine* and give it to the deacons, who in turn shall give it to the people. After all have been served, the minister shall say:

Jesus said, "Drink of it, all of you; for this is my blood of the covenant, which is poured out for many for the forgiveness of sins.

After a time of silence the minister shall say:

Behold, the Lamb of God, who takes away the sin of the world!

Lamb of God, who takes away the sin of the world, have mercy upon us.

Lamb of God, who takes away the sin of the world, grant us thy peace.

Most merciful Father, take our hands which have held holy things and work through them;

Take our lips which have tasted the signs of the body and blood of our Lord and speak through them;

Take our bodies which have received the bread and wine and make them fit temples of thy spirit;

Take our minds and think through them;

Take our hearts and fill them with thy love that we may truly serve thee in the world.   Amen.

O Lord, who made us a royal priesthood that we might offer intercessions for all men; hear us as we pray.

Here the deacon, following an ancient custom of the

* In a large congregation it may be necessary to break the bread and fill the cups before the service. Some symbolic breaking and pouring can then be carried out during the service.

church, presents the biddings for intercession. After each bidding the congregation prays silently, after which the minister collects the silent petition in an audible prayer; or a prayer of intercession, either extempore or as found in Part 3, selections 301-309, may be offered.

INTO THE WORLD

During the singing of a hymn or of the Nunc Dimittis, the deacons shall take the Bible and the remaining bread and wine from the Table to the place by the door.

Then shall the minister say:

Go forth into the world in peace; be of good courage; hold fast to that which is good; render to no man evil for evil; strengthen the fainthearted; support the weak; help the afflicted; honor all men; love and serve the Lord, rejoicing in the power of the Holy Spirit.

The grace of the Lord Jesus Christ and the love of God and the fellowship of the Holy Spirit be with you all. Amen.

or

The peace of the Lord Jesus Christ be with you all.

Peace be with you.

Brethren, Christ has risen.

The Lord has risen indeed. Hallelujah!

Christ has been raised from the dead, the first fruits of those who have fallen asleep.

Thanks be to God, who gives us the victory through our Lord Jesus Christ.

Worthy is the Lamb who was slain,

To receive power and wealth and might and honor and glory and blessing!

Salvation belongs to our God and to the Lamb! Amen!

Blessing and glory and wisdom and thanksgiving and honor and power and might be to our God for ever and ever. Amen.

The peace of God, which passes all understanding, keep your hearts and your minds in the knowledge and love of God, and of his Son Jesus Christ our Lord; and the blessing of God Almighty, the Father, the Son, and the Holy Spirit, remain with you always. Amen.

OUTLINE OF
THE SERVICE FOR THE LORD'S DAY
(without the Lord's Supper)

AFFIRMATION OF PURPOSE AND ENTRY OF SCRIPTURES
ADORATION
    Scripture sentences
    Hymn
    Prayer
    Ascription
CONFESSION
    Call
    Prayer
    Kyrie or *Agnus Dei*
    Assurance of forgiveness
    Praise: *Gloria Patri, Gloria in Excelsis,* or hymn
MINISTRY OF THE WORD
    Scripture lessons
    Prayer for illumination
    Sermon
    Affirmation of faith
OFFERTORY
    Presentation of gifts and self
    Prayer of dedication

29. THE SERVICE FOR THE LORD'S DAY
(without the Lord's Supper)

AFFIRMATION OF PURPOSE AND ENTRY OF SCRIPTURES

On a table near the door of the church shall be placed the Bible, and a receptacle where the people may leave their gifts as they enter.

Let there be silence as the people gather for worship. At the appointed hour, the people stand and the minister says:

Why are we gathered in this place at this hour?

We are gathered as the people of God to acknowledge him as Lord, to confess before him our sin, to offer him our sacrifice of praise and thanksgiving, to pray for the world, and to reconsecrate ourselves as his servants in the world.

Then let us worship the God before whom we stand.

The people are seated, and as a prelude is played the deacon brings the Bible to the Table or pulpit.

ADORATION

The minister or deacon from the Table or pulpit says one of the following (or the choir may sing an introit):

Our help is in the name of the Lord, who made heaven and earth.

Enter his gates with thanksgiving, and his courts with praise! Give thanks to him, bless his name! For the Lord is good; his steadfast love endures for ever, and his faithfulness to all generations.

Then shall a hymn of adoration be sung, followed by a prayer of adoration. The minister then says:

Worthy of praise from every mouth, of confession from every tongue, of worship from every creature, is thy glorious name, O Father, Son, and Holy Spirit:

Who didst create the world in thy grace and by thy compassion didst save the world and art even now in the world.

To thy majesty, O God, ten thousand times ten thousand bow down and adore, singing and praising without ceasing, and saying:

Holy, holy, holy, Lord God of hosts: heaven and earth are full of thy praises: Hosanna in the highest. Amen.

CONFESSION

The minister says:

If we say we have no sin, we deceive ourselves, and the truth is not in us. Let us, therefore, humbly confess our sin to God and seek his forgiveness through Jesus Christ our Savior.

Then shall be offered the prayer of confession extempore, or by the congregation as follows:

Almighty and most merciful Father; we have erred, and strayed from thy ways like lost sheep. We have followed too much the devices and desires of our own hearts. We have offended against thy holy laws. We have left undone those things which we ought to have done; and

we have done those things which we ought not to have done; and there is no health in us. But thou, O Lord, have mercy upon us, miserable offenders. Spare thou those, O God, who confess their faults. Restore thou those who are penitent; according to thy promises declared unto mankind in Christ Jesus our Lord. And grant, O most merciful Father, for his sake, that we may hereafter live a godly, righteous, and sober life, to the glory of thy holy name. Amen.

or

Almighty and most merciful God, we acknowledge and confess that we have sinned against thee in thought and word and deed; that we have not loved thee with our heart and soul, with all our mind and strength; and that we have not loved our neighbors as ourselves. Forgive us, O God, for what we have been and help us to become what we ought. Let love fill our lives that we give of ourselves even as Christ has given of himself for us. Amen.

After the prayer of confession there shall be silence in which each person confesses his own sin; then the following may be said or sung:

Lord, have mercy upon us.

Christ, have mercy upon us.

Lord, have mercy upon us.

or

O Lamb of God, who takest away the sins of the world,
Have mercy upon us.

O Lamb of God, who takest away the sins of the world,
Grant us thy peace.

The minister shall then say one of the following:

The saying is sure and worthy of full acceptance, that Christ Jesus came into the world to save sinners. Therefore, if any one is in Christ, he is a new creation; the old has passed away, behold, the new has come.

or

God shows his love for us in that while we were yet sinners Christ died for us. There is therefore now no condemnation for those who are in Christ Jesus.

O Lord, open thou our lips.
And our mouths shall show forth thy praise.

The Gloria Patri, the Gloria in Excelsis, or a hymn of praise is sung.

Here a welcome to the congregation and any necessary notices may be given and the gifts of the people gathered (if they have not previously been left at the door).

Ministry of the Word

The minister or deacon opens the Bible to the first lesson and says:

Hear the Word of God in the . . . .

An Old Testament and/or an Epistle lesson may be read followed by the singing or responsive reading of a Psalm.

After each lesson the reader says:

Here ends the reading of the lesson (Old Testament, Epistle, or Psalm).

The minister or deacon then opens the Bible to the Gospel lesson and says:

Hear the Word of God in the . . . .

Here the Gospel lesson is read.

After the reading of the Scriptures prayer is offered asking that the Holy Spirit bring understanding to the words which have been read.

The minister says, Let us pray:

Gracious Father, by thy Holy Spirit cause these words which have been read to become for us the very Word of life. Amen.

A sermon based upon one or more of the Scriptures read shall be preached.

After the sermon an invitation may be given to any who feel called to confess their faith in Christ or renew their obedience to him publicly. A hymn of invitation may be sung at this time.

The people may then stand and together affirm their faith, using the Apostles' or Nicene Creed, or an affirmation of faith of the congregation.

OFFERTORY

The minister shall say an offertory sentence. The gifts are then brought by the deacons to the Table as the Doxology or a suitable hymn is sung. After receiving the gifts the minister shall pray:

With these gifts we consecrate ourselves to thy service that thy Word may be heard in this place and throughout the whole world; through him who loved us and gave himself for us, even Christ Jesus, our Lord. Amen.

Then shall the prayers of thanksgiving, petition, and inter-cession be offered.

The minister, standing at the Table, shall say:

Lift up your hearts.

We lift them up unto the Lord.

Let us give thanks unto the Lord our God.

It is meet and right so to do.

Let us pray:

Almighty God, Father of all mercies, we thine unworthy servants do give thee most humble and hearty thanks for all thy goodness and lovingkindness to us and to all men. We bless thee for our creation, preservation, and all the blessings of this life; but above all, for thine inestimable love in the redemption of the world by our Lord Jesus Christ, for the means of grace, and for the hope of glory. And, we beseech thee, give to us a due sense of all thy mercies, that our hearts may be un-feignedly thankful, and that we show forth thy praise not only with our lips but in our lives, by giving up ourselves to thy service and by walking before thee in holiness and righteousness all our days; through Jesus Christ our Lord, to whom, with thee and the Holy Spirit, be all honor and glory, world without end. Amen.

O Lord, who made us a royal priesthood that we might offer intercessions for all men, hear us as we pray:

O God, the Creator and Preserver of all mankind, we humbly beseech thee for all sorts and conditions of men, that thou wouldst be pleased to make thy ways known unto them, thy saving health unto all nations. More especially we pray for the good estate of the universal

Church; may it be so guided and governed by thy good spirit that all who profess and call themselves Christians may be led into the way of truth, and hold the faith in unity of spirit, in the bond of peace, and in righteousness of life. Finally, we commend to thy fatherly goodness all those who are in any way afflicted or distressed in mind, body, or estate (especially . . .) may it please thee to comfort and relieve them, according to their several necessities; give them patience under their sufferings, and a happy issue out of all their afflictions. And this we beg for Jesus Christ's sake. Amen.

or

Here the deacon, following an ancient custom of the Church, presents the biddings for intercession. After each bidding the congregation prays silently, after which the minister collects the silent petition in an audible prayer; or a prayer of intercession, either extempore or as found in Part 3, selections 301-309, may be offered.

Into the World

During the singing of a hymn or the Nunc Dimittis, the deacons shall take the Bible from the Table to the place by the door.

Then shall the minister say:

Go forth into the world in peace; be of good courage; hold fast to that which is good; render to no man evil for evil; strengthen the fainthearted; support the weak; help the afflicted; honor all men; love and serve the Lord, rejoicing in the power of the Holy Spirit.

The grace of the Lord Jesus Christ and the love of God and the fellowship of the Holy Spirit be with you all. Amen.

or

The peace of the Lord Jesus Christ be with you all.

Peace be with you.

Brethren, Christ has risen.

The Lord has risen indeed. Hallelujah!

Christ has been raised from the dead, the first fruits of those who have fallen asleep.

Thanks be to God, who gives us the victory through our Lord Jesus Christ.

Worthy is the Lamb who was slain,

To receive power and wealth and wisdom and honor and glory and blessing!

Salvation belongs to our God and the Lamb! Amen!

Blessing and glory and wisdom and thanksgiving and honor and power and might be to our God for ever and ever. Amen.

The peace of God, which passes all understanding, keep your hearts and your minds in the knowledge and love of God, and of his Son Jesus Christ our Lord; and the blessing of God Almighty, the Father, the Son, and the Holy Spirit, remain with you always. Amen.

PART 3

MATERIALS

FOR PUBLIC WORSHIP

The materials for public worship follow the order of *The Service for the Lord's Day*. Both prayers and sentences are written for a variety of usages. A considerable amount of material for congregational participation has been included, but many of these responsive prayers and sentences can be adapted for use by the minister alone.

A number of affirmations of faith have been included. Among these are the Apostles' and Nicene Creeds, *A Statement of Faith* of the United Church of Christ, and several Scriptural affirmations. Many churches could here use their own covenants or affirmations. Affirmations are not intended to be creedal tests for church membership but common confessions on the part of a congregation concerning the Christian faith. They are appropriately used in worship to affirm the congregation's commitment to God as he is revealed in Christ.

69

In the prayers the formal *thee* and *thou* have generally been used to address deity. Those preferring the less formal *you* can readily make the substitution. It is best to strive for consistency and to keep the same form throughout the service. Some modern translations of the Bible use *you* when addressing deity. A Revised Standard Version concordance will help to identify the passages used in the Scripture sentences.

SCRIPTURE SENTENCES

Praise

30. Our help is in the name of the Lord, who made heaven and earth.

31. Unless the Lord builds the house, those who build it labor in vain.

32. This is the day which the Lord has made;
    let us rejoice and be glad in it.
    Blessed be he who enters
    in the name of the Lord!

33. O come, let us worship and bow down,
    let us kneel before the Lord, our Maker!
    For he is our God,
    and we are the people of his pasture,
    and the sheep of his hand.

34. Serve the Lord with gladness!
    Come into his presence with singing!
    Enter his gates with thanksgiving,
    and his courts with praise!
    Give thanks to him, bless his name!
    For the Lord is good;

his steadfast love endures for ever,
and his faithfulness to all generations.

This is the day which the Lord has made; 35.
let us rejoice and be glad in it.

Sing to the Lord, bless his name; 36.
tell of his salvation from day to day.
Declare his glory among the nations,
his marvelous works among all the peoples!
For great is the Lord, and greatly to be praised.

O give thanks to the Lord, for he is good; 37.
his steadfast love endures for ever!
Let Israel say,
"His steadfast love endures for ever."
Let the house of Aaron say,
"His steadfast love endures for ever."
Let those who fear the Lord say,
"His steadfast love endures for ever."

It is good to give thanks to the Lord, 38.
to sing praises to thy name, O Most High;
to declare thy steadfast love in the morning,
and thy faithfulness by night.

Know that the Lord is God! 39.
It is he that made us, and we are his;
we are his people, and the sheep of his pasture.

Bless the Lord, O my soul; and all that is within me, bless 40.
his holy name!
Bless the Lord, O my soul, and forget not all his benefits.

Enter his gates with thanksgiving, and his courts with 41.
praise! Give thanks to him, bless his name!

For the Lord is good; his steadfast love endures for ever, and his faithfulness to all generations.

42. Make a joyful noise to the Lord, all the lands! Serve the Lord with gladness! Come into his presence with singing!

43. My heart is ready, O God, my heart is ready!
I will sing, I will sing praises! Awake, my soul!
Awake, O harp and lyre! I will awake the dawn!
I will give thanks to thee, O Lord, among the peoples.

44. I will bless the Lord at all times; his praise shall continually be in my mouth.
O magnify the Lord with me, and let us exalt his name together!
Look to him, and be radiant.

45. Praise the Lord! Praise, O servants of the Lord, praise the name of the Lord!
Blessed be the name of the Lord from this time forth and for evermore!
From the rising of the sun to its setting the name of the Lord is to be praised!

46. O give thanks to the Lord, call on his name, make known his deeds among the peoples!
Sing to him; sing praises to him, tell of all his wonderful works!
Glory in his holy name; let the hearts of those who seek the Lord rejoice!

47. O sing to the Lord a new song; sing to the Lord, all the earth!

For great is the Lord, and greatly to be praised.
Honor and majesty are before him; strength and beauty
are in his sanctuary.

Praise the Lord! Praise God in his sanctuary; praise him   48.
in his mighty firmament!
Praise him for his mighty deeds; praise him according to
his exceeding greatness!

O magnify the Lord with me, and let us exalt his name   49.
together!

Thank the Lord for his steadfast love,   50.
for his wonderful works to the sons of men!
Extol him in the congregation of the people,
and praise him in the assembly of the elders.
Consider the steadfast love of the Lord.

I was glad when they said to me,   51.
"Let us go to the house of the Lord!"

Come, bless the Lord, all you servants of the Lord!   52.
Lift up your hands to the holy place, and bless the Lord!
May the Lord bless you from Zion, he who made heaven
and earth!

Praise the Lord!   53.
For it is good to sing praises to our God;
for he is gracious, and a song of praise is seemly.

Praise the Lord.   54.
Praise the name of the Lord,
give praise, O servants of the Lord,
you that stand in the house of the Lord,
in the courts of the house of our God!

Praise the Lord, for the Lord is good;
   sing to his name, for he is gracious!

55. The eyes of the Lord your God are always upon you,
   from the beginning of the year to the end of the year.
   Look carefully, then, how you walk; not as unwise men but
   as wise, making the most of the time.

56. Come to him, to that living stone, rejected by men but in
   God's sight chosen and precious; and like living stones
   be yourselves built into a spiritual house, to be a holy
   priesthood, to offer spiritual sacrifices acceptable to God
   through Jesus Christ.

57. This is the day which the Lord has made;
   let us rejoice and be glad in it.

58. Serve the Lord with gladness!
   Come into his presence with singing!
   Enter his gates with thanksgiving,
   and his courts with praise!
   O Lord, open thou my lips,
   and my mouth shall show forth thy praise.
   Glory be to the Father, and to the Son, and to the Holy
   Spirit;
   **at it was in the beginning, is now, and ever shall be;
   world without end.   Amen.**

59. Great is the Lord, and greatly to be praised!
   **Honor and majesty are before him; strength and beauty
   are in his sanctuary.**

60. Ascribe to the Lord the glory due his name; bring an
   offering, and come before him!

**Worship the Lord in holy array; tremble before him, all
the earth.**

O magnify the Lord with me, and let us exalt his name
together!
61.
**Holy, holy, holy is the Lord of hosts; the whole earth is
full of his glory.**

Worthy art thou, our Lord and God, to receive glory and
honor and power, for thou didst create all things, and by
thy will they existed and were created.
62.
**Holy, holy, holy is the Lord of hosts; the whole earth is
full of his glory.**

O come, let us sing to the Lord;
63.
let us make a joyful noise to the rock of our salvation!
Let us come into his presence with thanksgiving;
let us make a joyful noise to him with songs of praise!
For the Lord is a great God;
and a great King above all gods.

Praise the Lord, all nations! Extol him, all peoples!
64.
**For great is his steadfast love toward us; and the faith-
fulness of the Lord endures for ever. Praise the Lord!**

O give thanks to the Lord, for he is good; for his steadfast
love endures forever!
65.
**The Lord is good to all, and his compassion is over all
that he has made.**
Blessed be the Lord, the God of Israel, who alone does
wondrous things;
**Blessed be his glorious name for ever; may his glory fill
the whole earth!**

Enter into his gates with thanksgiving, and his courts with praise!

For the Lord is good; his steadfast love endures for ever, and his faithfulness to all generations.

66. O magnify the Lord with me,

   And let us exalt his name together!

Ascribe to the Lord, O families of the peoples. Ascribe to the Lord the glory due his name.

Hallelujah! For the Lord our God the Almighty reigns. Let us be glad and rejoice, and give honor to him.

Blessed be the name of God for ever and ever, to whom belong wisdom and might.

Be exalted, O God, above the heavens! Let thy glory be over all the earth!

Let the peoples praise thee, O God; let all the peoples praise thee!

Let the nations be glad and sing for joy, for thou dost judge the peoples with equity and guide the nations upon earth.

67. O sing to the Lord a new song; sing to the Lord, all the earth!

   Sing to the Lord, bless his name; tell of his salvation from day to day.

Declare his glory among the nations, his marvelous works among all the peoples!

For great is the Lord, and greatly to be praised; he is to be feared above all gods.

Honor and majesty are before him; strength and beauty are in his sanctuary.

Ascribe to the Lord the glory due his name.

Jesus said, "Where two or three are gathered in my name, there am I in the midst of them."   68.

"The hour is coming, and now is, when the true worshipers will worship the Father in spirit and truth, for such the Father seeks to worship him. God is spirit, and those who worship him must worship in spirit and truth."

We have a great high priest who has passed through the heavens, Jesus, the son of God.   69.

Let us then with confidence draw near to the throne of grace, that we may receive mercy and find grace to help in time of need.

I was glad when they said to me, "Let us go to the house of the Lord!"   70.

This is the day which the Lord has made; let us rejoice and be glad in it.

O come, let us worship and bow down, let us kneel before the Lord, our Maker!   71.

For he is our God, and we are the people of his pasture, and the sheep of his hand.

Seek the Lord while he may be found, call upon him while he is near; let the wicked forsake his way, and the unrighteous man his thoughts;   72.

Let him return to the Lord, that he may have mercy on him, and to our God, for he will abundantly pardon.

Our help is in the name of the Lord, who made heaven and earth.   73.

For God so loved the world that he gave his only Son, that whoever believes in him should not perish but have eternal life.

74. Where two or three are gathered in my name, there am I in the midst of them.

75. The Lord is near to all who call upon him; to all who call upon him in truth. He fulfills the desire of all who fear him; he also hears their cry, and saves them.

76. They who wait for the Lord shall renew their strength, they shall mount up with wings like eagles, they shall run and not be weary, they shall walk and not faint.

77. Behold, I stand at the door and knock; if any one hears my voice and opens the door, I will come in to him and eat with him, and he with me.

78. Ask, and it will be given you; seek, and you will find; knock, and it will be opened to you.

79. The Spirit and the Bride say, "Come." And let him who hears say, "Come." And let him who is thirsty come, let him who desires take the water of life without price.

80. Come to me, all who labor and are heavy-laden, and I will give you rest. Take my yoke upon you, and learn from me; for I am gentle and lowly in heart, and you will find rest for your souls. For my yoke is easy, and my burden is light.

81. Rejoice in the Lord always; again I will say, Rejoice. Have no anxiety about anything, but in everything by prayer and supplication with thanksgiving let your requests be made known to God. And the peace of God, which passes all understanding, will keep your hearts and your minds in Christ Jesus.

We have not a high priest who is unable to sympathize 82.
with our weaknesses, but one who in every respect has
been tempted as we are, yet without sinning. Let us then
with confidence draw near to the throne of grace, that we
may receive mercy and find grace to help in time of need.

Therefore, brethren, since we have confidence to enter 83.
the sanctuary by the blood of Jesus, by the new and living
way which he opened for us through the curtain, that is,
through his flesh, and since we have a great priest over
the house of God, let us draw near with a true heart in
full assurance of faith.

This is the message we have heard from him and proclaim 84.
to you, that God is light and in him is no darkness at all.
If we walk in the light, as he is in the light, we have
fellowship with one another, and the blood of Jesus his
Son cleanses us from all sin.

Grace to you and peace from God our Father and the 85.
Lord Jesus Christ.

PENITENCE

O Lord, open thou my lips, 86.
    and my mouth shall show forth thy praise.
For thou hast no delight in sacrifice;
    were I to give a burnt offering, thou wouldst not be
        pleased.
The sacrifice acceptable to God is a broken spirit;
    a broken and contrite heart, O God, thou wilt not
        despise.

With what shall I come before the Lord, and bow myself 87.
before God on high? He has showed you, O man, what is
good; and what does the Lord require of you but to do

justice, and to love kindness, and to walk humbly with
your God?

88. I will arise and go to my father, and I will say to him,
"Father, I have sinned against heaven and before you; I
am no longer worthy to be called your son."

89. If we say we have no sin, we deceive ourselves, and the
truth is not in us. If we confess our sins, he is faithful and
just, and will forgive our sins and cleanse us from all
unrighteousness.

90. Enter not into judgment with thy servant; for no man
living is righteous before thee. If thou, O Lord, shouldst
mark iniquities, Lord, who could stand? But there is forgiveness with thee, that thou mayest be feared.

91. Come now, let us reason together, says the Lord: though
your sins are like scarlet, they shall be as white as snow;
though they are red like crimson, they shall become like
wool.

92. The Lord is merciful and gracious, slow to anger and
abounding in steadfast love. The Lord is good to all, and
his compassion is over all that he has made.

93. Rend your hearts and not your garments.
Return to the Lord, your God, for he is gracious and
    merciful,
slow to anger, and abounding in steadfast love.

THE LORD'S SUPPER

94. Behold, I stand at the door and knock; if any one hears
my voice and opens the door, I will come in to him and
eat with him, and he with me.

Jesus said, "I am the living bread which came down from heaven; if any one eats of this bread, he will live forever; and the bread which I shall give for the life of the world is my flesh." 95.

The cup of blessing which we bless, is it not a participation in the blood of Christ? The bread which we break, is it not a participation in the body of Christ? Because there is one loaf, we who are many are one body, for we all partake of the same loaf. 96.

Beloved, let us love one another; for love is of God, and he who loves is born of God and knows God. In this the love of God was made manifest among us, that God sent his only Son into the world, so that we might live through him. 97.

Behold, how good and pleasant it is 98.
　　when brothers dwell in unity!
It is like the precious oil upon the head,
　　running down upon the beard,
upon the beard of Aaron,
　　running down on the collar of his robes!
It is like the dew of Hermon,
　　which falls on the mountains of Zion!
For there the Lord has commanded the blessing,
　　life for evermore.

What shall I render to the Lord for all his bounty to me? 99.
I will lift up the cup of salvation and call on the name of the Lord, I will pay my vows to the Lord in the presence of all his people.

O Lord, I am thy servant; thou hast loosed my bonds. I 100.
will offer to thee the sacrifice of thanksgiving and call on

the name of the Lord. I will pay my vows to the Lord in the presence of all his people.

101. Jesus said: "I am the bread of life; he who comes to me shall not hunger, and he who believes in me shall never thirst."

102. As Moses lifted up the serpent in the wilderness, so must the Son of man be lifted up, that whoever believes in him may have eternal life.

103. When he was at table with them, he took the bread and blessed, and broke it, and gave it to them. And their eyes were opened and they recognized him. Then they told how he was known to them in the breaking of the bread.

104. There is one God, and there is one mediator between God and men, the man Christ Jesus, who gave himself as a ransom for all.

105. The saying is sure and worthy of full acceptance, that Christ Jesus came into the world to save sinners.

106. God so loved the world, that he gave his only son:
     That whoever believes in him should not perish, but have eternal life.

107. God shows his love for us in that while we were yet sinners Christ died for us.
     Thanks be to God for his inexpressible gift.

108. Christ, our paschal lamb, has been sacrificed.
     Let us, therefore, celebrate the festival.
     Not with the old leaven, the leaven of malice and evil:
     But with the unleavened bread of sincerity and truth.

Thomas said to him, "Lord, we do not know where you 109.
are going; how can we know the way?"
> Jesus said to him, "I am the way, and the truth, and the
> life; no one comes to the Father, but by me."

Blessed are those who hunger and thirst for righteousness: 110.
> **For they shall be satisfied.**

O taste and see that the Lord is good! 111.
> **Happy is the man who takes refuge in him!**

VERSICLES

The Lord be with you. 112.
> **And with thy spirit.**

Let us pray.

O Lord, show thy mercy upon us.
> **And grant us thy salvation.**

O God, make clean our hearts within us.
> **And take not thy Holy Spirit from us.**

Lift up your hearts. 113.
> **We lift them up unto the Lord.**

O Lord, open thou our lips.
> **And our mouths shall show forth thy praise.**

Praise ye the Lord.
> **The Lord's name be praised.**

The Lord is nigh unto all them that call upon him, to all 114.
that call upon him in truth. He will fulfill the desire of
them that fear him; he also will hear their cry and will
save them.

The glory of the Lord Jesus Christ be with you.
> **And with thy spirit.**

115. Christ to thee our gifts we offer,
     Thine our praises ever be;
     Thine be glory and dominion,
     And eternal victory.

116. I was glad when they said unto me,
     let us go to the house of the Lord.
     The Lord is in his holy temple.
     Let all the earth keep silence before him.
     Surely the Lord is in this place;
     This is none other but the house of God.
     And this is the gate of heaven.

117. O magnify the Lord with me,
     And let us exalt his name together;
     For great is the Lord,
     And greatly to be praised.

118. From whence does my help come?
     My help comes from the Lord, who made heaven and
     earth.

119. O give thanks unto the Lord, for he is good:
     For his mercy endureth forever.
     O that men would praise the Lord for his goodness,
     And for his wonderful works to the children of men!

120. O sing unto the Lord a new song;
     Sing unto the Lord all the earth.
     Sing unto the Lord, bless his name;
     Show forth his salvation from day to day.
     For great is the Lord,
     And greatly to be praised.

O praise the Lord, all ye nations; 121.
  Laud him, all ye peoples.
For his loving-kindness is great toward us; and the truth
  of the Lord endures forever.
  Praise ye the Lord.

Praise ye the Lord, to whom all praise is due. 122.
  **Praised be the Lord to whom all praise is due forever
  and ever.**

Hear, O Israel: The Lord our God is one Lord. 123.
  **Praised be the Lord whose glorious name is forever and
  ever.**

Unto thee, O Lord, do I lift up my soul. 124.
  O my God, in thee have I trusted; let me not be ashamed.

O Lord, deal not with us according to our sin. 125.
  Neither reward us according to our iniquities.

O Lord, let thy mercy be shown upon us; 126.
  As we put our trust in thee.

Lord, have mercy upon us. 127.
  Christ, have mercy upon us.

Create in me a clean heart, O God; 128.
  Renew a right spirit within me.
Cast me not away from thy presence;
  And take not thy Holy Spirit from me.
Restore unto me the joy of thy salvation;
  And uphold me with thy free spirit.

PRAYERS OF ADORATION

129. Our Father, we are thy servants whom thou hast preserved and who live by thy power this day. We bless and glorify thee for thy providence, and humbly pray thee that this and all our days may be filled with praise to thee and devoted to thy service. **Amen.**

130. Great art thou, O Lord, and greatly to be praised. Great is thy power, and thy wisdom is infinite. Thee would we praise without ceasing. Thou callest us to delight in thy praise, for thou hast made us for thyself, and our hearts find no rest until they rest in thee. **Amen.**

131. Blessed be the God and Father of our Lord Jesus Christ! By his great mercy we have been born anew to a living hope through the resurrection of Jesus Christ from the dead, and to an inheritance which is imperishable, undefiled, and unfading. To him be glory this day and for-ever more. **Amen.**

132. We bless thee, O God. We adore thy power and magnify thy goodness. Our tongues sing of thy righteousness and tell of thy salvation from day to day. We give thanks to thee forever and ever. Praise be to thee, O God. **Amen.**

133. Glory be to thee, O Father Eternal, who didst send thy only Son into the world, that we might live through him. Glory be to thee, O Lord Jesus Christ, who hast brought life and immortality to light through the gospel. Glory be to thee, O Holy Spirit of God, who dost quicken us together with Christ and dost shed abroad his love in our hearts. Blessed be thou, Father, Son, and Holy Spirit, one God; and blessed be thy glorious name forever. **Amen.**

O God, eternal, and unchangeable, the same yesterday, 134. and forever: thou art glorious in holiness, full of love and compassion, abundant in grace and truth. All thy works praise thee in all places of thy dominion; and thy Son hath glorified thee upon earth. We adore thee, Father! **Amen.**

Worthy art thou, our Lord and God, to receive glory 135. and honor and power; for thou didst create all things, and by thy will they existed and were created. Great and wonderful are thy deeds, O Lord God the Almighty! Just and true are thy ways, O King of the ages! Who shall not stand in awe and glorify thy name, O Lord? For thou alone art holy. To thee be blessing and honor and glory and might for ever and ever. **Amen.**

O thou who art holy, the creator of all life and being; 136. the fount of all goodness and beauty; the source of truth and love: hallowed be thy name. For thine is the kingdom and the power and the glory, for ever and ever. **Amen.**

O God: Father, Son, and Holy Spirit, we join with thy 137. whole creation in giving thee praise. Holy, holy, holy, there is none beside thee. Thou art in all, beneath all, and beyond all. Thou wast, art, and evermore shalt be. Praise be to thee, O God. **Amen.**

Glory be to thee, O Father Almighty, who hast given 138. us thine only begotten Son, that we might live through him. Glory be to thee, O Lord Jesus Christ, who became man that we might become the sons of God. Glory be to thee, O Holy Spirit, who dost direct and rule our hearts. All glory be to thee, Father, Son, and Holy Spirit, one God, world without end. **Amen.**

139. How great thou art, O God! How small we are! Yet we would by thy mercy use our small thoughts and little words to praise thee. Magnify them that they may worthily glorify thy name and praise thy steadfast love toward the children of men. **Amen.**

140. Accept, O Lord, our gratitude for all the benefits thou hast given us, for the good things of this life and the hope of eternal joy. To thy holy name be ascribed honor and glory.

> **O let the sense of all thy blessings have this effect upon us: to make us daily more diligent in giving ourselves, all that we are, and all we have to thy glory. Amen.**

141. Worthy of praise from every mouth, of confession from every tongue, of worship from every creature, is thy glorious name, O Father, Son, and Holy Spirit:

> **who didst create the world in thy grace and by thy compassion didst save the world.**

To thy majesty, O God, ten thousand times ten thousand bow down and adore, singing and praising without ceasing, and saying:

> **Holy, holy, holy, Lord God of hosts; heaven and earth are full of thy praises; hosanna in the highest. Amen.**

142. Almighty God, most blessed and most holy, before the brightness of whose presence the angels veil their faces; with lowly reverence and adoring love we acknowledge thine infinite glory, and worship thee, Father, Son, and Holy Spirit.

> **Blessing and honor and glory and power be unto our God, for ever and ever. Amen.**

Worthy art thou, our Lord and God, to receive glory and 143.
honor and power,

> for thou didst create all things, and by thy will they
> existed and were created.

Great and wonderful are thy deeds, O Lord God the
Almighty!

> Just and true are thy ways, O King of the ages!

Who shall not read and glorify thy name, O Lord?
For thou alone art holy.

> To him who sits upon the throne and to the Lamb be
> blessing and honor and glory and might for ever and
> ever.   Amen.

Let the heavens praise thy wonder, O Lord, and let us 144.
sing to thy faithfulness in the assembly of the faithful.

> For who in the skies can be compared to thee, O Lord?
> Who among heavenly beings is like unto our God?

Blessed are the people who know the festal shout,
Who walk, O Lord, in the light of thy countenance.

> We exalt thy name all the day, and extol thy righteous-
> ness forever. Amen.

Thy steadfast love, O Lord, extends to the heavens, thy 145.
faithfulness to the clouds.

> Thy righteousness is like the mountains of God, thy
> judgments are like the great deep; man and beast thou
> savest, O Lord.

How precious is thy steadfast love, O God! The children
of men take refuge in the shadow of thy wings.

> They feast on the abundance of thy house, and thou
> givest them drink from the river of delights. For with
> thee is the fountain of life; in thy light do we see light.
> Praise be to thee, O Lord!   Amen.

146. Praise the Lord, all nations!

Extol him, all peoples!

For great is his steadfast love toward us; and the faithfulness of the Lord endures forever.

Praise the Lord! Amen.

PRAYERS OF INVOCATION

147. Almighty God, before whom all hearts be open, all desires known, and from whom no secrets are hid: cleanse the thoughts of our hearts by the inspiration of thy Holy Spirit, that we may perfectly love thee, and worthily magnify thy holy name; through Jesus Christ our Lord. **Amen.**

148. Deliver us, O Almighty God, when we draw nigh to thee, from coldness of heart and wanderings of mind; that with steadfast thought and kindled desire we may worship thee in spirit and in truth; through Jesus Christ our Lord. **Amen.**

149. We bring unto thee, O God, in ourselves the world of which we are a part. We confess that in the world we have lost thy way. Now we have come into thy house to find our way back to the road. Lead us into the paths of righteousness and into the ways of truth, and may we come to know him who is the way, the truth, and the life. **Amen.**

150. O thou who dost for ever stand outside the fast-closed doors of our hearts waiting to enter in, help us to throw aside the bolts. Come into our hearts that we may know thee and, having known thee, offer our praise and thanksgiving unto thee. **Amen.**

O God who art from eternity unto eternity, and art not 151.
at one time in one place because all times and all places
are in thee, we stand before thee weak and mortal amidst
the immensities of space. But blessed be thou, O Lord
God, that thou hast made us in thine own image and hast
breathed into us thine own life. Within this corruptible
thou hast planted incorruption and within this mortal immortality. So from our small space we dare lift our hearts
beyond all time and space to thee, the uncreated one, to
give thee praise and to beseech thee that the light of thy
countenance may shine upon the whole of our lives.
Amen.

O thou in whom we live and move and have our being, 152.
thou who hast made us so that our spirits are restless
until they find their rest in thee, help us to search within
until we find that beginning point where thou art. Help
us there to build an altar upon which we may offer praise
to thee. In our offering of praise cause us to find ourselves
so fully in thee that we know thee, whom to know is life
eternal. **Amen.**

O Lord, open thou our lips, 153.
> **that our mouths shall show forth thy praise.**

O Lord, open thou our minds,
> **that our thoughts shall be formed by thee.**

O Lord, open thou our hearts,
> **that we may receive the fullness of thy grace,**

And be pleased to grant that in this hour of worship we
may find our wholeness
> **by becoming whole in thee. Amen.**

Eternal Father, in this quiet hour we seek thee. From 154.
the fret and fever of the world's business, from the day's
discordant noises, from the praise and blame of men,

from the confused thoughts and vain imaginations of our hearts, we now turn aside to search out the quietness of thy presence.

Cause there to fall upon us now, our Father, a great sense of thy glory and power.

All week long we have toiled and striven; but now in stillness we would ponder the greatness of thy eternity.

Cause there to fall upon us now, our Father, a great sense of thy glory and power. Amen.

PRAYERS OF CONFESSION

155.   A GENERAL CONFESSION

Almighty and most merciful Father; we have erred, and strayed from thy ways like lost sheep. We have followed too much the devices and desires of our own hearts. We have offended against thy holy laws. We have left undone those things which we ought to have done; and we have done those things which we ought not to have done; and there is no health in us. But thou, O Lord, have mercy upon us, miserable offenders. Spare thou, those, O God, who confess their faults. Restore thou those who are penitent; according to thy promises declared unto mankind in Christ Jesus our Lord. And grant, O most merciful Father, for his sake, that we may hereafter live a godly, righteous, and sober life, to the glory of thy holy name. **Amen.**

156. Our heavenly Father, who by thy love hast made us, and through thy love hast kept us, and in thy love wouldst make us perfect, we humbly confess that we have not loved thee with all our heart and soul and mind and strength, and that we have not loved one another as Christ hath loved us. Thy life is within us, but our selfish-

ness hath hindered thee. We have resisted thy Spirit and gone our own ways. Forgive what we have been; help us to amend what we are; and in thy Spirit direct what we shall be; that thy image may come into full glory in us and in all men, through Jesus Christ our Lord. **Amen.**

Lord, we believe in thee; help thou our unbelief. Lord, 157. we love thee; yet not with perfect hearts. Lord, we long for thee; yet not with our full strength. Lord, we trust in thee; yet not with our whole selves. O Lord, our Christ, may we have thy mind and thy spirit. Make us contrite that we might be renewed from our sinful selves into new men and new women, according to thy will and for the sake of thy glory. **Amen.**

Almighty God, thou knowest that we have not lived the 158. life of which we are capable. Thou knowest that we have gifts which we have not used or that we have misused. Thou knowest that we have not loved thee above all lesser concerns, and that we have utterly failed to love our neighbor as ourselves. Thou knowest, O Lord, that we are not even able to love ourselves. Have mercy and forgive us, Lord, for Christ's sake. **Amen.**

Have mercy upon us, O God, according to thy loving- 159. kindness; according to the multitude of thy tender mercies blot out our transgressions. Wash us thoroughly from our iniquities, and cleanse us from our sin. For we acknowledge our transgressions, and our sin is ever before us. Create in us clean hearts, O God, and renew a right spirit within us. Cast us not away from thy presence; and take not thy Holy Spirit from us. **Amen.**

O Lord Jesus Christ, who didst give thy life for us that 160.

we might receive pardon and peace, mercifully cleanse us from all sin, and evermore keep us in thy favor and love, who livest and reignest with the Father and the Holy Spirit, ever one God, world without end. **Amen.**

161. We confess to God Almighty, the Father, the Son, and the Holy Spirit, and before the whole company of the faithful, that we have sinned exceedingly in thought, word and deed, through our fault, our own fault, our own most grievous fault. Wherefore we pray God to have mercy upon us.

Almighty God, have mercy upon us, forgiving us our sins and delivering us from evil, confirming and strengthening us in all goodness, and bringing us to everlasting life. **Amen.**

162. Our Father, we do not want to come to thee to confess our rebellion against thee. In shame we try to hide our wild spirits. Yet we are compelled to prostrate ourselves before thee, for there is nothing within us that can bring us peace. Have mercy upon us, O Lord, that by thy grace the warfare that we know so well may cease and we may worthily honor thy name and render unto thee an acceptable offering of our lives; through Jesus Christ, our Lord. **Amen.**

163. O thou Author of creation and Father of mankind, we acknowledge and confess that our hearts are unworthy to receive thee, for we have offended thee in word and thought and deed. We have made frail excuses when called to responsible decision. We have withheld ourselves from right duty by refusing to obey thy command to love. We have hidden our faces from thy truth which is light and consoled ourselves in darkness. But we pray thee, our Father, to deem us worthy to be restored to thyself. Save

us from our sin, blot out our guilt, and remold us into a new creation devoted to thy will and worthy of thy name; through Jesus Christ our Lord. **Amen.**

Our Father, we know that you would not love us for long, except that your love is unchanging. We trust that you will look upon us with a sense of humor, for even when we are trying to confess our sin, we put into words the petty while leaving the gross unspoken. Help us to overcome our clowning and get down to that which is real. Take from us the burden of that which does not matter. Free us from the bewildering array of problems of our own making. Help us to wake up to the fact that in Jesus Christ our sin is forgiven and if we but take up his way of love we are free. **Amen.** 164.

Eternal God, in whom we live and move and have our being, whose face is hidden from us by our sins, and whose mercy we forget in the blindness of our hearts; cleanse us, we beseech thee, from all our offenses, and deliver us from proud thoughts and vain desires, that with lowliness and meekness we may draw near to thee, confessing our faults, confiding in thy grace, and finding in thee our refuge and our strength; through Jesus Christ thy Son. **Amen.** 165.

Help us, our Father, to forgive men their wrongs against us, that in so doing we may ready ourselves to receive thy forgiveness. **Amen.** 166.

Forgive us, O God, for the protective shells which we build around ourselves to shield ourselves from our brothers' needs; through Jesus Christ, who was open to all men. **Amen.** 167.

Grant us forgiveness, our Father, for our part in those 168.

conditions which cause nations to war against one another. Remove from us the blindness which causes us to seek through war to preserve our liberties and yet in so doing destroy the freedom of others. **Amen.**

169. Forgive us, O God, when we fail to pray for our enemies, even as our Lord Jesus Christ prayed for his enemies on the cross. **Amen.**

170. We shudder in horror when we hear of the death of millions of Jews in the gas chambers of the Nazis; yet we are so ready to drop our napalm and anti-personnel bombs upon the villages and towns of our enemies. Can we be forgiven, O God? **Amen.**

171. Forgive us for our part in the brokenness of thy Church. Be merciful to us for our failure to take every opportunity to reach our hands out to our fellow Christians and in so doing make increasingly visible the oneness which we have in Christ. **Amen.**

172. Almighty God, Spirit of purity and grace, whose dwelling is with the humble and contrite heart, hear thy children's confession of sin and grant us thy mercy. For all that has been evil in our lives, for unholy thoughts and impure motives, for any scorn of goodness, trifling with truth, and indifference to beauty, for all our wanderings from the better way;

Forgive us, O Lord.

For lack of love toward thee whose love has never failed, for doubt of thy goodness and unbelief in thy providence, for ingratitude for blessings received and unwillingness to give of that which thou hast given, for any dullness of insight which has kept us unaware of thy glory, and for any disobedience unto such heavenly visions as we have been able to see;

Forgive us, O Lord, and may we henceforth love thee as we ought.

For all the wrong we have done our fellowmen: for unkind words and untruthful speech, for loss of temper and irritating conduct, for neglect of charity and failure in justice, for arrogant pride and contempt of the lowly, forgetfulness of others' pain and advantage taken of others' weakness; for whatever any person may rightfully hold against us;

Forgive us, O Lord, and help us to love our neighbor as ourselves.

For our faulty following of the Master, our slow faith in his power to save, our timid, hesitant answers to his call for service, our insensibility to the meaning of his cross; for all that mars our discipleship and makes it difficult for others to believe in him;

Forgive us, O Lord, and give us grace to follow the Master more steadfastly.

Help thy people, our Father, to be truly penitent, empower us to overcome all our temptations, enable us faithfully to live according to thy will, and create within us a growing likeness to Jesus Christ our Lord. **Amen.**

Out of the depths we cry to thee, O Lord! 173.

Lord, hear our voice! Let thy ears be attentive to our confessions and supplications!

(silent confession)

If thou, O Lord, shouldst mark iniquities who could stand? But there is forgiveness with thee, that thou mayest be feared.

We wait for the Lord, our souls wait, and in his word we hope.

O people, hope in the Lord! For with the Lord there is steadfast love, and with him is plenteous redemption. And he will redeem us from all our iniquities.

(silent prayer for forgiveness)

We pray in the name of Jesus Christ our Lord, who came into the world to save sinners. **Amen.**

174. Almighty God, Father of our Lord and Savior, hear now our common voice as we confess together our individual and our corporate sins.

Hear our prayer, merciful Father.

For all our failures to be obedient disciples,

Lord, have mercy upon us.

For the lustful thoughts of our minds, the selfish schemes of our hearts, the corrupt intents of our deeds, and the partial sincerity of our lives,

Lord, have mercy upon us.

For the walls we have consciously and unconsciously built between ourselves and thee,

Lord, have mercy and reconcile us to thee.

For the walls we have consciously and unconsciously built between ourselves and other people,

Lord, have mercy and reconcile us to them.

For all pride and self-centeredness, for all egocentricity, and for all selfish rationalizations,

Please, Lord, forgive us.

For all evils of the society to which we belong as responsible members, and for all times when we have ignored these evils, and for every instance when we have been afraid to speak the truth against evil,

Please, Lord, forgive us.

For all false gods which we have created, for all interests and objects which we have put above thee and thy will,

Lord, deliver us.

For every temptation to love our human ways more than we love thy truth and thy will,

Lord, deliver us.

Hear this prayer, our Father,

Help, save, pity, and defend us, O Lord.   Amen.

Have mercy on us, O God, according to thy steadfast love;   175.

According to thy abundant mercy blot out our transgressions.

Wash us thoroughly from our iniquity,

And cleanse us from our sin.

For we know our transgressions,

And our sin is ever before us.

Against thee only have we sinned,

And done that which is evil in thy sight.

So that thou art justified in thy sentence,

And blameless in thy judgment.

Create in us clean hearts, O God,

And put a new and right spirit within us.

Cast us not away from thy presence,

And take not thy Holy Spirit from us.

Restore to us the joy of thy salvation,

And uphold us with thy willing Spirit.   Amen.

I will arise and go to my Father, and I will say to him,   176.
"Father, I have sinned against heaven and before you; I am no longer worthy to be called your son." Let us seek

God's forgiveness through the confession of our sins. Let us pray:

> **Most merciful Father, we bow before thee and confess our sins. Like foolish children we have rebelled against thee and our true home; we have wandered into far countries seeking the gratification of our own desires; we have wasted thy good gifts in self-centered living; we have sought peace amidst the pigsties of alien places. This our rebellion we confess before thee. Lord, have mercy upon us and cause us to know with joy that our sins have been removed from us and that we have come once again to our true home. Amen.**

177. O thou whose tender mercies are over all thy works, humbly and sorrowfully we pray for thy forgiveness.

For every weakening and defiling thought to which our minds have given harbor,
> **Forgive us, Lord.**

For every word spoken hastily or in dark passion,
> **Forgive us, Lord.**

For every failure in self-control,
> **Forgive us, Lord.**

For every stumbling-block which by deed or example we have set in another's way,
> **Forgive us, Lord.**

For every lost opportunity to do good,
> **Forgive us, Lord.**

For loitering feet and procrastinating will,
> **Forgive us, Lord.**

Grant that as the days go by, thy Spirit may more and

more rule in our hearts, giving us victory over these and all other sinful ways. **Amen.**

We cannot truly praise God unless we come to him in humble confession. Let us therefore together confess our weaknesses and shortcomings before him. Let us pray: 178.

O Lord, we recognize that we have been created by thee, but we have fallen away from the good intent of thy creation.

> **Restore again thy image within us that we may know what it means to be thy children.**

We confess that we have not been obedient disciples.

> **Cause us to hear again thy call and follow thee.**

We acknowledge that we have loved ourselves too much and our brother too little.

> **Help us to hear and live thy commandment that we should love thee with heart, mind, and soul, and our neighbor as ourselves.**

All:

> **Forgive us, O Lord, and help us to find our peace in thee; through Christ our Lord.   Amen.**

WORDS OF ASSURANCE

The Lord is merciful and gracious. For as the heavens are high above the earth, so great is his steadfast love toward those who fear him; as far as the east is from the west, so far does he remove our transgressions from us. 179.

The sacrifice acceptable to God is a broken spirit; a broken and a contrite heart, O God, thou wilt not despise. 180.

The Lord redeems the life of his servants; none of those who take refuge in him will be condemned. 181.

182. The Lord is near to the broken-hearted, and saves the crushed in spirit.

183. How precious is thy steadfast love, O God! The children of men take refuge in the shadow of thy wings. They feast on the abundance of thy house, and thou givest them the river of thy delights. For with thee is the fountain of life; in thy light do we see light.

184. Hear also these words of Scripture: The Lord is gracious, merciful, and slow to anger, and abounding in steadfast love.

185. Hear what comfortable words our Savior Christ says to all that truly turn to him: Come to me, all who labor and are heavy-laden, and I will give you rest.

186. If we confess our sins, he is faithful and just, and will forgive our sins and cleanse us from all unrighteousness.

187. There is therefore now no condemnation for those who are in Christ Jesus, who walk not according to the flesh, but according to the Spirit.

188. The saying is sure and worthy of full acceptance, that Christ Jesus came into the world to save sinners.

189. Ask, and it will be given you; seek, and you will find; knock, and it will be opened to you. For every one who asks receives, and he who seeks finds, and to him who knocks it will be opened.

190. This is the message we have heard from him and proclaim to you, that God is light and in him is no darkness at all. If we walk in the light, as he is in the light, we

have fellowship with one another, and the blood of Jesus his Son cleanses us from all sin.

God will supply every need of yours according to his riches in glory in Christ Jesus. 191.

May our Lord Jesus Christ himself, and God our Father, who loved us and gave us eternal comfort and good hope through grace, comfort your hearts and establish them in every good work and word. 192.

God shows his love for us in that while we were yet sinners Christ died for us. God so loved the world that he gave his only Son, that whoever believes in him should not perish but have eternal life. There is therefore now no condemnation for those who are in Christ Jesus. 193.

If any man sin, we have an advocate with the Father, Jesus Christ the righteous. And he is the expiation for our sins, and not for ours only but also for the sins of the whole world. The grace of our Lord Jesus Christ be with us all. 194.

Hear the words of Scripture: If you forgive men their trespasses, your heavenly Father also will forgive you. 195.

PRAYERS FOR ILLUMINATION

Our Father, open our eyes that we may behold the unexpected from thy Word. Bring us to an understanding of thy laws and write them upon our hearts. We have chosen the way of thy truth; measure us therefore in this moment by thy Holy Word. Amen. 196.

O Lord, thou who desirest truth in the inner man, may thy Word be so spoken this day that it shall find rootage 197.

within and be brought to fruition in our life with our neighbor. Amen.

198. O Lord, through the words that shall be spoken this day, and through the stirrings of thy Spirit in our thoughts and hearts, remind us of thy power and authority, that we may newly commend ourselves into thy hands. Amen.

199. O thou who fed the multitude upon the hillside, so feed us now with thy word of life that we too may be filled. Amen.

200. O Lord, open wide the window of our spirits and fill us with thy light; open wide the door of our hearts, that we may receive thy presence in the sharing of thy Word. Amen.

201. O God, prepare now our minds and hearts, that through thy Word Christ may dwell within us and ever rule over our thoughts and affections as the Lord and Master of our lives. Amen.

202. Be present, O God, with this thy congregation, and with thy minister; that neither may thy Word be fruitless nor thy worship barren; but that we, laboring together with thee, may, by the gracious aid of thy Spirit, lay hold upon thy righteousness and take courage in thy power. Amen.

203. O God, author of eternal light, send forth thy spirit upon us that our lips may praise thee, our lives may bless thee, and our meditations glorify thee; through Jesus Christ our Lord. Amen.

204. Almighty God, we ask thee to send forth thy truth into

our hearts, and to pour upon us the glory of thy brightness; through Christ our Lord. Amen.

O God of Grace, enable us to hear anew thy word of 205.
truth, and grant that we may so act upon it that we may
become as Christ to our neighbor. Amen.

O Lord our God, open our eyes, that we may behold 206.
wondrous things out of thy law; and let the words of our
mouths and the meditation of our hearts, be acceptable
in thy sight, O Lord, our rock and our redeemer. Amen.

Blessed Lord, who hast given holy Scriptures for our 207.
learning, grant that we may in such wise hear them that
we become inwardly renewed and outwardly thy servants
in the world. Amen.

May thy Word be for us this day a lamp upon the way 208.
and a light upon the path that, having heard, we may go
forth from this place confident that we walk with thee.
Amen.

We confess, Father, that it is often hard for us to keep 209.
our minds fixed upon thy Word. So easily do we wander
into paths of inattention. Make us alert and ready and
willing to hear and, having heard, to understand. Amen.

How hard it is to both speak and hear thy Word, O Lord! 210.
Break down pride and bring humility upon both speaker
and hearer, that clear channels for thy truth may be
found. Amen.

Give us, O God, the grace to listen. May we hear beyond 211.
the many loud words which are spoken thy still small

voice. May its whisperings become for us the thunder of thy presence. Amen.

212. Eternal God, take the halting human words which are about to be spoken and make of them a vessel for thy holy word. Rough hewn though they be, may these words become for us by thy Holy Spirit the words of life. Amen.

213. Fulfill now, O Lord, we beseech thee, thy gracious promise that thy Word shall not return unto thee empty, but shall accomplish that which thou dost purpose and prosper in that for which thou hast sent it; for thy name's sake. Amen.

214. O God, who didst command the light to shine out of darkness, through thy word shine into our hearts, to give the light of the knowledge of thy glory in the face of Jesus Christ. Amen.

215. Spirit of truth, as we turn to thy Word, guide us into all truth. Scatter our darkness and let the light of thy countenance be upon us. In thy wisdom make us wise. Deepen our understanding that we may come to know him who is the way, the truth, and the life, even Christ Jesus, our Lord. Amen.

AFFIRMATIONS OF FAITH*

216.   THE APOSTLES' CREED

I believe in God the Father Almighty, Maker of heaven and earth:

   And in Jesus Christ his only Son our Lord: who was

*The affirmations of faith are not intended to be tests of belief, but expressions of the faith of Christians of many eras and places.

conceived by the Holy Spirit, born of the Virgin Mary: suffered under Pontius Pilate, was crucified, dead, and buried: He descended into hell; the third day he rose again from the dead: He ascended into heaven, and sitteth on the right hand of God the Father Almighty: From thence he shall come to judge the living and the dead.

I believe in the Holy Spirit: the holy catholic Church; the communion of saints: the forgiveness of sins: the resurrection of the body: and the life everlasting. Amen.

THE NICENE CREED 217.

I believe in one God the Father Almighty, Maker of heaven and earth, and of all things visible and invisible:

And in one Lord Jesus Christ, the only-begotten Son of God; begotten of his Father before all worlds, God of God, Light of Light, very God of very God; begotten, not made; being of one substance with the Father; by whom all things were made: Who for us men and for our salvation came down from heaven, and was incarnate by the Holy Spirit of the Virgin Mary, and was made man: and was crucified also for us under Pontius Pilate; He suffered and was buried: and the third day he rose again according to the Scriptures: and ascended into heaven, and sitteth on the right hand of the Father: and he shall come again, with glory, to judge both the living and the dead; whose kingdom shall have no end.

And I believe in the Holy Spirit, the Lord and Giver of Life, who proceedeth from the Father and the Son; who with the Father and Son together is worshiped and glorified; who spake by the prophets: And I believe one catholic and apostolic Church: I acknowledge one baptism for the remission of sins: and I look for the resurrection of the dead: and the life of the world to come. Amen.

218.   A Statement of Faith, United Church of Christ

We believe in God, the Eternal Spirit, Father of our Lord Jesus Christ and our Father, and to his deeds we testify:

He calls the worlds into being, creates man in his own image and sets before him the ways of life and death.

He seeks in holy love to save all people from aimlessness and sin.

He judges men and nations by his righteous will declared through prophets and apostles.

In Jesus Christ, the man of Nazareth, our crucified and risen Lord, he has come to us and shared our common lot, conquering sin and death and reconciling the world to himself.

He bestows upon us his Holy Spirit, creating and renewing the Church of Jesus Christ, binding in covenant faithful people of all ages, tongues, and races.

He calls us into his Church to accept the cost and joy of discipleship, to be his servants in the service of men, to proclaim the gospel to all the world and resist the powers of evil, to share in Christ's baptism and eat at his table, to join him in his passion and victory.

He promises to all who trust him forgiveness of sins and fullness of grace, courage in the struggle for justice and peace, his presence in trial and rejoicing, and eternal life in his kingdom which has no end.

Blessing and honor, glory and power be unto him. Amen.

219.   Scriptural Affirmation

God is spirit, and those who worship him must worship in spirit and truth. God is light and in him is no darkness at all. God is love and every one that loves is begotten of

God and knows God. Love never fails. There is no fear in love, but perfect love casts out fear. So then we are debtors, not to the flesh, to live according to the flesh, but we received the spirit of sonship. Being therefore always of good courage, we walk by faith, not by sight, and we make it our aim to please him. For we know that in everything God works for good with those who love him, who are called according to his purpose. Amen.

SCRIPTURAL AFFIRMATION

220.

Where the Spirit of the Lord is, there is the one true Church, apostolic and universal, whose holy faith let us now reverently and sincerely declare:

Minister and Congregation:

We believe that God is spirit, and those who worship him must worship in spirit and truth.

We believe that God is light, and that if we walk in the light, as he is in the light, we have fellowship with one another.

We believe that God is love, and that everyone who loves is born of God and knows God.

We believe that Jesus Christ is the Son of God, and that God gave us eternal life, and this life is in his Son.

We believe that he is the resurrection and the life, and whoever believes in him, though he die, yet shall he live.

We believe that we are children of God, and that he has given us his Spirit.

We believe that, if we confess our sins, God who is faithful and just, will forgive our sins and cleanse us from all unrighteousness.

We believe that the world passes away and the lust of it but he who does the will of God abides for ever.   Amen.

OFFERTORY SENTENCES

221. You shall give to him freely, and your heart shall not be grudging when you give to him; because for this the Lord your God will bless you in all your work and in all that you undertake.

222. Bring the full tithes into the storehouse, that there may be food in my house.

223. Let your light so shine before men, that they may see your good works and give glory to your Father who is in heaven.

224. For what does it profit a man, to gain the whole world and forfeit his life? For what can a man give in return for his life?

225. Remember the words of the Lord Jesus, how he said, "It it more blessed to give than to receive!"

226. Having gifts that differ according to the grace given to us, let us use them: if service, in our serving; he who contributes, in liberality; he who gives aid, with zeal; he who does acts of mercy, with cheerfulness.

227. On the first day of every week, each of you is to put something aside and store it up, as he may prosper.

228. He who sows sparingly will also reap sparingly, and he who sows bountifully will also reap bountifully. Each one must do as he has made up his mind, not reluctantly or under compulsion, for God loves a cheerful giver.

229. As we have opportunity, let us do good to all men, and especially to those who are of the household of faith.

Do not neglect to do good and to share what you have, for such sacrifices are pleasing to God. 230.

If anyone has the world's goods and sees his brother in need, yet closes his heart against him, how does God's love abide in him? 231.

We are to do good, to be rich in good deeds, liberal and generous, thus laying up for ourselves a good foundation for the future, so that we may take hold of the life which is life indeed. 232.

As you wish that men would do to you, do so to them. 233.

You know the grace of our Lord Jesus Christ, that though he was rich, yet for your sake he became poor, so that by his poverty you might become rich. 234.

Who then will offer willingly, consecrating himself today to the Lord? 235.

Thine, O Lord, is the greatness, and the power, and the glory, and the victory, and the majesty; for all that is in the heavens and in the earth is thine; both riches and honor come from thee, and thou rulest over all. 236.

All things come from thee, and of thy own have we given thee. 237.

The earth is the Lord's and the fulness thereof, the world and those who dwell therein. 238.

Make your vows to the Lord your God, and perform them; let all around him bring gifts to him. 239.

111

240. Ascribe to the Lord the glory due his name; bring an offering, and come into his courts!

241. Everyone to whom much is given, of him will much be required.

242. It is required of stewards that they be found trustworthy.

243. They gave according to their means, and beyond their means, of their own free will; but first they gave themselves to the Lord.

244. Each one must do as he has made up his mind, not reluctantly or under compulsion, for God loves a cheerful giver.

245. Bear one another's burdens, and so fulfill the law of Christ. Let him who is taught the Word share all good things with him who teaches.

246. Honor the Lord with your substance and with the first fruits of all your produce.

247. Every man shall give as he is able, according to the blessing of the Lord your God which he has given you.

248. You shall open wide your hand to your brother, to the needy, and to the poor in the land.

PRAYERS OF DEDICATION

DEDICATION OF SELF

249. Father in heaven, we confess Jesus Christ as Savior of men and the light of the world; together we acknowledge his right to command; we commit ourselves anew to bear

witness to him among men; we offer ourselves to serve all men in love; we accept afresh our calling to make visible our unity in him; we pray for the gift of the Holy Spirit for our task. Through thy holy name, hear us. **Amen.**

250. O Lord, our heavenly Father, we offer and present to thee ourselves, our souls and bodies, to be a reasonable, holy, and living sacrifice to thee. Take us as we are and make us more fit for thy service. Use us for thyself and for the edification of thy church. We are not our own, but thine, bought with a price; therefore claim us as thy right, keep us as thy charge, use us as thou wilt and when thou wilt, to the glory of thy holy name and the good of our fellowship; through Jesus Christ our Lord. **Amen.**

251. O Christ, our only Savior, so dwell within us that we may go forth with the light of hope in our eyes, the fire of inspiration on our lips, thy Word on our tongues, and thy love in our hearts. **Amen.**

252. Heavenly Father, thou who hast given us life, enable us to glorify thee through worthy service. Take first place in our lives, and forbid, we pray thee, that any personal ambition or unworthy purpose should tempt us to become unmindful of the stewardship thou hast committed to our hands. Forbid that we should sit idly by, merely as on-lookers, when there is so much to be done; in Christ's name. **Amen.**

253. O thou who dwellest in every humble heart, and dost consecrate it for thy sanctuary: hallow, we pray thee, our hearts within us, that they may be houses of prayer, the dwelling place of thy Spirit, wherein thou dost reveal thy holy mysteries; through Jesus Christ our Lord. **Amen.**

254. O God, who makest all things work together for good to them that love thee; pour into our hearts the unchanging tenderness of thy love, that those desires which spring from thine inspiration may not be disturbed by any temptation; through Jesus Christ our Lord. **Amen.**

255. O thou who hast taught us that we are most truly free when we lose our wills in thine, help us to gain this liberty by continual surrender to thee; through Jesus Christ our Lord. **Amen.**

256. Accept, O Lord, our gratitude for all the benefits thou hast given us, for the good things of this life and the hope of eternal happiness. To thy holy name be ascribed the honor and glory. Let the sense of all thy blessings have this effect upon us—to make us daily more diligent in devoting ourselves, all we are, and all we have to thy glory. **Amen.**

257. Even before a word is on our lips, O Lord, thou knowest it altogether. Therefore, Lord, we pray that thou wilt get beyond our mouths to remold our hearts that we may know the blessings of the pure in heart; through Jesus Christ the one righteous man, we pray. **Amen.**

258. Open our ears, O God, that we may hear thy voice calling us to be disciples of thy Son Jesus Christ. As we hear his call coming through the voices of the oppressed, the sick, those in prison, those discriminated against because of race, and those caught in the bleak toils of poverty, help us to have courage to answer: Send us. We pray through Jesus Christ. **Amen.**

259. Open our minds, O God, to truth. Help us not to cling so to the past that we are unwilling to be·moved by that

which is new. Make us hospitable to the thoughts of others even when such thoughts call into question our own positions. Help us ever to seek him who is the truth. **Amen.**

Give us hands open to the world, ready to share the benefits which we have so bountifully received from thee. Transform all inclinations to miserliness into a spirit of generosity. Help us to use our worldly goods not for ourselves alone but that through them thy name may be glorified; through Jesus Christ. **Amen.** 260.

Give us grateful hearts, our Father, for all thy mercies, and make us mindful of the needs of others; through Jesus Christ our Lord. **Amen.** 261.

DEDICATION OF GIFTS

O God, our Father, be pleased to accept this offering of our money as the symbol of our love and devotion; and give thy servants grace so to use it that thy name may be honored among men, and the happiness and prosperity of thy Church increased; through Jesus Christ our Lord. **Amen.** 262.

O Lord, we pray that these gifts may be accepted as the symbols of our lives. As we dedicate our gifts, we dedicate our lives for thy service. **Amen.** 263.

Almighty God, our heavenly Father, who hast not spared thine own Son but delivered him up for us all, and who, with him, hast freely given us all things: receive these offerings which we bring and dedicate to thee; and enable us, with all our gifts, so to yield ourselves to thee that with body, soul, and spirit we may truly and freely serve thee, and in thy service find our deepest joy; through Jesus Christ our Lord. **Amen.** 264.

265. Our Father, giver of every good and perfect gift, in gratitude we lay these our gifts before thee. With these offerings we consecrate ourselves to thy service. Use us and that which we have given of our substance for thy work in the world; this we pray in the name of thy one priceless gift, Jesus Christ our Lord. **Amen.**

266. O God, who givest us so much, help us to love thee more than we love thy bounties. Show us how to use all that we have and are, as good stewards in thy Church and in thy kingdom. We ask this in Jesus' name. **Amen.**

267. O God, who needest not be enriched with any gifts that we may bring, yet who lovest a cheerful giver: receive these our offerings, our souls and our bodies, a living sacrifice, holy and acceptable to thee; through Jesus Christ our Lord. **Amen.**

268. Accept, O Lord, these offerings which thy people make unto thee, and grant that the causes to which they are devoted may prosper under thy guidance, to the glory of thy name; through Jesus Christ our Lord. **Amen.**

269. Almighty God our Father, we present our gifts to thee as a symbol of the dedication of our lives to thy service through thy Church; bless their use and our service both within the Church and in the world; through Jesus Christ our Lord. **Amen.**

270. Thou who didst come down from heaven to bring a blessing to the fallen race; thou who didst wander here upon the earth, unappreciated, betrayed, mocked, condemned —but ever giving of thy blessing; thou who in the act of blessing wast parted from thine own as thou didst ascend again into heaven, thou our Savior and Redeemer, bless

us now as we are here assembled for the holy Supper in remembrance of thee. Oh, when at every meal something is wanting if the blessing is lacking, what then is this holy meal of grace without thy blessing? It does not even exist, for it is indeed the Supper of blessing; through him who is the source of all blessing, even Jesus Christ. **Amen.**

Holy Father, Creator, Redeemer, and King, we offer unto thee this bread and this wine, thanking thee for all the food thou hast provided for us out of the earth; and we present unto thee these our gifts, blessing thee for the strength and skill to do our daily work; and together with them we offer and present unto thee ourselves, beseeching thee so to strengthen and sanctify us by thy Holy Spirit that all our meals may be thy sacraments, all our work thy worship, and our bodies a living sacrifice, holy and acceptable unto thee; through Jesus Christ our Lord. **Amen.** 271.

To thy Table, Lord, we bring money, bread, and wine, and with these material signs we bring ourselves. Consecrate the money to thy service in this place and throughout the world. Take the common bread and wine and make of them the means whereby once again we may come to know in ourselves thy Son. Take us and make of us a living sacrifice, holy and acceptable to thee; through Jesus Christ. **Amen.** 272.

PRAYERS OF PETITION

We bow our knees unto thee, Father for whom the whole family in heaven and earth is named, that thou wouldst grant us, according to the richness of thy glory, to be strengthened with might by thy Spirit in the inner man; that Christ may dwell in our hearts by faith; that we, being rooted and grounded in love, may be able to 273.

117

comprehend with all saints what is the breadth and length, and depth, and height; and to know the love of Christ, which passeth knowledge, that we might be filled with all the fullness of God. **Amen.**

274. Almighty Father, who of thy great love to men didst give thy dearly beloved Son to die for us, grant that through his cross our sins may be put away and remembered no more against us; and that, cleansed by his blood and mindful of his sufferings, we may take up our cross daily and follow him in newness of life, until we come to his everlasting kingdom; through the same Son Jesus Christ our Lord. **Amen.**

275. Almighty God, who dost freely pardon all who repent and turn to thee, fulfill in every contrite heart thy promise of redeeming grace. Absolve us from all our sins, and deliver us from the workings of an evil conscience; through the perfect sacrifice of Christ our Lord. **Amen.**

276. O God the Lord, strong to deliver and mighty to save, who hast been the refuge and dwelling place of thy people in all generations: perfect in us, we beseech thee, the work of thy converting grace, and be pleased to confirm in us every good purpose and deed, that having been called into the way of righteousness, we may have power to continue steadfastly in the same until the day of Jesus Christ, to whom, with thee and the Holy Spirit, be all honor and praise, world without end. **Amen.**

277. O Lord Jesus Christ, give us wisdom, we beseech thee, to build our house upon the rock and not upon the sand: that should the floods of doubt, the rains of affliction, and the winds of loneliness beat upon us, we may not fall because we are founded upon thee, the Rock. **Amen.**

..., O Lord, to know that which is worth knowing, 278.
... that which pleaseth thee most, to esteem that
...which to thee is precious. Give us the right judg-
...to discern between that which lasts and the ever-
...ing, and, above all, to seek after the good pleasure
of thy will. **Amen.**

Father in heaven, our intercession is that to them that 279.
labor and are heavy laden thou wouldst give rest for their
souls; and yet this is hardly an intercession, for who might
count himself so sound that he need only pray for others?
We pray on our own accounts that thou wouldst give our
spirits rest. O God, help us to rest our restless selves in
thee. **Amen.**

Our Father, thou who dost love us beyond all our know- 280.
ings, hold not our sins up against us but hold us up
against our sins, so that the thought of thee when it
wakens in our soul should not remind us of what we have
committed but of what thou didst forgive, not of how we
went astray but of how thou didst save us. **Amen.**

Teach us, good Lord, to serve thee as thou deservest; to 281.
give and not count the cost; to fight and not heed the
wounds; to toil and not seek for rest; to labor and ask for
no reward save that of knowing that we do thy will;
through Jesus Christ our Lord. **Amen.**

O thou who dwellest in every humble heart, and dost 282.
consecrate it for thy sanctuary: hallow, we pray thee, our
hearts within us, that they may be houses of prayer, the
dwelling places of thy Spirit wherein thou dost reveal thy
holy mysteries; through Jesus Christ our Lord. **Amen.**

O Lord Jesus Christ, save us from the error of wishing to 283.

119

admire thee instead of being willing to follow to resemble thee. **Amen.**

284. Teach us, O God, not to torture ourselves with our sense of guilt, nor to wear ourselves out through feverish religious activities, but rather teach us to breathe deeply in faith. **Amen.**

285. O thou who hast caused thy Word to be read, thy love to be declared, thy comfort to be promised, and hast made our hearts to desire the peace which thou alone canst give, we ask thee not to lift us out of the world, but to prove thy power within the world; not for tasks more suited to our strength, but for strength more suited to our tasks. Grant us now the vision that moves, the strength that endures, and the grace of our Lord Jesus Christ. **Amen.**

286. Remove from us the sudden anger or secret hate which destroys our brother,

    O Lord we pray thee.

Take from us the contemptuous pride which bruises the self-respect of our brother,

    O Lord we pray thee.

Help us to stand beside our suffering brother and help him bear his burden,

    O Lord we pray thee.

If a brother needs us, make us ready to yield our help ungrudgingly,

    O Lord we pray thee.

Grant that we may look into the face of all men through the eyes of our brother, Jesus Christ.

    Hear us, O God, and grant us thy grace.   Amen.

Lord, be merciful unto us;

Heal our souls, for we have sinned against thee.

O Lord, show thy mercy upon us

And grant us thy salvation.

Turn again, O Lord,

And grant us thy salvation.

Let thy mercy, O Lord, be upon us

As we put our trust in thee.   Amen.

Be pleased, O Lord, to hear our humble supplication, and to keep us in thy way.

From indolence and weakness of purpose, from indifference, carelessness, and insincerity,

O Lord, deliver us.

From despondency and lack of faith, from cowardice and self-conceit,

O Lord, deliver us.

From dishonesty, extravagance, and debt, and all injustice to others,

O Lord, deliver us.

From all temptation to put pleasure above duty, and from all frailty of the flesh,

O Lord, deliver us.

In all times of ignorance or perplexity, in all times of mistake or misunderstanding,

Help us, O Lord.

That we may love thee in our fellow men, and find thee in our work and prayers,

We beseech thee to hear us, O Lord.

O God, the protector of all that trust in thee, without whom nothing is strong, nothing is holy; increase and multiply upon us thy mercy, that, thou being our ruler and guide, we may so pass through things temporal that we finally lose not the things eternal; through Jesus Christ our Lord, to whom with the Father and the Holy Spirit, one God, be honor, glory, dominion, and praise for ever and ever. **Amen.**

PRAYERS OF REMEMBRANCE AND THANKSGIVING

289.
A GENERAL THANKSGIVING

Almighty God, Father of all mercies, we, thine unworthy servants, do give thee most humble and hearty thanks for all thy goodness and loving-kindness to us and to all men. We bless thee for our creation, preservation, and all the blessings of this life; but above all, for thine inestimable love in the redemption of the world by our Lord Jesus Christ, for the means of grace, and for the hope of glory. And, we beseech thee, give to us a due sense of all thy mercies, that our hearts may be unfeignedly thankful; and that we show forth thy praise, not only with our lips but in our lives, by giving up ourselves to thy service and by walking before thee in holiness and righteousness all our days; through Jesus Christ our Lord, to whom, with thee and the Holy Spirit, be all honor and glory, world without end. **Amen.**

290. Almighty and most merciful Father, from whom cometh every good and perfect gift; we give thee praise and hearty thanks for all thy mercies. For thy goodness that hath created us, thy bounty that hath sustained us, thy fatherly discipline that hath chastened and corrected us, thy patience that hath borne with us, and thy love that hath redeemed us, we praise thee, O Lord. For thy Son our Savior, for thy Spirit our Comforter, for thy Church

our home, for the lives of all good and godly men, and for the hope of the life to come, we praise thee, O God. Grant unto us, with all thy gifts, a heart to love and praise thee; and enable us to show our thankfulness for thy benefits by giving up ourselves to thy service, and cheerfully conforming in all things to thy blessed will; through Jesus Christ our Lord. **Amen.**

291. Most merciful Father, from whom come all the blessings of the light, and who in darkness still art near; all praise and thanks be unto thee for all thy dealings with us which manifest thy goodness, and for those also in which thy love is hidden from our eyes. We thank thee for thy holy Word delivered to thy Church, for the faith which it has conveyed to men from one generation to another, and for the mercies by which it has enlarged and comforted our souls. For these and all thy other benefits, we give thee thanks, O Father; through Jesus Christ our Lord. **Amen.**

292. Lift up your hearts:

We lift them up unto the Lord.

Let us give thanks unto the Lord our God:

It is meet and right so to do.

What shall I render unto the Lord for all his benefits toward me? I will offer to thee the sacrifices of thanksgiving.

Thine, O Lord, is the greatness and the power and the victory and the majesty!

For thy perfect wisdom and perfect goodness; for the fullness of thy love revealed to us through Christ Jesus our Savior:

We praise and worship thee, O Lord.

For thy calling and the opportunities in our lives to serve thee in our brothers, for experiences of learning, for the fellowship of this congregation:

We lift our thanks to thee.

For all who preach the gospel, for those who bear witness to Christ in foreign lands, and for all who work toward the restoration of the unity of thy Church:

We now thank thee, O God, and praise thy glorious name through Jesus Christ our Lord. Amen.

293. O give thanks to the Lord, for he is good:

For his steadfast love endures forever.

Let us pray:
For accepting us despite ourselves,
For thy grace that continually renews hope in us and remakes our lives:

We thank thee, our Father.

For thy providence which sustains and supports us,
For thy love that chastises and heals us:

We thank thee, our Father.

For minds that make us restless until we know the truth and for faith that promises triumph over doubt:

We thank thee, our Father.

For the labor of scholars that adds to our understanding and for the inspiration that comes from those of simple trust:

We thank thee, our Father.

For fleeting glimpses of reality, for visions we cannot describe, for depths we can but feel:

We thank thee, our Father. Amen.

O God our Father, merciful and gracious; hear the thanksgivings with which we come before thee, in the name of
Jesus Christ, thy Son.

For the wonder of thy beauty, manifest in the world; for
thy wisdom inspiring the works of men; and for thy
fatherly love shown forth to us in Christ Jesus:

Praise be to thee, O God.

For the happiness of our earthly life; for home and friends;
and for the joy of loving and being loved:

Praise be to thee, O God.

For the power to love thee, for the right to pray to thee,
and for thine answers to our prayers:

Praise be to thee, O God.

For thy love in stooping to our humanity throughout
the ages, revealing the fullness of thy grace and truth; and
for all prophets, saints, benefactors, and lovers of God and
men, who have seen the vision of thy glory:

Praise be to thee, O God.

But, above all, for Jesus Christ thy Son, the Word Incarnate, who came to end the reign of sin and death and
to bring in the reign of righteousness and life:

Praise be to thee, O God. Amen.

Hear, O God, our prayers of thanksgiving:

For the revelation of thyself to us. *(Silent prayer)*

Hear, O God, our prayers of thanksgiving:

**For that which thou hast done for us in thy Son Jesus
Christ.** *(Silent prayer)*

Hear, O God, our prayers of thanksgiving:

For thy daily mercy and grace. *(Silent prayer)*

Hear, O God, our prayers of thanksgiving:

For thy call to discipleship; for the answer we must give.
(Silent prayer)

Accept our praise, O God,

To thy glory, for ever and ever, world without end. Amen.

296. Almighty and eternal God, faced with the uncertainties of life and because of the mysteries which surround our whole existence, we sometimes find it difficult to praise thee. Grant us faith to respond to thy mighty deeds, words, and grace, that we may be able to affirm and bless thee as our Father.

Thou didst call the world into being and summon man into life.

We thank thee that we and the whole created order have our being in thee.

Thou didst give a sure promise to the people thou didst choose, and although they did not remain constant in faithfulness, thou didst remain faithful and sought to bring them back unto thee.

We thank thee that thou didst send thy prophets to show thy people the way, and we would know the ways of thy loving-kindness and faithfulness through them.

Thou didst disclose thyself at the incarnation in the humblest of births, and in the human form of thy Son Jesus Christ thou presented man with the way, the truth, and the life.

We thank thee that we have seen thee in thy Son as he became servant unto the world.

Through his agony on the cross for us, we see perfect obedience, and through his resurrection from the dead, power and life were bestowed by thy Holy Spirit upon the fellowship of the Church.

We praise thee and thank thee, for we have been given thy grace and power; we are a part of thy creation which thou didst call into being; we are a part of mankind which thou didst create; the promises thou didst give thou gavest to us; and it was for us that thy Son lived and died and bestowed the Spirit at his exaltation, that we might be called apart from the world for the world.

All these mighty deeds, our Father, are present before us now at this Table. The elements of thy creation as well as ourselves we present unto thee for thy sanctification. Thou who didst manifest thyself in human form at the incarnation, so now manifest thyself in these elements of bread and wine that we may know thee. May we in love and fellowship with our neighbor find the true meaning of life in the participation at thy Table. For it is in the name of Jesus Christ, present here, that we pray. **Amen.**

297. O Lord Jesus Christ, be present with us now, as thou wast with thy disciples in the upper room. Do thou, who art the giver of this feast and the feast itself, preside at thine own Table; and give us of thyself, who art the bread of life, that we may be nourished unto life eternal.
We lift up our hearts and give thanks for thy providence and the riches of thy grace; above all, for the unspeakable gift of salvation in Jesus Christ thy Son.

Not as we ought, but as we are able, we bless thee for his holy incarnation, for his perfect life and ministry on earth, for his agony and death on the cross, and for his glorious resurrection and reign at thy right hand. Holy, holy Lord God of hosts, heaven and earth are full of thy glory. Glory be to thee, O Lord most high.

Bestow unto us now, we beseech thee, thy gracious presence; and so sanctify by thy Word and Spirit these gifts of bread and wine which we now set apart to their sacred use, that we partaking of them may receive by faith and participate in the body and blood of Jesus Christ, crucified for us, with all his benefits, to our spiritual nourishment and growth in grace, and to the glory of thy holy name.

Accept, we beseech thee, O Lord, this our sacrifice of praise and thanksgiving, and receive us as we dedicate ourselves anew to thee; through Jesus Christ our Lord. Amen.

298. We give thanks unto thee, O holy Lord, Father Almighty, everlasting God, for the universe which thou hast created, for the heavens and the earth, and for every living thing. We thank thee that thou hast formed us in thine image and made us for thyself. We bless thee that when we rebelled against thee, thou didst reveal thy righteous will and steadfast love by the law and the prophets.

Above all, we thank thee for the gift of thy Son, the Redeemer of all men, who was born of Mary, lived on earth in obedience to thee, died on the cross for our sins, and rose from the dead in victory; who rules over us as Lord of all, prays for us continually, and will return again in triumph.

We thank thee for thy Holy Spirit and thy holy Church, for the means of grace and the promise of eternal life. With patriarchs and prophets, apostles and martyrs, with thy Church on earth and with all the company of heaven, we magnify and praise thee, we worship and adore thee, O Lord Most Holy:

Holy, holy, holy, Lord God of hosts; heaven and earth are full of thy glory; glory be to thee, O Lord most high. Blessed be he who comes in the name of the Lord. Hosanna in the highest.

Here we offer ourselves in obedience to thee, through

128

the perfect offering of thy Son Jesus Christ, giving thee thanks that thou hast called us to be a royal priesthood, a holy nation, thine own people: and to thee, O Father, as to the Son and the Holy Spirit, be ascribed blessing and honor and glory and power forever and ever.

Our Father, who art in heaven . . .

Let us give thanks to the Lord: 299.

Let us remember the skills by which we make our living and the remuneration gained from these *(silence)*.

Almighty God and Father, who in creation hast given us every good skill and ability by which we might labor in our daily life, hear our common prayer of thanks. Though we work in mill, office, school, home, or elsewhere, and though our position be great or minor, and though our earnings be large or small, and even though presently we might be without work and seeking employment, nevertheless, Father, we give thanks for every skill thou hast given us; and we pray thee for guidance in the conduct of our work and for an understanding of the meaning and necessity of our labor; for the sake of Jesus Christ our Lord.

Let us remember with gratitude the relations we enjoy with others *(silence)*.

Almighty God and Father, who hast given us the ability to make and to break the ties of friendship and affection with others, we give thee thanks for those ties which brighten and deepen our lives. Grant, O Lord, that we might have the spirit to make these happy relationships even more stable and to rebuild those indifferent or hostile relationships which divide us from others. May we have the strength to follow thy commandment of love in every part of our lives; for the sake of Jesus Christ our Lord.

Let us remember with gratitude the work of the Church *(silence)*.

Almighty God, who hast called from the world a Church to be a fellowship of those doing thy work and who hast given this Church strength to meet its responsibilities, we give thanks for our membership in thy Church and our participation in thy work in the world. Grant, Lord, that we might be faithful in service, earnest in witness, and true in faith, to thy glory and for the sake of Jesus Christ our Lord.

Let us remember with gratitude the gospel *(silence)*.

Almighty God, who hast come to us in the person of Jesus Christ and who hast revealed to us through his life and teachings the sense and purpose of our own lives, we give thee deepest thanks for our having heard the good news of the gospel. Grant, Lord, that we might continue strong in this faith and might ever be eager to share it with other men and women, for the sake of Jesus Christ our Lord.

Let us give thanks for the celebration of this meal *(silence)*.

Almighty God, who hast given us these elements of bread and wine as a living remembrance of our Savior, we come with thanks to the Table of our Lord. Open our hearts and minds to receive this sacrament, and grant that we might be strengthened by our fellowship in it, to thy glory and for the sake of Jesus Christ our Lord.

Let us pray as Jesus taught us. Our Father . . .

Let us give thanks to the Lord our God *(silence).*

Let us give thanks for our daily work, for the skills and responsibilities we exercise, and for the opportunity to labor together in home, office, school, mill, and elsewhere for the common good.

We give thee thanks, O Lord our God, and pray thy blessing.

Let us give thanks for wives and husbands, for mothers and fathers, for brothers and sisters, for relatives, for friends, for fellow workers and fellow students, for those who serve us in many ways, and for each other; and let us pray for each of them.

We give thee thanks, O Lord our God, and pray thy blessing.

Let us give thanks for the substance of life: for food and drink; for clothing and shelter; for medicine and doctors; and for every other benefit and comfort to our bodies; and let us pray that all men might have these to use in a right and proper way.

We give thee thanks, O Lord our God, and pray thy blessing.

Let us give thanks for peace: in our homes and places of daily work, in our clubs and groups, on our streets and alleys, in our city and nation, and throughout the world; and let us pray that this rare blessing may increase.

We give thee thanks, O Lord our God, and pray thy blessing.

Let us give thanks for the mission of the Church in the world; and let us pray that her witness and service may be made known in every part of life.

We give thee thanks, O Lord our God, and pray thy blessing.

(Here may special thanks be given for various specifics.)
Let us give thanks for this holy meal, for the fellowship of each other at the Table and for the living memory of our Lord; and let us pray that these elements may be used to the glory of God.

We give thee thanks, O Lord our God, and pray thy blessing. Our Father . . .

PRAYERS OF INTERCESSION

301.   A General Intercession

O God, the Creator and Preserver of all mankind, we humbly beseech thee for all sorts and conditions of men that thou wouldst be pleased to make thy ways known unto them, thy saving health unto all nations. More especially we pray for the good estate of the universal Church that it may be so guided and governed by thy good Spirit, that all who profess and call themselves Christians may be led into the way of truth, and hold the faith in unity of spirit, in the bond of peace, and in righteousness of life. Finally, we commend to thy fatherly goodness all those who are in any way afflicted or distressed in mind, body, or estate (especially . . .); that it may please thee to comfort and relieve them, according to their several necessities; giving them patience under their sufferings and a happy issue out of all their afflictions. And this we beg for Jesus Christ's sake. **Amen.**

302.   Almighty Father, who hast given us confidence to come boldly before thee with our petitions and intercessions, we bring thee our needs and the needs of the world. In this time of world tension, when men are being taught to hate and to kill one another, we desperately pray for thy Spirit to bring peace and encourage reconciliation. Guide

all men and agencies committed to international understanding, and inspire leaders of all nations to prepare a way by which all people might walk together; through Jesus Christ our Lord. **Amen.**

Merciful Father, who hast promised us that no power 303. can separate us from thy love in Christ Jesus, be with us now in our miseries and needs. If we mourn, comfort us; if we are sick, heal us; if we despair, encourage us; if we fall, strengthen us; and if we are selfish, rebuke us. Give thy love to those not present amongst us according to their needs (especially those we name now . . .); and give us sensitivity and power to minister in thy name and with thy Spirit to all others in need; through Jesus Christ our Savior. **Amen.**

God of our fathers, we beseech thee to hear our prayer 304. for thy Church. Fill it with truth and peace. Where it is corrupt, purify it; where it is in error, correct it; where it is slow to speak and act, speed it by thy strength; where it is rejected, help it to understand the rejection; where men misjudge it, let it not misjudge them; where it is divided, unite it; and whether it is right or wrong, love it at all times; through Jesus Christ our Lord. **Amen.**

O Lord, who hast made us a royal priesthood that we 305. might offer intercessions for all men; hear us when we pray:

That it may please thee to lead thy Church universal in the right way:

We beseech thee to hear us, gracious Lord.

That it may please thee to illumine all ministers, missionaries, evangelists, and teachers with true knowledge and right understanding of thy Word, that by their preaching

133

and living they may set it forth, and show it accordingly:

We beseech thee to hear us, gracious Lord.

That it may please thee to endue the President of the United States and our legislators with wisdom and understanding, and to give grace to our judges and magistrates to execute justice and to maintain truth:

We beseech thee to hear us, gracious Lord.

That it may please thee to give to all nations unity, peace, and concord.

We beseech thee to hear us, through Jesus Christ our Lord. Amen.

306. Almighty God, who in Jesus Christ hast taught us to pray and promised that anything we ask in his name will be given us, so guide us by thy Holy Spirit that our prayers for others may serve thy will and show thy steadfast love; through the same Jesus Christ our Lord. **Amen.**

Let us pray for the world:

Lord of all the worlds that are, Savior of men, we pray for the whole creation: order the unruly powers; crush every tyranny; rebuke injustice; feed and satisfy the longing peoples, that in freedom all thy children may enjoy this good world which thou hast made and glory in thy salvation; through Jesus Christ our Lord. **Amen.**

Let us pray for the Church:

Most gracious God, who hast set one Table before us and called us into fellowship with thee, we pray that the Church, gathered by thy Word and Spirit, may be a faithful witness to thee in all the world; through Jesus Christ our Lord. **Amen.**

Let us pray for peace:

Eternal God, send peace on earth, and by thy grace put down the pride, greed, and anger that turn man against man, and nation against nation. Speed the day when wars are ended and all men call thee Father; through Jesus Christ our Lord. **Amen.**

Let us pray for enemies:

O thou whom we cannot love unless we love our brother, remove from us and all men both hate and prejudice, that thy children may be reconciled with those whom they fear, resent, or threaten and thereafter may live in peace; through Jesus Christ our Lord. **Amen.**

Let us pray for those in authority:

Almighty God, Lord of the nations, direct all those who govern us; thy servant *(name of the President)*, the President of the United States, and those with authority in every land; that they may be led by thy wisdom and rule with justice and mercy; through Jesus Christ our Lord. **Amen.**

Let us pray for the sick:

Merciful God, who dost bear the pain of the world, look with compassion upon those who are sick (and especially upon . . .), that they may be strengthened by thy presence and ministered to by thy grace; through Jesus Christ our Lord. **Amen.**

Let us pray for the sorrowing:

God of comfort, stand beside those who sorrow (especially . . .), that they may be sure that neither life nor death, nor things present, nor things to come, shall be able to separate them from thy love; through Jesus Christ our Lord. **Amen.**

Let us pray for family and friends:

O God, our Father, bless us and those we love, our friends and families, that, drawing close to thee, we may be drawn closer to each other; through Jesus Christ our Lord. **Amen.**

Almighty God, who hast given us grace at this time with one accord to make our common supplications unto thee, and dost promise that where two or three are gathered together in thy name thou wilt grant their requests; fulfill now, O Lord, the desires and petitions of thy servants, as may be most expedient for them; granting us in this world knowledge of thy truth, and in the world to come life everlasting. **Amen.**

307. Almighty God, who hast taught us to pray in trust and confidence, hear our voice as we collect and bring to thee our needs and our wishes and our hopes for thy world. We ask thee to receive these prayers for ourselves and for others, and to do thy will with them. Give us patience to endure in faith thy silence; and sight and ears to see and hear with joy thy acts and voice, wherever it might please thee so to act and to speak; through Jesus Christ our Lord. **Amen.**

Let us pray for the world, that peace and brotherhood might come to all men *(silence).*

Almighty Father, thou who alone art the Creator and the Ruler of this world and its people, we pray that peace will increase in our time as men everywhere learn to practice their common brotherhood. May it please thee to guide the leaders of every land into policies by which all nations might live together as friends, and may people everywhere seek together to eliminate wars, starvation, illness, and sufferings in every part of the earth; through Jesus Christ our Lord. **Amen.**

Let us pray for our community, that selfish interests might end, that walls between people might be broken, and that we might live together in peace and equality *(silence)*.

Lord of Life, who desirest all men to live in peace with their neighbors and to work together for the common good, grant that in this community the unredeemed powers of selfishness might be destroyed and that men might no longer be devils to each other. May the walls which divide us be broken, and may the bonds which unite us be built stronger, that we might all live together in peace, the rich and the poor, the strong and the weak, the healthy and the sick, the black and the white, the young and the old; through Jesus Christ our Lord. **Amen.**

Let us pray for the Church universal and for this congregation, that as a family of God's chosen people we might overcome all bitterness and bickering among ourselves and might go out to do the will of him who has called us and who has made us one *(silence)*.

Lord of the Church, who hast called us and made us one people, we pray for the power, courage, and insight to perform thy work and witness in thy world. Where we are corrupt, purify us; where we are wrong, guide us; where we are right, strengthen us; where we are in need, provide for us; where we are divided and torn apart, heal our wounds; through Jesus Christ our Lord. **Amen.**

Let us pray for those in need: the sick in mind and body and spirit; the poor; the bereaved; the hopeless; and especially those among them who are known to us *(silence)*.

Father of mercy, whose love is ever with us in our times of need, we pray for those friends and strangers who know misery and sorrow this day. Give them a living sense of thy presence and love, and grant us the compassion and sensitivity to minister to them in thy name; through Jesus Christ our Lord. **Amen.**

Let us pray for one another, that at home, at school, at leisure, and at work we might live as men and women who have been made new in Christ Jesus *(silence)*.

O God, who hast promised to be with us as we strive to live according to our calling in Christ Jesus, now strengthen, encourage, rebuke, and comfort us according to our needs as we seek to live and labor faithfully in thy name; give us grace that we might become the instruments for making real in the world these our prayers; through Jesus Christ our Lord. **Amen.**

308. Our Father, we are so in love with ourselves that we forget that thou hast commanded us to love one another even as thou dost love us. Take our self-love and by thy grace make it love for our neighbor. We pray for him. Help us to stand by his side as Christ's man in the world that, even though he does not know thee, he can in us discern love; through him who loved us and gave himself for us, even Christ our Lord, we pray. **Amen.**

309. O thou who art the Father of all, we pray for the children of the world. We know that thou dost have a special love for these little ones. Deepen our concern for all

children, and if there are those with special needs bring those needs before us that we might be thy instruments to meet them. Help us to feed the hungry, clothe the naked, teach the unlearned, befriend the lonely, give shelter to the homeless, and bring healing to the sick. Through these ministries may these thy little ones come to know and love thee; we pray in the name of Jesus, who loved children and said, "Let them come to me." **Amen.**

ASCRIPTIONS OF GLORY

Now to him who by the power at work within us is able to do far more abundantly than all that we ask or think, to him be glory in the Church and in Christ Jesus to all generations, for ever and ever. **Amen.** 310.

Now to him who is able to keep you from falling and to present you without blemish before the presence of his glory with rejoicing, to the only God, our Savior through Jesus Christ our Lord, be glory, majesty, dominion, and authority, before all time and now and for ever. **Amen.** 311.

Now unto the blessed and only Sovereign, the King of kings, the Lord of lords, who alone has immortality and dwells in unapproachable light, whom no man has ever seen or can see; to him be honor and eternal dominion. **Amen.** 312.

To him who loves us and has freed us from our sins by his blood and made us a kingdom, priests to his God and Father, to him be glory and dominion for ever and ever. **Amen.** 313.

Glory be to the Father, and to the Son, and to the Holy Spirit; as it was in the beginning, is now, and ever shall be, world without end. **Amen.** 314.

315. To the King of ages, immortal, invisible, the only God, be honor and glory for ever and ever. **Amen.**

316. Now to the King eternal, immortal, invisible, the only wise God, be honor and glory, praise and adoration, dominion and power, world without end. **Amen.**

317. To the Father, Son, and Holy Spirit, three persons and one God, be ascribed as is most due, the kingdom, the power, and the glory, for ever and ever, world without end. **Amen.**

318. Now to the God of all grace, who has called us into his eternal glory by Christ Jesus, be glory and dominion and power, for ever and ever. **Amen.**

PRAYERS OF DISMISSAL AND BLESSING

319. The grace of the Lord Jesus Christ, and the love of God, and the fellowship of the Holy Spirit be with you all. **Amen.**

320. Grace to you and peace from God our Father and the Lord Jesus Christ. **Amen.**

321. The Lord bless you and keep you: The Lord make his face to shine upon you, and be gracious to you: The Lord lift up his countenance upon you, and give you peace. **Amen.**

322. Now may the God of peace who brought again from the dead our Lord Jesus, the great shepherd of the sheep, by the blood of the eternal covenant, equip you with everything good that you may do his will, working in you that which is pleasing in his sight, through Jesus Christ; to whom be glory for ever and ever. **Amen.**

The peace of God, which passes all understanding, will 323.
keep your hearts and minds in Christ Jesus; the blessing
of God Almighty, the Father, the Son, and the Holy
Spirit, be amongst you, and remain with you always.
Amen.

Arise, shine; for your light has come, and the glory of 324.
the Lord has risen upon you. The Lord will be your everlasting light, and your God will give you glory. **Amen.**

May the God of steadfastness and encouragement grant 325.
you to live in such harmony with one another, in accord
with Christ Jesus, that together you may with one voice
glorify the God and Father of our Lord Jesus Christ.
Amen.

May the Lord of peace himself give you peace at all times 326.
and always. The Lord be with you all. **Amen.**

May our Lord Jesus Christ himself, and God our Father, 327.
who loved us and gave us eternal comfort and good hope
through grace, comfort your hearts and establish them in
every good work and word. **Amen.**

Finally, brethren, whatever is true, whatever is honorable, 328.
whatever is just, whatever is lovely, whatever is gracious,
if there is any excellence, if there is anything worthy of
praise, think about these things. What you have learned
and received and heard and seen, do; and the God of
peace will be with you. **Amen.**

May thy peace go with us, O God. Grant us the assurance 329.
that nothing shall deprive us of that peace; neither ourselves, nor our foolish, earthly desires, nor wild longings,
nor the anxious cravings of hearts. **Amen.**

330. Go in peace; and the blessing of God Almighty, the Father, the Son, and the Holy Spirit be upon you, and remain with you always. **Amen.**

331. Grace, mercy, and peace from God the Father, Son, and Holy Spirit, be with you henceforth and for ever. **Amen.**

332. Go in peace; publish the gospel; visit the sick; comfort the dispirited; and may the love of God go with us all. **Amen.**

333. Go now in love, as those called to do his work. And may his peace, grace, and mercy abide in you. **Amen.**

334. As we depart, he departs with us to guide, sustain, and grant us the power to carry out his will. **Amen.**

335. Almighty God, who callest us both to worship and to work, our worship now is ended. Grant, we pray, that as we turn again to the tasks that lie before us, our work may not betray our worship, nor our worship loose its reins upon our work; through Jesus Christ our Lord. **Amen.**

336. As we have praised thee with our lips, our Father, so now we would praise thee with our lives. In office or home, in schoolroom or store, in factory or open field—let all our words and deeds be an offering to thee, until we worship thee wholly in our work, and in working magnify thy holy name; through Jesus Christ our Lord. **Amen.**

337. Go forth in peace, but not in complacency; be strong, but not arrogant; have convictions, but be understanding of the beliefs of others; be eager to love, but not meddlesome; proud enough not to scorn yourselves, but suffi-

ciently humble not to be jealous of your neighbors; through Jesus Christ our Lord. **Amen.**

As thou, O Lord, hast blessed our coming in, now bless 338. our going forth; and grant that when we leave thy house we may not leave thy presence, but be thou ever near unto us and keep us near unto thee; through Jesus Christ our Lord. **Amen.**

The Lord our God be with us as he was with our fathers, 339. that he may incline our hearts to walk in all his ways. **Amen.**

THE LORD'S PRAYER

Our Father who art in heaven, 340.
Hallowed be thy name.
Thy kingdom come,
Thy will be done,
   On earth as it is in heaven.
Give us this day our daily bread;
And forgive us our debts,
   As we also have forgiven our debtors;
And lead us not into temptation,
   But deliver us from evil.
*For thine is the kingdom and the power
   And the glory, forever. **Amen.**
     Revised Standard Version

Our Father which art in heaven, 341.
Hallowed be thy name.
Thy kingdom come. Thy will be done
   In earth, as it is in heaven.

*Many ancient authorities omit "For thine is the kingdom and the power and the glory, forever. Amen."

143

Give us this day our daily bread.
And forgive us our debts,
   As we forgive our debtors.
And lead us not into temptation,
   But deliver us from evil:
For thine is the kingdom, and the power,
   And the glory, for ever. **Amen.**
King James Version

342.   Our Father, who art in heaven,
Hallowed be thy Name.
Thy kingdom come.
Thy will be done
   On earth, as it is in heaven.
Give us this day our daily bread.
And forgive us our trespasses,
   As we forgive those who trespass against us.
And lead us not into temptation;
   But deliver us from evil:
For thine is the kingdom, and the power,
   And the glory, for ever and ever. **Amen.**
The Book of Common Prayer

TRADITIONAL USAGES

343.   SANCTUS

Holy, holy, holy, Lord God of hosts,
Heaven and earth are full of thy glory:
Glory be to thee, O Lord most high. **Amen.**

344.   AGNUS DEI

O Lamb of God, that takest away the sins of the world,
   have mercy upon us.
O Lamb of God, that takest away the sins of the world,
   have mercy upon us.

O Lamb of God, that takest away the sins of the world, grant us thy peace.

Sursum Corda 345.

Lift up your hearts.

We lift them up unto the Lord.

Let us give thanks unto the Lord our God.

It is meet and right so to do.

Gloria in Excelsis 346.

Glory be to God on high, and on earth peace, good will towards men.

We praise thee, we bless thee, we worship thee, we glorify thee, we give thanks to thee for thy great glory, O Lord God, heavenly King, God the Father Almighty.

O Lord, the only-begotten Son, Jesus Christ; O Lord God, Lamb of God, Son of the Father, that takest away the sins of the world, have mercy upon us. Thou that takest away the sins of the world, have mercy upon us.

Thou that takest away the sins of the world, receive our prayer. Thou that sittest at the right hand of God the Father, have mercy upon us.

For thou only art holy; thou only art the Lord; thou only, O Christ, with the Holy Spirit, art most high in the glory of God the Father. Amen.

Nunc Dimittis 347.

Lord, now lettest thou thy servant depart in peace, according to thy word. For mine eyes have seen thy salvation, which thou hast prepared before the face of all people; to be a light to lighten the Gentiles and to be the glory of thy people Israel.

Glory be to the Father, and to the Son, and to the Holy

145

Spirit; as it was in the beginning, is now, and ever shall be, world without end.   Amen.

348.   VENITE

O come let us sing unto the Lord; let us heartily rejoice in the strength of our salvation.

Let us come before his presence with thanksgiving; and show ourselves glad in him with psalms. For the Lord is a great God; and a great King above all gods.

In his hand are all the corners of the earth; and the strength of the hills is his also.

The sea is his and he made it; and his hands prepared the dry land.

O come, let us worship and fall down, and kneel before the Lord our Maker.

For he is the Lord our God; and we are the people of his pasture, and the sheep of his hand.

O worship the Lord in the beauty of holiness; let the whole earth stand in awe of him. For he cometh, for he cometh to judge the earth: and with righteousness to judge the world, and the peoples with his truth.

Glory be to the Father and to the Son, and to the Holy Spirit; as it was in the beginning, is now and ever shall be, world without end.   Amen.

349.   JUBILATE DEO

O be joyful in the Lord, all ye lands: serve the Lord with gladness, and come before his presence with a song.

Be ye sure that the Lord he is God; it is he that hath made us, and not we ourselves: we are his people, and the sheep of his pasture.

O go your way into his gates with thanksgiving, and into

his courts with praise: be thankful unto him, and speak good of his name.

For the Lord is gracious, his mercy is everlasting: and his truth endureth from generation to generation. Glory be to the Father, and to the Son, and to the Holy Spirit; as it was in the beginning, is now, and ever shall be, world without end. Amen.

BENEDICTUS

350.

Blessed be the Lord God of Israel; for he hath visited and redeemed his people;

And hath raised up a mighty salvation for us, in the house of his servant David;

As he spake by the mouth of his holy prophets, which have been since the world began;

That we should be saved from our enemies, and from the hand of all that hate us.

To perform the mercy promised to our forefathers, and to remember his holy covenant;

To perform the oath which he sware to our forefather Abraham, that he would give us;

That we being delivered out of the hand of our enemies might serve him without fear;

In holiness and righteousness before him, all the days of our life.

And thou child, shalt be called the prophet of the Highest: for thou shalt go before the face of the Lord to prepare his ways;

To give knowledge of salvation unto his people for the remission of their sins,

Through the tender mercy of our God; whereby the day-spring from on high hath visited us;

To give light to them that sit in darkness, and in the shadow of death, and to guide our feet into the way of peace.

Glory be to the Father and to the Son, and to the Holy Spirit; as it was in the beginning, is now and ever shall be, world without end. Amen.

351.   MAGNIFICAT

My soul doth magnify the Lord, and my spirit hath rejoiced in God my Savior.

For he hath regarded the lowliness of his handmaiden. For behold, from henceforth all generations shall call me blessed.

For he that is mighty hath magnified me; and holy is his Name.

And his mercy is on them that fear him, throughout all generations.

He hath showed strength with his arm; he hath scattered the proud in the imagination of their hearts.

He hath put down the mighty from their seat, and hath exalted the humble and meek.

He hath filled the hungry with good things; and the rich he hath sent empty away.

He remembering his mercy hath holpen his servant Israel; as he promised to our forefathers, Abraham and his seed for ever.

352.   TE DEUM LAUDAMUS

We praise thee, O God; we acknowledge thee to be the Lord.

All the earth doth worship thee, the Father everlasting.

To thee all angels cry aloud;

The heavens and all the powers therein;

To thee cherubim and seraphim continually do cry, "Holy, Holy, Holy, Lord God of Sabaoth!"

Heaven and earth are full of the majesty of thy glory.

The glorious company of the apostles praise thee.

The goodly fellowship of the prophets praise thee.

The noble army of martyrs praise thee.

The holy Church throughout all the world doth acknowledge thee;

The Father of an infinite majesty;

Thine adorable true and only Son;

Also the Holy Spirit: the Comforter.

Thou are the King of Glory, O Christ. Thou art the everlasting Son of the Father.

When thou tookest upon thee to deliver man, thou didst humble thyself to be born of a virgin.

When thou hadst overcome the sharpness of death, thou didst open the Kingdom of Heaven to all believers.

Thou sittest at the right hand of God, in the glory of the Father.

We believe that thou shalt come to be our Judge.

We therefore pray thee: help thy servants, whom thou hast redeemed with thy precious blood.

Make them to be numbered with the saints, in glory everlasting.

O Lord, save thy people and bless thine heritage.

Govern them and lift them up for ever.

Day by day we magnify thee;

And we worship thy name for ever, world without end.

Vouchsafe, O Lord, to keep us this day without sin.

O Lord have mercy upon us, have mercy upon us.

O Lord, let thy mercy be upon us, as our trust is in thee.

O Lord in thee have I trusted; let me never be confounded.

PART 4

SENTENCES AND PRAYERS
FOR THE CHRISTIAN YEAR

The Christian year, beginning with the first Sunday in Advent, celebrates the events of the gospel. Through the seasons of Advent, Christmas, Epiphany, Lent, Passiontide, Easter, Ascension, and Pentecost the story of God's acts in Christ, the coming of the Holy Spirit, and the establishment of the Church are told. In the remainder of the Christian year during the Trinity or Kingdomtide season, the Church looks particularly at God's mission to the world.

A collection of sentences and prayers for these seasons of the Christian year are given. These by no means exhaust the richness of material that can be provided for each season. But when they are combined with the use of the lectionary, they will give to the congregation an orderly presentation of God's acts in the world and a recurring reminder of what he has done to show his love among men.

ADVENT

353. Let the heavens be glad, and let the earth rejoice before the Lord, for he comes to judge the earth. He will judge the world with righteousness, and the peoples with his truth.

354. It is full time now for you to wake from sleep. The night is far gone, the day is at hand. Let us then cast off the works of darkness and put on the armor of light.

355. Hosanna to the Son of David! Blessed be he who comes in the name of the Lord! Hosanna in the highest!

356. A voice cries: "In the wilderness prepare the way of the Lord, make straight in the desert a highway for our God.

   Every valley shall be lifted up, and every mountain and hill be made low; the uneven ground shall become level, and the rough places a plain.

   And the glory of the Lord shall be revealed, and all flesh shall see it together, for the mouth of the Lord has spoken."

357. There shall come forth a shoot from the stump of Jesse, and a branch shall grow out of his roots.

   And the spirit of the Lord shall rest upon him, the spirit of wisdom and understanding, the spirit of counsel and might, the spirit of knowledge and the fear of the Lord.

PRAYERS

358. Blessed be thou, O eternal Lord God:

In whom the heavens rejoice and the earth is glad, for
thou shalt judge the world in righteousness.

Blessed be thou, O Christ our Savior:

Who will come in power and great glory to perfect thy
kingdom, and to bring in thy ransomed with the songs
of everlasting joy.

Blessed be thou, O holy and gracious Spirit:

Who dost quicken our hearts and fill our mouths with
praise.

Glory be to thee, O God, for ever and ever. Amen.

We praise thee for all thy comings among the children
of men, but especially do we praise thee for thy coming
in Jesus Christ our Lord. Help us to live in faithful expec-
tation of his full and final triumph over all the powers
that oppose him and to look with hope to that day when
all the nations will be his kingdom and he will reign as
King of kings and Lord of lords. Amen. **359.**

Almighty God, who comes to men in their deepest
moment of need and who ever comes to him who calls
upon thee, hear our petitions and supplications. Thou
who spoke of old through the prophets, make plain to us
their message that we may come to know it in our day, **360.**

We beseech thee, O Lord.

For thy grace, that we might have open hearts to receive
him whose coming we celebrate in this season,

We beseech thee, O Lord. Amen.

Our heavenly Father, our spirits turn at this season not
only to the coming of thy Son into history in the form of
a babe, but also to thy coming in thy Spirit. We beseech
thee, O Lord, to pour thy Spirit upon all who walk in **361.**

darkness. Grant thy power to the weak; thy love to those who hate; and thy peace to those who know only the ugliness of strife, struggle, and turmoil. If it be thy will, our Father, make us instruments of thy power and love and peace for those who know thee not. Hear thou our prayer, Wonderful Counselor, Mighty God, Everlasting Father, Prince of Peace. **Amen.**

362. O Lord, send us forth into the world in thy name. Bestow upon us thy power, that our weakness may become strength. Grant unto us thy love, that our hatred may be overcome. And pour forth thy peace, that our anxieties may find comfort in thee; through Jesus Christ our Lord. **Amen.**

CHRISTMAS

Sentences

363. Blessed be the Lord God of Israel, for he has visited and redeemed his people.

364. Glory to God in the highest, and on earth peace among men with whom he is pleased.

365. In many and various ways God spoke of old to our fathers by the prophets; but in these last days he has spoken to us by a Son.

366. The Word became flesh and dwelt among us, full of grace and truth.

367. The people who walked in darkness have seen a great light; those who dwelt in a land of deep darkness, on them has light shined.

Behold, a virgin shall conceive and bear a son, and his 368. name shall be called Emmanuel (which means God with us).

Behold, I bring you good news of a great joy which will 369. come to all the people; for to you is born this day in the city of David a Savior, who is Christ the Lord.

PRAYERS

O Father Almighty, thou didst send thy son Jesus Christ 370. into the world to be born of woman that we might have life:

Glory to thee.

O Jesus Christ, thou didst take upon thee the form of a servant, and wast made in the likeness of men:

Glory to thee.

O Holy Spirit, thou didst overshadow Mary, that she might bring forth her first-born son:

Glory to thee.

Grant that our praise may be worthy of thy manifold grace and that by thy Holy Spirit thy Son may be born in our hearts. **Amen.**

Almighty and Eternal God, who didst create light and 371. life, even as we come into thy presence we would hide ourselves from thee in shame. Our thoughts, words, and deeds are dark shadows upon us. Like the men of old, we have strayed from thy ways, losing sight of thy light.

Thou who came as light into our dark world, we have failed in times past to perceive thee; so even now we fail in our perception of thy marvelous gift of light.

Remove from us the shadows that we might stand in

the radiance of him who is the light of the world; even Jesus Christ our Lord. **Amen.**

372. Lift up your hearts:

   We lift them up unto the Lord.

Let us give thanks unto the Lord our God:

   It is meet and right so to do.

We praise thee, our Father, for all the joy of this season. We sing gladly our hymns and carols. We give our gifts to one another in joy. But above all we thank thee for the matchless gift of thy Son, Jesus Christ. We praise thee that thou didst see fit to have him come into the world in the form of a child, to be born as a man among men. We thankfully acknowledge him as Wonderful Counselor, Mighty God, Prince of Peace. Give us words worthy of so great a gift. Give us lives that will in their deeds fully praise thee. Give us love that we may love him who has loved us and who gave himself for us, even Christ our Lord; and to thee be all praise, glory, dominion, and power, now and forevermore. **Amen.**

373. O thou holy Father, who didst present man with the great and glorious gift of thy Son Jesus Christ, we humbly bow and present the meagerness of our gifts and with them our lives. Count not this offering for its worth, but take that which we give and ourselves for thy service; through Jesus Christ our Lord. **Amen.**

374. Almighty and Everlasting God, who didst send thy Son into the world not alone for us but for all mankind, we beseech thee to hear the prayers of thy servants as we lift up our hearts in intercession for the world.

Let us pray for the child who has no welcome room in the world (*silence*).

Let us pray for those in the world who suffer from hunger *(silence)*.

Let us pray for those in the world who suffer from injustice *(silence)*.

Let us pray for those in the world who suffer from ignorance and meaninglessness *(silence)*.

Thou hast heard the prayers of thy people, O Lord. We who are thy servants and the servants of our brothers do humbly beseech thy power and love, so to guide all mankind in such a brotherhood that the homeless may be housed, starvation may be alleviated, justice may be upheld for all, the ignorant may be enlightened by wisdom, and meaning in life may be found for those from whom meaning has departed; through Jesus Christ our Lord. **Amen.**

O thou who didst in humility come to man as a babe, so grow in our hearts that with thy peace and grace we might go forth into the world resolved in our faith to meet the issues of life with courage and humbleness. **Amen.** 375.

EPIPHANY

Sentences

Jesus said: I am the light of the world; he who follows me will not walk in darkness, but will have the light of life. 376.

The star which they had seen in the East went before them, till it came to rest over the place where the child was. And going into the house they saw the child with Mary his mother, and they fell down and worshiped him. 377.

Arise, shine; for your light has come, and the glory of 378.

the Lord has risen upon you. And nations shall come to your light, and kings to the brightness of your rising.

379. O holy Father, we confess that both as individuals and as a Church, we have been too much preoccupied with ourselves and too little concerned for the welfare of others. Thou hast taught us to help to bear the burdens of our brethren in Christ; but often we have failed to support the weak, to help the needy, and to encourage the disheartened. Thou hast commanded us to let our light shine out in the world; but we have failed to bear witness to Christ before men, and to seek them that are lost. For all our disobedience, carelessness, and lovelessness, we implore thy forgiveness. Cleanse us from our sin, and so strengthen and assist us by thy grace that we may henceforth fulfill the law of Christ; for his dear sake. **Amen.**

380. O thou who didst cause thy star to shine on kings in realms afar, ordain, we pray, that all the kingdoms of the world become the kingdom of thy Son. Teach us to speak the word of thy gospel in the strange lands of business and science, of literature and art, of people that have never heard thy name and nations that have judged thee by the enemies they thought to be thy friends. Refute the prejudice that makes us hate our brothers; upset the selfishness that blinds us to the debt we owe thy heavy-burdened children; disturb the complacency that keeps us from thy service; and stabbing us awake, redeem us from the sleep of death. Through Christ, in whom thou didst manifest thyself to mankind, we pray. **Amen.**

381. As the wise men of old came themselves bearing gifts, so we come unto thee with our gifts. Accept them that they may be transformed into the light of the gospel that the

158

world might believe and come to know him whom to know is life eternal, even Christ Jesus, our Lord. **Amen.**

O Lord our God, who didst bring the gentile kings to 382. seek and adore the Christ child, we pray thee to lead thy Church into all the dark places of the earth, bearing the torch of Christ's light, so that the day may speedily come when all the men of the earth shall do homage to the King of kings; even Jesus Christ our Lord.

O Lord our God, hear the prayer of thy servants.

O Lord our God, who didst lead the kings of the east to bow the knee before the majesty of the infant Jesus, grant that the President of the United States and all the rulers of the earth may sit at his feet and learn the ways of him who is the Prince of peace; even Jesus Christ our Lord.

O Lord our God, hear the prayer of thy servants.

O Lord our God, guide and prosper, we pray thee, those who are laboring for the spread of thy gospel among the nations; grant that the whole world may be filled with the knowledge of thy truth.

O Lord our God, hear the prayer of thy servants; through Jesus Christ thy Son.   Amen.

LENT

Sentences

Draw near to God and he will draw near to you. Humble 383. yourselves before the Lord and he will exalt you.

The Lord is merciful and gracious, slow to anger and 384. abounding in steadfast love. If we confess our sins, he is faithful and just, and will forgive our sins and cleanse us from all unrighteousness.

385. For thus said the Lord God, the Holy One of Israel, "In returning and rest you shall be saved; in quietness and in trust shall be your strength."

386. The apostles returned to Jesus; and he said to them, "Come away by yourselves to a lonely place, and rest a while."

387. I will arise and go to my father, and I will say to him, "Father, I have sinned against heaven and before you; I am no longer worthy to be called your son."

388. Rend your hearts and not your garments. Return to the Lord your God, for he is gracious and merciful, slow to anger, and abounding in steadfast love.

389. Train yourself in godliness; for while bodily training is of some value, godliness is of value in every way, as it holds promise for the present life and also for the life to come.

390. Jesus said: "If any man would come after me, let him deny himself and take up his cross daily and follow me."

391. Is not this the fast that I choose: to loose the bonds of wickedness, to undo the thongs of the yoke, to let the oppressed go free, and to break every yoke?

Is it not to share your bread with the hungry, and bring the homeless poor into your house; when you see the naked, to cover him, and not to hide yourself from your own flesh?

392. Then shall your light break forth like the dawn, and your healing shall spring up speedily; your righteousness shall go before you, the glory of the Lord shall be your rear guard.

Then you shall call, and the Lord will answer; you shall cry, and he will say, Here I am.

PRAYERS

O thou who dost in utter faithfulness stand outside the 393. closed doors of the hearts of men, knocking again and again, give us the will to open our lives to thee. Make thy home within our hearts that we may love thee even as thou hast loved us; through Jesus Christ, our Lord. **Amen.**

Father Almighty, we know that we have been made for 394. thy glory; yet we have gone into hiding; we have tried to keep away from thy presence. Forgive us and bring us once again to the place where we may see thee and sing praises to thy majesty; through Jesus Christ. **Amen.**

We know, O God, that only the pure in heart shall see 395. thee. Help us in this season to remove from our lives all the dark shadows that would hide thee from us. Make us so clean within that our outward acts will witness to thy grace; through Jesus Christ, who was tempted as we are, yet without sin. **Amen.**

Even as Christ set his face to go up to Jerusalem, so we 396. would renew our discipleship and take up the cross and follow him. Help us to make the cross meaningful by putting right before self-interest, by putting our neighbors before ourselves, by putting principle above reputation, and by putting love of thee above love of self; through Jesus Christ, our Lord. **Amen.**

In this season of self-discipline, when we are giving 397. thought to our discipleship, make us aware that being a disciple means to follow Jesus Christ as he seeks to be servant of all. Thus we would remember: all who are removed from home and friends and must live among strangers; all who are hungry or without adequate shelter; all who because of color of skin are kept from full participation in the whole of life; all who restlessly toss through the long hours of the night because of anxiety or fear; all who face the perils of war; all who walk through the valley of the shadow of death. Give us not only the sensitive awareness to pray for these but the grace to serve them in their need; through him who loved us and gave himself for us, even Christ our Lord. **Amen.**

398. O Lord, who for our sake didst fast forty days and forty nights; give us grace to discipline ourselves during this season so that our bodies, minds, and spirits may become fitting vessels for thy grace. Lead us into the paths of righteousness for thy name's sake. **Amen.**

399. O thou who didst show thy love for mankind in the gift of thy Son Jesus Christ and hast brought him to our remembrance through thy Spirit, we raise our voices in praise to thee for his days upon the earth, for his victory over temptation, for his acts of love and mercy, for his plain teaching concerning thy way, for his faithfulness even to death, for his victory in the cross and resurrection. Thanks be to thee, O God, for thy unspeakable gift in Jesus Christ; to whom with thee and the Holy Spirit be given glory, power, and dominion, for ever and ever. **Amen.**

PASSIONTIDE

SENTENCES

400. When the days drew near for him to be received up, he set his face to go to Jerusalem.

Whoever would be great among you must be your servant, and whoever would be first among you must be your slave; even as the Son of man came not to be served but to serve, and to give his life as a ransom for many. 401.

The very stone which the builders rejected has become the head of the corner; this was the Lord's doing, and it is marvelous in our eyes. 402.

Hosanna to the Son of David! Blessed be he who comes in the name of the Lord! Hosanna in the highest! Say to the daughter of Zion, "Behold, your salvation comes; behold, his reward is with him, and his recompense before him." Blessed be the King who comes in the name of the Lord! 403.

Blessed is he who comes in the name of the Lord: 404.
Hosanna in the highest.
Lift up your heads, O gates! and be lifted up, O ancient doors!
That the King of glory may come in!
Who is the King of glory?
The Lord of hosts, he is the King of glory!

The crowds that went before him and that followed him shouted, "Hosanna to the Son of David! Blessed be he who comes in the name of the Lord! Hosanna in the highest!" 405.

He was despised and rejected by men; a man of sorrows, and acquainted with grief. 406.

He was wounded for our transgressions, he was bruised for our iniquities; upon him was the chastisement that made us whole, and with his stripes we are healed. 407.

163

408. Is it nothing to you, all you who pass by? Look and see if there is any sorrow like my sorrow.

409. If any man would come after me, let him deny himself and take up his cross and follow me. For whoever would save his life will lose it; and whoever loses his life for my sake and the gospel's will save it.

410. God shows his love for us in that while we were yet sinners Christ died for us.

411. Let us run with perseverance the race that is set before us, looking to Jesus the pioneer and perfecter of our faith, who for the joy that was set before him endured the cross, despising the shame, and is seated at the right hand of the throne of God.

412. For to this you have been called, because Christ also suffered for you, leaving you an example, that you should follow in his steps.

413. God so loved the world that he gave his only Son, that whoever believes in him should not perish but have eternal life.

414. Christ, our paschal lamb, has been sacrificed. Let us, therefore, celebrate the festival, not with the old leaven, the leaven of malice and evil, but with the unleavened bread of sincerity and truth.

415. Hear the words of our Lord Jesus: "I am the good shepherd. The good shepherd lays down his life for the sheep."

416. In this is love, not that we loved God but that he loved us and sent his Son to be the expiation for our sins. Be-

loved, if God so loved us, we also ought to love one another.

Let us confess our sin before God.   417.

God so loved the world, that he gave his only Son;

That whoever believes in him should not perish, but have eternal life.

God shows his love for us in that while we were yet sinners Christ died for us:

Thanks be to God for his inexpressible gift.

O Savior of the world, who by thy cross hast redeemed us:

Save us and help us, we humbly beseech thee, O Lord.

We confess that all we like sheep have gone astray, we have turned everyone to his own way:

Have mercy upon us.

We have crucified thee, the Lord of glory, afresh, and put thee to open shame:

Have mercy upon us.

Lamb of God, that takest away the sins of the world:

Have mercy upon us.

Lamb of God, that takest away the sins of the world:

Have mercy upon us, and grant us thy peace.   Amen.

Almighty God, whose most dear Son went not up to joy   418.
but first suffered pain, and entered not into glory before
he was crucified; mercifully grant that we, walking in the
way of the cross, may find it none other than the way of
life and peace; through the same, thy Son, Jesus Christ
our Lord. **Amen.**

Our Father, as on this day we keep the special memory   419.

of our Redeemer's entry into the city, so grant, O Lord, that now and ever he may triumph in our hearts. Let the King of grace and glory enter in, and let us lay ourselves and all we are in full and joyful homage before him; through the same Jesus Christ our Lord. **Amen.**

420. O Lord, we do not understand our own actions; for we do not do what we want, but we do the very thing we hate. We can will what is right, but we cannot do it. We do not do the good we want to do; but the evil we do not want, that is what we do. Father, we believe; help our unbelief! **Amen.**

421. Almighty and everlasting God who, of thy tender love toward mankind, hast sent thy Son, our Savior Jesus Christ, to take upon himself our flesh and to suffer death upon the cross, that all mankind should follow the example of his great humility; mercifully grant that we may both follow the example of his patience and also be made partakers of his resurrection; through the same Jesus Christ our Lord. **Amen.**

422. Almighty Father, who knows our temptations to give up our disciplines of faithfulness, that we might enjoy selfish pleasures rather than thy truth, rebuke us in our unfaithfulness and give us strength to return steadfastly to the way of discipleship; through Jesus Christ our Lord. **Amen.**

423. Our Father, thou knowest how much we desire to accept an easier way than that of becoming a disciple. Mercifully forgive our wanderings and lead us in the way of the cross; through our Lord Jesus Christ. **Amen.**

424. Merciful God, whose Son Jesus steadfastly walked the road to Jerusalem knowing full well that a cross stood at

the journey's end; grant us courage that we, like Jesus, might walk toward the cross which he has appointed for us, strengthened by the same Jesus, who is our sure Master and Lord. **Amen.**

425. Almighty God, who knowest how exposed we are to the temptations of the world, grant us nevertheless the strength to follow our Master down the road to discipleship, even though surely we shall meet the cross on that road; through the same Jesus Christ. **Amen.**

426. Too often, our Father, when we are asked to say Yes to some high cause, we pray that if it be thy will thou wouldst take this cup from us. O God, give us courage to be able to say, "Not our wills, but thine be done;" through Jesus Christ who was faithful even to death, yea the death on the cross. **Amen.**

427. Our Father, even as Christ before his passion prayed for his disciples and all who would believe through their word, so we would join him in intercession for our brethren. Especially do we commend to thy care all who face great temptation, all who stagger under burdens too heavy for them to bear, all whose spirits are broken by the heavy weight of debt, all who live in surroundings that breed ignorance and evil, all who face the bitter barbs of their neighbors because of color or creed. Open to them thy ways and grant that we may walk with them therein to bear with them their burdens; through Jesus Christ who bore the cross. **Amen.**

428. Thanks be to thee, O God, for Jesus Christ, who for the joy that was set before him endured the cross.
Thanks be to thee, O God, for Jesus Christ, who in the

cross triumphed over sin and death, principalities and powers, and over all who would seek to set aside thy will in the world.

Thanks be to thee, O God, for Jesus Christ, who in the cross showed thy great love for us in that he died for the ungodly; yea, even while we were yet sinners he died for us.

Thanks be to thee, O God, who in Jesus Christ calls us to take up the cross and follow him. Grant that we may with joy give answer and in truth become his disciples; in his name we pray. **Amen.**

429. Help us, O God, to take towel and basin and in humbleness of spirit to wash the feet of those in need; through Jesus Christ, who came and served. **Amen.**

430. Help us, O God, to join thee in thy weakness as seen in thy Son Jesus Christ, who was scourged, spat upon, crucified, and died that the full limits of thy love might be made known. **Amen.**

431. Help us, O God, to join thy Son Jesus Christ in his great sorrow for the city. In spite of all of our knowledge, ghettos remain; life is made cheap through crime, drugs, prejudice, and prostitution; children are hungry and do not learn to read; garbage is piled in the streets; and rats roam through the dwellings. Forgive us God even as we weep. **Amen.**

EASTER

SENTENCES

432. The Lord has risen!

The Lord has risen indeed: Hallelujah!

"I am the first and the last;" says the Lord, "I died, and behold I am alive for evermore."	433.

Christ holds his priesthood permanently, because he continues forever. Consequently he is able for all time to save those who draw near to God through him, since he always lives to make intercession for them.	434.

Jesus said: "I am the resurrection and the life; he who believes in me, though he die, yet shall he live, and whoever lives and believes in me shall never die."	435.

Jesus came and stood among them and said to them, "Peace be with you." When he had said this, he showed them his hands and his side. Then the disciples were glad when they saw the Lord.	436.

Christ has been raised from the dead, the first fruits of those who have fallen asleep. Thanks be to God, who gives us the victory through our Lord Jesus Christ.	437.

Christ being raised from the dead will never die again; death no longer has dominion over him. The death he died he died to sin, once for all, but the life he lives he lives to God.	438.

Christ, our paschal lamb, has been sacrificed. Let us, therefore, celebrate the festival.	439.

The stone which the builders rejected has become the chief corner-stone. This is the Lord's doing; it is marvelous in our eyes.	440.

Blessed be the God and Father of our Lord Jesus Christ! By his great mercy we have been born anew to a living	441.

hope through the resurrection of Jesus Christ from the dead.

442. If then you have been raised with Christ, seek the things that are above, where Christ is, seated at the right hand of God.

PRAYERS

443. The Lord has risen indeed:

> **Hallelujah!**

Christ has been raised from the dead, the first fruits of those who have fallen asleep.

> **Thanks be to God, who gives us the victory through our Lord Jesus Christ. Amen.**

444. Praise be to thee, O Father Almighty, who didst bring forth thy Son from the dead and hast exalted him to eternal glory. Praise be to thee, O Lord Jesus Christ, thou who art the resurrection and the life.

Praise be to thee, O Holy Spirit, who dost make God alive in our hearts.

All praise and thanksgiving be to thee, O most blessed Trinity, now and forevermore, world without end. **Amen.**

445. Our Father, as we stand before the empty tomb we, like Mary and the disciples, find it hard to believe that Christ rose from the dead. Forgive our unbelief. Take from our minds the dark shadows of doubt and help us to find in the midst of the secularity of our day the spirit of the living Christ. For our unfaithfulness to him in our world, we ask pardon. Judge us not by our bad intentions nor by our poor performances, but only by thy mercy; through Christ our Lord. **Amen.**

We offer our praise and thanksgiving to thee for Jesus 446.
Christ our Lord. We thank thee that thou didst see fit to
illumine our human life by his presence amongst us. We
thank thee for the song of joy at his birth; for the days
of his youth and manhood; for his teaching and example;
for his deeds of love and mercy; for his commitment even
to the death on the cross; but above all on this the day of
his resurrection we thank thee for his triumph over death
and for the hope that because he lives, we shall live also,
and that neither death nor life, nor things present nor
things to come, shall be able to separate us from thy love,
which is in Christ Jesus our Lord; through whom we pray.
Amen.

Almighty God, who brought again from the dead our 447.
Lord Jesus Christ, grant us grace to believe in his victory
and faith and to make it our own. Help us in the days of
our flesh to be more ready to minister like Christ than to
be ministered to; give us a ready heart to bear the heavy
burdens of others; keep our tempers cool and our spirits
calm; make us brave to fight for right and to stand firm
against those who would oppress the weak; cause us in
all our ways to say with him, "Not my will, but thine be
done." Give us grace to know him as our living Lord and
strength to follow in his footsteps; in his name we pray.
Amen.

May the God of peace who brought again from the dead 448.
our Lord Jesus, the great shepherd of the sheep, by the
blood of the eternal covenant, equip us to do his work in
the world, working in us that which is pleasing in his
sight, through Jesus Christ.

To whom be glory for ever and ever. Amen.

ASCENSION

449. God has gone up with a shout, the Lord with the sound
of a trumpet. Sing praises to our God, sing praises! Sing
praises to our King, sing praises! For God is the king of
all the earth; sing praises with a psalm! God reigns over
the nations; God sits on his holy throne.

450. Lift up your heads, O gates! and be lifted up, O ancient
doors!
That the King of glory may come in.
Who is this King of glory?
The Lord of hosts, he is the King of glory.

451. Thus it is written that Christ should suffer and on the
third day rise from dead, and
**That repentance and forgiveness of sins should be
preached in his name to all nations.**
You are a witness to these things you have in Christ Jesus,
who, though he was in the form of God, did not count
equality with God a thing to be grasped,
**but emptied himself taking the form of a servant, being
born in the likeness of men.**
And being found in human form he humbled himself and
became obedient unto death, even death on a cross. Therefore, God has highly exalted him and bestowed on him
the name which is above every name,
**that at the name of Jesus every knee should bow and
every tongue confess that Jesus Christ is Lord.**

452. Jesus said, "And I, when I am lifted up from the earth,
will draw all men to myself."

172

Eternal God, our Father, with thanksgiving we come to 453.
him, to that Living Stone, rejected by men but in thy
sight chosen and precious, to offer our prayers and supplications. Grant that through him our unworthy brokenness may find worth in thy sight and that thou who hast
called us into thy eternal glory in Christ will restore, establish, and strengthen us. To thee be dominion for ever
and ever. **Amen.**

O God our Father, who hast exalted thy Son Jesus Christ 454.
and bestowed on him a name which is above every name,
to thee we offer our thanks and pray for that day when at
the name of Jesus every knee should bow, in heaven and
on earth and under the earth, and every tongue confess
that Jesus Christ is Lord; to the glory of thee, our God
and Father. **Amen.**

Since then we have a great high priest who has passed 455.
through the heavens, Jesus, the Son of God, we with
confidence draw near to thy throne of grace, our Father.
Grant that we may receive mercy and find grace to help
in our time of need. Help us to come to know the presence
of him who said: "Lo, I am with you always, even to the
close of the age." **Amen.**

PENTECOST

SENTENCES

In the last days it shall be, God declares, that I will pour 456.
out my Spirit upon all flesh, and your sons and your
daughters shall prophesy, your old men shall dream
dreams, and your young men shall see visions.

The fruit of the Spirit is love, joy, peace, patience, kind- 457.

ness, goodness, faithfulness, **gentleness, self-control**; against such there is no law. If we live by the Spirit, let us also walk by the Spirit.

458. The hour is coming, and now is, when the true worshipers will worship the Father in spirit and truth, for such the Father seeks to worship him.

   God is spirit, and those who worship him must worship in spirit and truth.

459. God's love has been poured into our hearts through the Holy Spirit which has been given to us.

460. Do you not know that you are God's temple and that God's Spirit dwells in you?

461. For all who are led by the Spirit of God are sons of God. When we cry, "Abba! Father!" it is the Spirit himself bearing witness with our spirit that we are children of God.

462. This is the day which the Lord has made.

   We will rejoice and be glad in it.

   This is the day of which Jesus declared: "You shall receive power when the Holy Spirit has come upon you.

   And you shall be my witnesses in Jerusalem and in all Judea and Samaria and to the end of the earth."

463. Where the Spirit of the Lord is, there is freedom.

   There are varieties of gifts, but the same Spirit.

464. As many as are led by the Spirit of God, they are the sons of God.

The Spirit itself gives witness to our spirit, that we all are the children of God.

The Spirit and the Bride say, "Come." And let him who   465.
hears say, "Come." And let him who is thirsty come, let
him who desires take the water of life without price.

Prayers

We offer unto thee, our Father, praise for the gift of thy   466.
Spirit. When we are lonely the Spirit comes to be our
friend. When we are filled with doubt and unbelief the
Spirit speaks the word of truth. When we burn with hatred
the Spirit brings to us the gift of love. For thy Spirit we
praise thee, O God our Redeemer. **Amen.**

Spirit of truth, Spirit of love, Spirit of Christ, Spirit of   467.
God, thou Holy Spirit, we adore thee for thy manifold
gifts to us. Enkindle our hearts and enable our lips to
sing forth praise worthy of thy great power. **Amen.**

Pour forth thy Spirit, O Father, upon all flesh, that discord   468.
and strife may be brought to an end. Deliver men everywhere from all contempt for others not of their race, color,
condition, or creed. Quicken by thy gospel true brotherhood among all peoples, and bring them to true unity in
thy Spirit; through Jesus Christ our Lord. **Amen.**

Most merciful Father, like the prodigal we come before   469.
thee to say that we have sinned and are no longer worthy
to be called thy children. Against thee we have rebelled.
Yet in our distant land thou through thy Spirit didst say
to us, "Come home." By that same Spirit make us clean
that we may stand before thee once again to affirm our
sonship and to receive from thee the blessings of thy

household; through Jesus Christ, who promised the abiding presence of thy Spirit, we pray. **Amen.**

470. Through thy Spirit, our Father, move across the world and speak to all sorts and conditions of men. By thy Spirit befriend all who are far from home and lonely. Give to all whose minds are clouded with doubt and disturbed by disbelief thy Spirit of truth. To all who have lost a loved one bring the Spirit's comfort. May the healing strength of thy Spirit be given to all who suffer illness or injury. Grant to all who create in the realms of art and science the Spirit's inspiration. By thy Spirit open to all ministers and missionaries thy Holy Word. Defend thy Church from all perils by the sword of the Spirit; through that same Spirit, we pray. **Amen.**

471. O heavenly Father, we pray for thy holy Church universal; send down upon her ministers and people thy Holy Spirit; give to them wisdom and grace; enlighten them with the knowledge of thy Word; inflame them with a pure zeal for thy glory; and grant that by their faithful witness and work thy Church may be strengthened and thy kingdom made known in the world:

   We beseech thee to hear us, O Lord.

   Grant thy blessing to all those who translate, print, and circulate the Holy Scriptures; may thy Spirit inspire them with true knowledge and skill, with patient zeal and love:

   We beseech thee to hear us, O Lord.

   Strengthen with thy Spirit all our brethren, thy servants the missionaries. Make them mighty in thy truth and love, help them to set forth Christ as thy power unto salvation:

   We beseech thee to hear us, O Lord. Amen.

TRINITY

Sentences

Holy, holy, holy is the Lord of hosts; the whole earth is full of his glory. 472.

"I am the Alpha and the Omega," says the Lord God, who is and who was and who is to come, the Almighty. 473.

Holy, holy, holy is the Lord God Almighty, who was and is and is to come. 474.

Through Christ we have access in one Spirit to the Father. 475.

But you, beloved, build yourselves up on your most holy faith; pray in the Holy Spirit; keep yourselves in the love of God; wait for the mercy of our Lord Jesus Christ unto eternal life. 476.

The grace of the Lord Jesus Christ and the love of God and the fellowship of the Holy Spirit be with you all. 477.

Why are we gathered at this place at this hour? 478.

We are gathered as the people of God, to come to know and serve and praise him as he is seen in Jesus Christ and made known by the Holy Spirit.

Then let us acknowledge the God before whom we stand.

In the name of the Father and of the Son and of the Holy Spirit. Amen.

Prayers

Father, Son, and Holy Spirit, thou one God, we adore thee for the manifold ways in which thou hast made thy- 479.

177

self known to the children of men. Magnify our thanksgiving that it may be worthy of thy greatness, and help us so to sing thy praises that the men of the world may truly know how great thou art. **Amen.**

480. Blessed be thou, O eternal Lord God:
> **In whom the heavens rejoice and the earth is glad, for thou shalt judge the world in righteousness.**

Blessed be thou, O Christ our Savior:
> **Who wilt come in power and great glory to perfect thy kingdom, and to bring in thy ransomed with songs of everlasting joy.**

Blessed be thou, O holy and gracious Spirit:
> **Who dost quicken our hearts and fill our mouths with praise.**

Glory be to thee, O God, thou who art one, yet three, for ever and ever. **Amen.**

481. Let us give glory to God.
> **Glory be to the Father, and to the Son, and to the Holy Spirit.**

As it was in the beginning, is now and ever shall be,
> **World without end. Amen.**

482. The Lord be with you.
> **And with thy spirit.**

Let us pray.

Almighty and everlasting God by whose Spirit the whole body of the Christ is governed and sanctified, receive our supplications and prayers which we offer before thee for all estates of men in thy holy Church, that every member of the same, in his vocation and ministry, may in truth and with godliness serve thee; through our Lord and Savior, Jesus Christ. **Amen.**

Beloved in Christ, in communion with the saints of all 483. ages let us make bold to offer our prayers of intercession unto Almighty God: Father, Son, and Holy Spirit.
O God, we pray for the Church, which is set today amid the perplexities of a changing order and face to face with a great new task.

    Be with thy Church, O Lord.

Grant her a new birth through the travail of repentance and humiliation. Put upon her lips the ancient gospel of her Lord.

    Be with thy Church, O Lord.

Help her to proclaim boldly the coming of the kingdom of God and the doom of all that resist it.

    Be with thy Church, O Lord.

Fill her with the prophet's scorn of tyranny, and with a Christlike tenderness for the heavy-laden and downtrodden. Give her faith to espouse the cause of the people.

    Be with thy Church, O Lord.

Bid her cease from seeking her own life, lest she lose it. Make her valiant to give up her life to humanity, as did her crucified Lord in whose name we pray.

    Be with thy Church, O Lord. Amen.

Lord of the outcast and the downtrodden, we commend 484. to thee all who are in sickness, peril, or sorrow; all little children; all old, frail folk.

    By thy Spirit hear our prayers, O merciful and gracious Father, for the love of thy Son our Savior Jesus Christ.

Let the sorrowful sighing of the prisoners come before thee, and according to the greatness of thy power comfort thou those who are preparing to die.

By thy Spirit hear our prayers, O merciful and gracious Father, for the love of thy Son our Savior Jesus Christ. Amen.

PART 5

SENTENCES, SCRIPTURES,
AND PRAYERS FOR
SPECIAL DAYS AND OCCASIONS

While these days and occasions do not belong to the Christian year, they have become a part of the recurring cycle of the Church's worship. They provide occasions wherein the Church reminds itself of God's special mercies as well as its own involvement in human society.

Inasmuch as these days are not in the lectionaries (Part 8), special Scripture selections have been included.

OLD YEAR

SENTENCES

The eyes of the Lord your God are always upon you, from the beginning of the year to the end of the year. 485.

Lord, thou hast been our dwelling place in all generations. From everlasting to everlasting thou art God. 486.

487. The Lord will keep your going out and your coming in from this time forth and for evermore.

Scripture Selections

Deuteronomy 8. Psalms 42. 46. 90. 91. 103. 121. 130. 139. 146. Isaiah 40:25-31. Matthew 25:14-30. 25:31-46. Luke 12:32-48. Hebrews 12:18-29. 1 Peter 1:1-25. 2 Peter 3:8-18.

Prayers

488. Eternal Father, as another year draws to its close, we give thee thanks for all the ways by which thou hast led us. For thy goodness that hath created us, for thy bounty that hath sustained us, for thy fatherly discipline that hath corrected us, and for thy patience that hath sustained us:

We thank thee, O God.

For the worship and uplifting fellowship of thy Church, for the light and inspiration of thy Word, and for the comfort and guidance of thy Holy Spirit:

We thank thee, O God.

For all the truth we have learned, for all the good deeds thou hast enabled us to do, for all victories won and for all blessings of life whether recognized or unperceived:

We thank thee, O God.

For our Lord Jesus Christ, who has called us into his way, his truth, and his life, and has shown unto us thy holy love:

We thank thee, O God, to whom be all praise and thanksgiving, now and forevermore. Amen.

489. O thou who art more ready to forgive than we are to confess, we come before thee in the closing hours of this year acknowledging our failures to be true disciples of thy Son Jesus Christ. We have followed our own selfish ways

rather than walking with him who is the true way. We have come to thee for grace without being gracious to our brothers. In the world we have pursued human interests rather than witnessing to thy will for man. Forgive us, O Lord, and help us amend our ways in the year to come; through Jesus Christ, our Lord. **Amen.**

Our heavenly Father, as this old year passes we acknowl- 490.
edge thy presence not only as Lord of the past but also as Lord of the present and future; we acknowledge that thou dost make all things new. We beseech thee to use us as thy instruments in thy work in the world. Empower us, through thy grace, so to know the past that in the present we may search out thy ways for the future. Make of us strong witnesses to our faith; use us that others in despair may perceive hope in thee; and as we have caught thy love, may we in turn fulfill all love in our relationships with thee, with our brother, and with ourselves, that thy kingdom come and thy will be done; through Jesus Christ our Lord. **Amen.**

O God, whose days are without end, and whose mercies 491.
cannot be numbered; we turn to thee who hast made us a royal priesthood that we might offer intercessions for all men. Hear us as we pray:

For all whose lives this past year have known the hard-ships of poverty, the injustice of prejudice, and the dis-comfort of unkindness; grant that with the coming of the new year they may be relieved of those burdens which can be lifted and be given patience to bear those which continue to press down upon them:

We beseech thee to hear us, O Lord.

For the leaders of the nations who have dealt with the hard and desperate problems of our world; grant that they may seek out thy will, and having found it be conformed to its ways:

We beseech thee to hear us, O Lord.

For thy Church, whose voice at times is so small and unwilling to speak, grant a new vision and courage to witness and work in the world:

We beseech thee to hear us, O Lord.

For all in pain and distress of body and mind, for the desolate and the brokenhearted; bring before their eyes their crucified Savior and his glorious resurrection that in him they may know of their victory:

We thy servants beseech thee to incline thine ear, O Lord. Amen.

NEW YEAR

Sentences

492. Teach us to number our days that we may get a heart of wisdom. Let the favor of the Lord our God be upon us, and establish thou the work of our hands upon us.

493. Behold, now is the acceptable time; behold, now is the day of salvation.

494. The old has passed away, behold, the new has come. All this is from God, who through Christ reconciled us to himself and gave us the ministry of reconciliation.

495. We do not lose heart. Though our outer nature is wasting away, our inner nature is being renewed every day.

496. They who wait for the Lord shall renew their strength, they shall mount up with wings like eagles, they shall run and not be weary, they shall walk and not faint.

Thus says the Lord: "Behold, I am doing a new thing; I   497.
will make a way in the wilderness and rivers in the desert."

He who sat upon the throne said, "Behold, I make all   498.
things new. I am the Alpha and the Omega, the beginning and the end."

SCRIPTURE SELECTIONS

Genesis 1:1–2:3. Joshua 1:1-8. Psalms 1. 25. 27. 34. 62.
103. 121. 146. Proverbs 3:1-18. Isaiah 40:21-31. Matthew 6:25-34. Luke 12:22-48. 19:11-27. 2 Corinthians
5:1-10. Ephesians 6:10-20. Philippians 4:4-20. Hebrews
11.

PRAYERS

O thou God of holy love, we acknowledge that at the   499.
beginning of this year our lives do not stand before thee
as a book unwritten. Much that we shall do has already
been spelled out before the year has begun. Inscribed
deep within are old habits and familiar behavior patterns.
We know that these in large part will write for us the
history of this coming year. Cause us as we live to be
aware of thy forgiving grace, and when we have written a
life page full of the errors of our misdeeds help us to
acknowledge ourselves for what we are and to seek thy
love; through Jesus Christ, our Lord. **Amen.**

Eternal God, who didst lay the foundations of the earth,   500.
and whose mercy is from everlasting to everlasting, in this
beginning of the new year we raise our voices in thanksgiving unto thee.

For the old which we cherished so much and to which
we even now would cling:
   We praise thy name and give thee thanks.

185

For the new, with its untold promise and its possibilities of good:

We praise thy name and give thee thanks.

For the knowledge that whether it be in the old or the new, thou art ever with us making all things new:

We praise thy name and give thee thanks.

For thy love which never fails, and that even in our faithlessness and disobedience thou dost continue thy kindness toward us:

We praise thy name and give thee thanks.

For thy strength that sustains us in weakness, for thy patience which bears with us in sin, for thy guidance which leads us in perplexity, and for thy comfort which helps us in distress:

We praise thy name and give thee thanks.

Most of all, for thy forgiveness and grace in Jesus Christ, for the abiding presence of thy Holy Spirit, for our fellowship with thee and with one another in thy Church, and for our assurance of eternal life in thy heavenly kingdom:

We praise thy name and give thee thanks.

Therefore we worship and adore thee, O Lord our God, of whom, and through whom, and to whom are all things.

To thee be glory for ever. Amen.

501. Eternal Father, teach us in the days of this year to discover the preciousness of time. Keep us from squandering our hours in senseless thought and useless activities. Help us through good books, high conversation, and creative action to so number our days that we may get a heart of wisdom and a life devoted to thy reconciling ministry in the world; through Jesus Christ. **Amen.**

MISSION IN OUR LAND

SENTENCES

There was a little city with few men in it; and a great 502.
king came against it and besieged it, building great siege-
works against it. But there was found in it a poor wise
man, and he by his wisdom delivered the city. The words
of the wise heard in quiet are better than the shouting of
a ruler among fools.

I will restore your judges as at the first, and your coun- 503.
selors as at the beginning. Afterward you shall be called
the city of righteousness, the faithful city.

How beautiful upon the mountains are the feet of him 504.
who brings good tidings, who publishes peace, who brings
good tidings of good, who publishes salvation, who says to
Zion, "Your God reigns."

Bear one another's burdens, and so fulfill the law of 505.
Christ. As we have opportunity, let us do good to all men,
especially to those who are of the household of faith.

You are a chosen race, a royal priesthood, a holy nation, 506.
God's own people, that you may declare the wonderful
deeds of him who called you out of darkness into his
marvelous light.

Jesus said: "The harvest is plentiful, but the laborers are 507.
few; pray therefore the Lord of the harvest to send out
laborers into his harvest."

SCRIPTURE SELECTIONS

Isaiah 6. 11. 42:1-9. 54. 55. Jeremiah 1:1-10. Ezekiel
37:1-14. Hosea 6. Malachi 3. Matthew 9:35—10:6. Luke

10:1-22. John 1:35-51. 17:2-26. Acts 1:1-19. 8. Romans 12. 1 Corinthians 12. 2 Corinthians 8. 9. Galatians 6. 1 John 4:7-21.

PRAYERS

508. Too often, our Father, we have tried to be Christian with our words alone and have forgotten that the disciples of Jesus Christ are known also by their fruits. We have praised thee with fervor within the sanctuary but out on the streets we have walked past human need. We have spoken of mission but forgotten that thy Son and our Lord went into all the cities, villages, and towns of his home country to preach the gospel, heal the sick, and comfort the sorrowing. Forgive us, Father, that we have neglected so great a salvation; and grant that through Jesus Christ our Lord we may become disciples in deed as well as word. **Amen.**

509. We thank thee, our Father, for Jesus Christ thy Son, who in the days of his earthly ministry saw fit to walk the crowded streets of the city and the narrow paths of the countryside, and there to minister to human need. We thank thee that he called his disciples into that same ministry and that even now men and women are serving in his name amidst the squalor and rebellion of the inner city, as well as on the sparsely settled prairies and amidst the distant mountain ranges. We thank thee that even though we cannot stand beside them we can have a part in their ministry through our intercessions for them and by sharing with them of our substance. We thank thee for missionaries in our land whose vision and work has brought the light of the gospel to all sorts and conditions of men. Accept our thanksgivings through Jesus Christ thy Son. **Amen.**

We beseech thee, O God, to broaden our vision and 510.
deepen our commitment. Take our eyes away from ourselves and our own interests and help us to see the needs
of others and the conditions of life which they face. Bring
us into the inner city. Help us to see the squalor of the
slums, the underfed and frightened children, the bitter
and rebellious youth, the frustrated and bewildered parents, the old ones who impatiently wait to welcome death's
relief. Revive within us the spirit of him who served the
poor, the lonely, the fearful, even Christ Jesus our Lord.
Amen.

Our Father, we commend to thy tender care all in this 511.
land whose lives are eaten away by fear, all whose lot
is made bitter because of the race to which they belong,
all for whom poverty is not only a word but a reality, all
who live in houses owned by landlords whose only concern
is for profit and not the welfare of their tenants, all children who must grow up in ignorance because of inade-
quate or overcrowded schools, all who live in the luxury
of suburbia and who hide from the realities of the inner
city, all who live on the broad and open plains yet whose
vision is so limited that they cannot see the desperate
conditions of many of their fellow human beings. Give to
each in his need thy mercy, and through that same mercy
cause thy Church throughout this land to rise from its
preoccupation with its own inner life and get out into the
world where men need help, there to minister in thy
name; through Jesus Christ our Lord. **Amen.**

We ask, O God, thy blessing upon all those who have 512.
dedicated their lives to the ministry of mission in our
land. As they work in the inner city, on the reservations,
in the local churches, in schools and colleges, or in whatever place and with all sorts and conditions of men, we

pray that their insight and strength may continue to deepen and their dedication and labor may continue to bring the word of peace to those to whom they have been called; in the name of him who called all of his people to be his witnesses, both in Jerusalem and Judea as well as the uttermost parts of the earth. **Amen.**

BAPTISM

513. Then Jesus came from Galilee to the Jordan to John, to be baptized by him. John would have prevented him, saying, "I need to be baptized by you, and do you come to me?" But Jesus answered him, "Let it be so now; for thus it is fitting for us to fulfill all righteousness." Then he consented. And when Jesus was baptized, he went up immediately from the water, and behold, the heavens were opened and he saw the Spirit of God descending like a dove, and alighting on him; and lo, a voice from heaven, saying, "This is my beloved Son, with whom I am well pleased."

514. Now when all the people were baptized, and when Jesus also had been baptized and was praying, the heaven was opened, and the Holy Spirit descended upon him in bodily form, as a dove, and a voice came from heaven, "Thou art my beloved Son; with thee I am well pleased."

515. "Truly, truly, I say to you, unless one is born of water and the Spirit, he cannot enter the kingdom of God. That which is born of the flesh is flesh, and that which is born of the Spirit is spirit. Do not marvel that I said to you, 'You must be born anew.' The wind blows where it wills, and you hear the sound of it, but you do not know whence

190

it comes or whither it goes; so it is with every one who is born of the Spirit."

And Peter said to them, "Repent, and be baptized every 516. one of you in the name of Jesus Christ for the forgiveness of your sins; and you shall receive the gift of the Holy Spirit." So those who received his word were baptized, and there were added that day about three thousand souls. And they devoted themselves to the apostles' teaching and fellowship, to the breaking of bread and the prayers.

And now why do you wait? Rise and be baptized, and 517. wash away your sins, calling on his name.

Do you not know that all of us who have been baptized 518. into Christ Jesus were baptized into his death? We were buried therefore with him by baptism into death, so that as Christ was raised from the dead by the glory of the Father, we too might walk in newness of life.

If you confess with your lips that Jesus is Lord and be- 519. lieve in your heart that God raised him from the dead, you will be saved. For man believes with his heart and so is justified, and he confesses with his lips and so is saved. The scripture says, "No one who believes in him will be put to shame."

For just as the body is one and has many members, and 520. all the members of the body, though many, are one body, so it is with Christ. For by one Spirit we were all baptized into one body—Jews or Greeks, slaves or free—and all were made to drink of one Spirit.

For in Christ Jesus you are all sons of God, through faith. 521.

For as many of you as were baptized into Christ have put on Christ. There is neither Jew nor Greek, there is neither slave nor free, there is neither male nor female; for you are all one in Christ Jesus.

522. You were buried with him in baptism, in which you were also raised with him through faith in the working of God, who raised him from the dead.

523. Fight the good fight of the faith; take hold of the eternal life to which you were called when you made the good confession in the presence of many witnesses.

524. Baptism now saves you, not as a removal of dirt from the body but as an appeal to God for a clear conscience, through the resurrection of Jesus Christ, who has gone into heaven and is at the right hand of God, with angels, authorities, and powers subject to him.

SCRIPTURE SELECTIONS

Mark 1:1-13. Acts 8:26-40. 9:1-19. 10:34-38. 16:11-15. 16:16-34. 19:1-7. Ephesians 4:1-6. 5:21-33. Colossians 3:1-17. Titus 3:4-7. Hebrews 10:19-25. 1 John 5:6-12.

PRAYERS

525. Almighty and everlasting God, we give thee humble and hearty thanks for our Savior Jesus Christ, who died for our sins, was buried, and was raised. Graciously accept, we beseech thee, these thy servants that they, coming to thee in baptism, may be united with Christ in his Church, and receive according to thy promise the forgiveness of their sins, and the gift of the Holy Spirit. Grant that they, putting on the Lord Jesus Christ, may receive out of his fullness and evermore abide in him. Keep

them strong in faith, steadfast in hope, abounding in love. Bestow upon them the manifold gifts of thy grace, that they may serve thee profitably in thy Church. Defend them in all trials and temptations, and grant that, persevering to the end, they may inherit eternal life; through Jesus Christ our Lord. **Amen.**

Send thy blessing, we beseech thee, O Lord, upon these 526. thy servants, who today acknowledge before men their desire to be disciples of Jesus Christ. Strengthen them by thy Spirit, that they may live always worthy of the confession which they have made. Teach them to serve thee with loyal and steadfast hearts; to give and not to count the cost; to fight and not to heed the wounds; to strive and not to seek for rest; to labor and to ask for no reward, save that of knowing that they do thy will; through Jesus Christ our Lord. **Amen.**

Grant, O Lord, that these who have in baptism made 527. public confession of the lordship of Jesus Christ may in their lives in the world continually show that they are his disciples so that through their witness men may come to believe in him whom to know is life eternal, even Christ our Lord. **Amen.**

May we, O Lord, in witnessing anew the coming of these 528. baptized to thee, renew our covenant with thee that we may continue to walk in newness of life; through the grace of our Lord Jesus Christ. **Amen.**

We thank thee, our Father, for every renewal which comes 529. in life. May this baptism be for these who are to be baptized a springtime which will prepare them for a summer of growth and an autumn of abundant harvest. Plant within them the seeds of thy Spirit that their lives may

bear richly the fruits of that same Spirit; through Jesus
Christ our Lord. **Amen.**

EDUCATION

Sentences

530. Remember also your Creator in the days of your youth.

531. The fear of the Lord is the beginning of knowledge; fools
despise wisdom and instruction.

532. The Lord gives wisdom; from his mouth come knowledge
and understanding; he stores up sound wisdom for the
upright; he is a shield to those who walk in integrity,
guarding the paths of justice.

533. Trust in the Lord with all your heart, and do not rely on
your own insight. In all your ways acknowledge him, and
he will make straight your paths.

534. Keep hold of instruction, do not let go; guard her, for she
is your life.

535. The child grew and became strong, filled with wisdom;
and the favor of God was upon him.

536. You then, my son, be strong in the grace that is in Christ
Jesus, and what you have heard from me before many
witnesses entrust to faithful men who will be able to
teach others also.

537. Do your best to present yourself to God as one approved,
a workman who has no need to be ashamed, rightly
handling the word of truth.

Teach what befits sound doctrine. Show yourself in all respects a model of good deeds, and in your teaching show integrity, gravity, and sound speech. 538.

Scripture Selections

Psalm 19. Proverbs 1:1-9. 1:20-33. 4:1-9. Matthew 4:23—5:11. 10:1-4, 24-25. 2 Timothy 2:1-15. Titus 2:1-8.

Prayers

O God, who in times past didst through thy holy prophets 539. teach men thy will and way, we praise thee that thy voice has not grown silent, but that thou hast given unto us teachers to open before us thy truth and lead us into right paths; through Christ our Lord, we pray. **Amen.**

O God, our Father merciful and gracious, hear the thanks- 540. givings with which we come before thee, in the name of Jesus Christ thy Son.

For thy providence which sustains and supports us; for thy love which chastens and heals us:

We thank thee, our Father.

For minds that make us restless until we know the truth; for faith that promises triumph over doubt:

We thank thee, our Father.

For fleeting glimpses of reality, for visions we cannot describe, for depths we can but feel:

We thank thee, our Father.

For the labor of scholars that adds to our understanding; for the inspiration we receive from those of simple trust:

We thank thee, our Father.

For all who are faithful teachers of thy truth; and especially those who have taught us to know and understand thy way:

We thank thee, our Father.

For the writers and publishers of books and magazines which help those who teach and those who learn to come to a clearer understanding of thy Word:

We thank thee, our Father.   Amen.

541. Our Father, thou who hast brought us to this time and place, guide us into all truth. Scatter our darkness and let the light of thy countenance be upon us. Cause us to be faithful to the insights which have come to our fathers and have been transmitted to us through thy chosen teachers; yet help us to break free from tradition when new and nobler vistas of truth open before us.

By thy Spirit hear our prayer, O merciful and gracious Father, for the love of thy Son our Savior, Jesus Christ.

Our Father, thou who hast brought us to this time and place, renew within us that calling which came to those in times past to teach thy truth to the children of men. Help us to provide worthily a place and books and teachers. Be gracious unto all who come to this place to study, to teach, and to administer. From their work together may there come amongst us a true school of thy Word and thy Spirit.

By thy Spirit hear our prayer, O merciful and gracious Father, for the love of thy Son our Savior, Jesus Christ.

Our Father, thou who hast brought us to this time and place, enable us to glorify thee through worthy service. Give us ears to hear through the words of faithful teachers the call of thy Son Jesus Christ, as he summons us through the voices of the oppressed, the sick, those in prison, those discriminated against because of their race, those killed and mutilated in war, and those caught in the bleak toils of poverty. Forbid that we should only listen to thy teachings and not obey them.

By thy Spirit hear our prayer, O merciful and gracious Father, for the love of thy Son our Savior, Jesus Christ. Amen.

CHRISTIAN HOME AND FAMILY LIFE

SENTENCES

Love is patient and kind; love is not jealous or boastful; it is not arrogant or rude. Love does not insist on its own way. Love bears all things, believes all things, hopes all things, endures all things. Love never ends. 542.

Honor your father and your mother, that your days may be long in the land which the Lord your God gives you. 543.

Unless the Lord builds the house, those who build it labor in vain. 544.

A wise son makes a glad father, but a foolish son is a sorrow to his mother. 545.

Hear, O Israel: The Lord our God is one Lord; and you shall love the Lord your God with all your heart, and with all your soul, and with all your might. And these words which I command you this day shall be upon your heart; and you shall teach them diligently to your children, and shall talk of them when you sit in your house, and when you walk by the way, and when you lie down, and when you rise. 546.

Jesus said, "Let the children come to me, do not hinder them; for to such belongs the kingdom of God." 547.

548. A good wife who can find? Her children rise up and call her blessed; her husband also, and he praises her.

Scripture Selections

Genesis 2:18-24. Deuteronomy 6:1-9. Psalm 128. Proverbs 31: 10-31. Mark 9:14-29. Luke 1:46-55. 2:41-52. 1 Corinthians 13. Hebrews 11:1-3, 8-12. 13:1-6.

Prayers

549. O thou who art the Father of all and for whom every fatherhood on earth is named, we adore thee for thy goodness unto thy children. Praise be to thee, both now and forevermore. **Amen.**

550. Gracious God, our Father, we thank thee that thou didst choose the humble home of a village carpenter to cradle the infant Jesus, and that in this home he grew and became strong, filled with wisdom, and that thy favor was upon him. Grant that the love seen so plentifully in Mary and the care and concern of Joseph for the child Jesus may be ours, and that our children may grow and become strong, filled with wisdom, and in thy favor. **Amen.**

551. On this day, our Father, as we offer thanksgiving for thy gracious gift of home and family, we would remember before thee:
> those who live in broken homes;
> those who do not know the strong love of a father or the gentle concern of a mother;
> those whose homes are blighted by poverty, or damaged by alcoholism or drugs;
> those homes where having everything of this world's goods has driven out all spirituality.

For all homes and families we pray. We beseech thee, loving Father, that all homes and families may be strengthened by thy grace, that they may in thee find their full measure of fulfillment. This we ask through Jesus Christ, our Lord. **Amen.**

CHURCH ANNIVERSARY

SENTENCES

How lovely is thy dwelling place, O Lord of hosts! 552.

I was glad when they said to me, "Let us go to the house 553. of the Lord!"

Jesus said: "Where two or three are gathered in my name, 554. there am I in the midst of them."

All who believed were together. And they devoted them- 555. selves to the apostles' teaching and fellowship, to the breaking of bread and the prayers.

No other foundation can any one lay than that which is 556. laid, which is Jesus Christ.

Come to Jesus Christ, to that living stone, rejected by 557. men but in God's sight chosen and precious; and like living stones be yourselves built into a spiritual house, to be a holy priesthood, to offer spiritual sacrifices acceptable to God through Jesus Christ.

Christ loved the Church, and gave himself up for her. 558.

SCRIPTURE SELECTIONS

Psalms 84. 111. 122. 133. 147. Jeremiah 31:31-34. Matthew 7:24-27. Matthew 16:13-28. John 10:1-18. John 15:1-17. John 17. Acts 2. Romans 12. 1 Corinthians 12. Ephesians 2. 3. 4:1-16. Colossians 3:1-17. Hebrews 10:19-25. Hebrews 11. 1 Peter 2:1-10.

559. Almighty God, who hast set the one foundation of every church, renew our human temple that it may, through us, continue to serve thee. Be with us in our tasks of decision making and program planning, that we may reflect the light of thy spirit. Have mercy on us that we may go boldly into the world preaching and teaching thy Word. Grant that as we come to this time of celebration we will not be so blinded by ourselves that we will not see thee and thy will. This do we ask in the name of our Lord Jesus Christ. **Amen.**

560. O God, who by thy grace in Jesus Christ hast made us to share in a high and heavenly calling, we confess to thee our grievous sins as members of thy Church. We have not led a life worthy of this high calling; we have been overprotective of ourselves, and not concerned enough for others. We have used thy word of truth to accomplish our own ends, and not to fulfill thy will. We have been noisy when we should have been silent. We have not obeyed thy Word read and preached to us. We have misused thy grace received in the sacraments, and we have not loved one another as thou didst show thy love for us in the saving act of Christ. O God, Father and Head of the Church, cleanse us and keep us accountable to thee. Through Jesus Christ our Lord and in his name we pray. **Amen.**

561. Almighty God, who hast built thy Church upon the one sure foundation, Jesus Christ our Lord, we lift up our hearts this day in gratitude to thee. We give thanks for this day and the meaning it has in our lives. We thank thee for thy Word which has been preached in this church, and for the sacraments symbolic of our membership in the

body of Christ. We thank thee for the good fellowship of thy people; and for the eternal blessing of grace which thou hast given us through thy Son, Christ. We thank thee for this church building, this congregation as a whole, and each of its members. We bless thy holy name for those who have established this community and built this house of prayer. Unto thee O God, in the unity of the Holy Spirit, be praise and glory in the Church, throughout all ages. Through Jesus Christ our Lord, we adore thee. **Amen.**

O God, who hast brought us into fellowship with one 562. another through thy Son Jesus Christ our Lord: grant us grace and mercy to continue in this ministry together. Help us to do thy will when all else seems more expedient. Direct our thoughts to thee through the reading and preaching of Holy Scripture, that we may always stand in the light of thy Son Jesus Christ. Bless us in our weakness, O God, that we may better love and serve one another. Make holy our willingness to be obedient to thee. We ask through Jesus Christ our Lord. **Amen.**

On this day as we rejoice in the years of blessing in this 563. church, we commend to thee, Almighty God, the whole Christian Church throughout the world. Bless all who call upon the name of our Lord Jesus Christ that they may find strength in that calling. May thy grace fill every member, so that they who know thy Holy Spirit may ever love thy name. Look in mercy at the many wrongs that thy Church has committed, and be gracious in thy judgment. If it be good in thy sight, heal the outward division of thy people and may the one true Church exalt thy name and show forth thy love. Go before thy Church that the world may know thy kingdom is truly at hand. This we ask through Jesus Christ our Lord. **Amen.**

LABOR DAY

SENTENCES

564. In the beginning God created the heavens and the earth.

565. So we built the wall; and all the wall was joined together to half its height. For the people had a mind to work.

   So the wall was finished. And all the nations perceived that this work had been accomplished with the help of our God.

566. The Lord your God has blessed you in all the work of your hands.

567. Commit your work to the Lord, and your plans will be established.

568. There is nothing better than that a man should enjoy his work.

569. According to the work of a man God will requite him.

SCRIPTURE SELECTIONS

Genesis 1:1—2:3. Deuteronomy 25:13-16. 2 Kings 12:9-12. Nehemiah 4. Ecclesiastes 3. Matthew 20:1-16. 1 Corinthians 3:5-16.

PRAYERS

570. We rejoice, O God, in thy marvelous works, the works of thy hand. To thee it is most fitting to offer our thanks and to declare thy steadfast love in the morning, and thy faithfulness by night. Praise is due to thee, O God; and to thee shall vows be performed. **Amen.**

571. For thy creation, the work of thy hands, with all of its marvelous complexities and its indescribable beauties:

202

We thank thee, O Lord.

For Jesus Christ, the carpenter of Nazareth, who with skilled hands built houses, shaped tables and chairs, and showed by his good example that a workman need not be ashamed of his labor:

We thank thee, O Lord.

For Paul the Apostle who, even though his call was to preach the gospel to the whole world, found his living with needle, thread, and cloth in the making of tents:

We thank thee, O Lord.

For all honest workers who with hand and heart, mind and body seek to be colaborers with thee in the fulfillment of thy creation:

We thank thee, O Lord. Amen.

572. We pray for all workers. Grant that they may find joy in their labor and receive a sense of having done well in thy sight and in the eyes of their fellows. Cause them to give a full measure of their labor to those who have hired them.

We pray for all employers. Grant that they be motivated by justice in dealing with their employees. Impress upon them a sense of responsibility for the welfare of all who work for them.

We pray for all unemployed. Grant that opportunity and justice may so reign in the land that all who are able may find work.

We pray for all who are discriminated against in employment because of race or color or creed. Grant that laws may be enacted to restrain injustice, but above all may the hearts of men be so opened that they will employ and be employed solely for their skills and willingness to labor.

We pray for labor unions. May they not only seek the welfare of their members, but seek equal opportunity for all and a just distribution of the goods of society.

These mercies we ask in the name of Jesus Christ our Lord. **Amen.**

WORLD WIDE COMMUNION
AND CHRISTIAN UNITY

Sentences

573. Sing to the Lord a new song; sing to the Lord, all the earth!

574. Behold, how good and pleasant it is when brothers dwell in unity!

575. Jesus said, "I do not pray for these only, but also for those who are to believe in me through their word, that they may all be one; even as thou, Father, art in me, and I in thee, that they also may be in us, so that the world may believe that thou hast sent me."

576. And day by day, attending the temple together and breaking bread in their homes, they partook of food with glad and generous hearts, praising God and having favor with all the people.

577. Lead a life worthy of the calling to which you have been called, with all lowliness and meekness, with patience, forbearing one another in love, eager to maintain the unity of the Spirit in the bond of peace.

578. There is one body and one Spirit, just as you were called to the one hope that belongs to your call, one Lord, one

faith, one baptism, one God and Father of us all, who is above all and through all and in all.

His gifts were that some should be apostles, some prophets, some evangelists, some pastors and teachers, for the equipment of the saints, for the work of the ministry, for building up the body of Christ, until we all attain to the unity of the faith and of the knowledge of the Son of God. 579.

Speaking the truth in love, we are to grow up in every way into him who is the head, into Christ, from whom the whole body, joined and knit together by every joint with which it is supplied, when each part is working properly, makes bodily growth and upbuilds itself in love. 580.

He who loves his brother abides in the light, but he who hates his brother is in the darkness and walks in the darkness, and does not know where he is going. 581.

Scripture Selections

Psalms 96. 133. Isaiah 26:12-19. 61. 65:17-25. Jeremiah 31:31-34. Joel 2:23-29. Matthew 16:13-20. John 10:11-16. 15:1-12. 17:18-26. Romans 12. 1 Corinthians 12. Ephesians 4:1-16. Colossians 1. 3:1-17. 1 John 4. Revelation 1:8, 12-20.

Prayers

Save us, O Lord our God, 582.

And gather us from among the nations,

That we may give thanks to thy holy name

And glory in thy praise. Amen.

In the presence of our Lord Jesus Christ, let us confess our sins against unity: 583.

For the little importance that we have given to this Word proceeding from thy heart, "Other sheep I have which are not of this fold; them also I must bring; they shall hear my voice"

We beseech thee to pardon us, O Lord.

For our controversies, sometimes full of irony, narrow-mindedness, or exaggeration with regard to our Christian brethren, for our stubbornness and harsh judgments

We beseech thee to pardon us, O Lord.

For the many times that we have looked at the speck in the eye of our fellow Christian, rather than at his sincere faith and perseverance and good will

We beseech thee to pardon us, O Lord.

For all restrictive measures unjustly made against others

We beseech thee to pardon us, O Lord.

For all self-sufficiency and pride which we have shown to our Christian brethren and for all our lack of understanding toward them

We beseech thee to pardon us, O Lord.

For all those things in our conduct and example by which we have obstructed our own witness and hindered the work of unity among our brethren

We beseech thee to pardon us, O Lord.

For our neglect of frequent, fervent, and brotherly prayer for them

We beseech thee to pardon us, O Lord.   Amen.

584. Almighty God, who hast gathered thy people throughout the ages and in all the world into one Church, forgive us the painful divisions and wounds which we, thy children, have inflicted upon this thy household of faith. Grant us the grace to overcome our human errors and prejudices

that we might walk together in the unity of our one Master; in whose name we pray. **Amen.**

May the Holy Spirit guide our prayer toward Jesus Christ 585.
and the Father:
Beyond the frontiers of language, race, and nation
Unite us, Lord Jesus.

Beyond our ignorances, our prejudices, and our instinctive enmities
Unite us, Lord Jesus.

Beyond our intellectual and spiritual barriers
Unite us, Lord Jesus.

O God, for thy greater glory
Gather together all separated Christians.

O God, that goodness and truth may prevail
Gather together all separated Christians.

O God, that there may be only one flock and one shepherd
Gather together all separated Christians.

O God, that human pride may be confounded
Gather together all separated Christians.

O God, that peace may at last reign on earth
Gather together all separated Christians.

O God, for the greater joy of thy Son
Gather together all separated Christians.   Amen.

For the unity of all Christian people; for their renewal 586.
and sanctification in truth and love; for all movements
and organizations serving Christian unity; for responsible
teaching within the churches; for faithfulness in common
and private prayer
Lord, have mercy. Christ, have mercy. Lord, have mercy.

For all Christians, that they may feel deeply the pain of their division and may trust in God's power to heal them; for persecuted churches and those which are suffering; for the witness of the Church amid the contradictions of the world; for all enemies and opponents of the Church

Lord, have mercy. Christ, have mercy. Lord, have mercy.

For the Roman Catholic Church; for all its members, each in his vocation and ministry; for the continued guidance of the Holy Spirit as the Roman Church seeks renewal

Lord, have mercy. Christ, have mercy. Lord, have mercy.

For the Orthodox Churches; for the ancient Oriental Churches; for the Anglican Communion; for the Old Catholic Church; for the United Churches; that the members of these churches may faithfully serve the peace and unity of all Christians and of all mankind

Lord, have mercy. Christ, have mercy. Lord, have mercy.

For the Lutheran Churches; for the Presbyterian and Reformed Churches; for the Baptist Churches; for the Methodist Church; for the Disciples of Christ; for the United Church of Christ; that all may walk in the Spirit and grow in the knowledge and love of God and in care for mankind

Lord, have mercy. Christ, have mercy. Lord, have mercy.

For the proclamation of the good news of Jesus Christ in all lands; for a renewal of missionary responsibility in the churches; for all those who take seriously the command to go and preach the gospel and who give their strength to this task; for unity in the Christian mission

Lord, have mercy. Christ, have mercy. Lord, have mercy.

For the peace of the whole world; for governments and international organizations; that the peace of Christ may prevail in all racial and national conflicts; for justice for the oppressed, the hungry, and those dispossessed of their rights; for the witness of the Church in the life of all

Lord, have mercy. Christ, have mercy. Lord, have mercy. Amen.

Lord of the Church, who hast called us to be thy people, 587. we rejoice that on this day the unity of thy Church is being shown as the faithful throughout the whole earth sit at the Lord's Table and partake of this holy meal. We pray that all Christian people might increase in their faith and witness and that every wall which still separates them one from another and brings disunity to thy Church on earth will be broken down; through Jesus Christ our Lord. **Amen.**

Eternal Father, who created this world and all who live 588. within it, grant thy peace this day to all Christians who gather faithfully to eat at thy Table. May we ever continue to grow in mutual love and esteem, under the guidance of thy Spirit, that thy one kingdom might be seen among us; through Jesus Christ our Lord. **Amen.**

Grant us this day, O Lord, an awareness of our member- 589. ship in the whole body of Christ. Give us a sense of being in every nation, among every race, and with every kind of person in the one fellowship of Jesus Christ. **Amen.**

Bless those, Father, who eat this day at other Tables. For- 590. give each of us for the scandal which leads us to make our Tables private rather than open to all members of thy Church, and give us such insight as to overcome this scandal in the days ahead. In Jesus Christ, who called us to be one, we pray. **Amen.**

Almighty God who calls us together, remind us as we 591. come to eat and drink at thy Table that we are one, in all nations, in all races, and in all churches, so far as we believe truly and serve faithfully. Bless those separated from us, and grant us renewed determination to break down the tragic barriers between us. May we, particularly in this community, do everything possible, by thy grace and according to thy will, to achieve a manifestation of our unity in Christ; for we pray in his name. **Amen.**

592. The cup of blessing which we bless, is it not a participation in the blood of Christ? The bread which we break, is it not a participation in the body of Christ? Because there is one loaf, we who are many are one body, for we all partake of the same loaf.

As this bread was once scattered upon the mountains, and has now been gathered into one, so may thy Church be gathered into the unity of thy kingdom: All glory be unto thee, O Lord, for ever and ever!

> **Gather thy Church, O Lord, from the four winds, into the kingdom of thy love.**

Holy Father, we thank thee for thy holy name which thou hast imprinted upon our hearts and for the knowledge of faith and immortality which thou hast brought to light through Jesus, thy Servant.

> **Gather thy Church, O Lord, from the four winds, into the kingdom of thy love.**

Have mercy, O Lord, upon thy Church;
Deliver her from all evil,
And perfect her in thy love.
Gather her out of the nations
Into that unity which thou has prepared,
And unto thee be the power and the glory,
For ever and ever!

> **Gather thy Church, O Lord, from the four winds, into the kingdom of thy love.**

Come, Lord Jesus, come!
Glory be to thee for ever and ever and ever. **Amen.**

Gather thy Church, O Lord, from the four winds, into the kingdom of thy love.

Our Father . . .

593. O God, who in thy Son Jesus Christ didst form thy Church to be of one heart and of one soul, in the power of the resurrection and in the fellowship of the Holy Spirit; renew her evermore in her first love and grant such a measure of it to us thy servants that we may go forth to serve thee as thou willest and where thou showest, through Jesus Christ our Lord. **Amen.**

594. Let us now strive to walk worthy of the calling with which we have been called, with all humility and meekness, with patience, bearing with one another in love, careful to preserve the unity of the Spirit in the bond of peace; one body and one spirit; even as we have been called in one hope of our calling; one Lord, one faith, one baptism; one God and Father of all, who is above all, and throughout all, and in us all. **Amen.**

MISSION OVERSEAS

SENTENCES

595. The people who walked in darkness have seen a great light; those who dwelt in a land of deep darkness, on them has light shined.

596. Thus says God, the Lord, "I am the Lord, I have called you in righteousness, I have taken you by the hand and kept you; I have given you as a covenant to the people, a light to the nations, to open the eyes that are blind, to

bring out the prisoners from the dungeon, from the prison those who sit in darkness."

597. Jesus said: "All authority in heaven and on earth has been given to me. Go therefore and make disciples of all nations, baptizing them in the name of the Father and of the Son and of the Holy Spirit, teaching them to observe all that I have commanded you; and lo, I am with you always, to the close of the age."

598. Jesus said: "Go into all the world and preach the gospel to the whole creation. He who believes and is baptized will be saved."

599. We know that this is indeed the Savior of the world.

600. Jesus said: "I am the light of the world; he who follows me will not walk in darkness, but will have the light of life."

601. Jesus said: "I have other sheep, that are not of this fold; I must bring them also, and they will heed my voice. So there shall be one flock, one shepherd."

602. God made from one every nation of men to live on all the face of the earth, having determined allotted periods and the boundaries of their habitation, that they should seek God, in the hope that they might feel after him and find him. Yet he is not far from each one of us, for "In him we live and move and have our being."

SCRIPTURE SELECTIONS

Genesis 12:1-9. Psalms 67. 72. 96. 126. Isaiah 6. 42:1-13. 49:1-13. 60:1-7. Jeremiah 1:1-10. Jonah 1. 3. Matthew 9:35—10:16. 28:16-20. Luke 10:1-12. John 17:6-21.

20:19-23. Acts 1:1-11. 12:23—13:3. 16:9-15. 17:22-34.
Romans 10:1-17. 15:14-33. 1 Corinthians 9. 2 Corinthians
5:11-22.

Prayers

O God our Father, thou who hast called us to be a light 603.
to the nations, how we have failed thee! We have taken
thy light and put it under the bushel basket of our selfishness. We have failed to see that thou hast chosen us not
because we deserve it, but because thou hast a mission
for us in the world. Forgive us, O God, and grant us grace
to be witnesses to thy Son Jesus Christ; through whom
we pray. **Amen.**

Eternal God, who made the world and everything in it, 604.
and who didst give to all men life and breath and everything and hast made from one every nation of men to
live on all the face of the earth, we praise thee and
thank thee for the calling wherein thou hast called some
to be special witnesses to the marvels of thy grace. We
thank thee for prophets and apostles who have in times
past spoken thy truth, for the ambassadors of Christ in
every age and our own who have in obedience to the
commission to thy Church gone forth into distant lands
to bring light and healing to those who dwell in darkness and in the shadow of death, and for that numberless
throng who have believed because of their words and
deeds. Above all we thank thee for Jesus Christ, who
was sent by thee as thy witness in the world and who
has given unto man the hope that the kingdoms of this
world shall become thy kingdom, and peace and love
shall be the common lot of all men. **Amen.**

We thank thee, our Father, for thy Son, who taught us 605.

213

that our field is the world. We marvel how the whole world was encompassed in his view, even as he walked within the narrow boundaries of Palestine. We cast down our eyes in shame for the isolated and parochial smallness of our own vision. Grant unto us broad vistas that we may see in this our age the wide doors of opportunity standing open before us. We pray that with the new means of transportation and with television and telstars we may seize the increasing opportunities to send forth thy truth and to participate in new and strengthened witness and Christian service to the ends of the earth; through him who has already gone before us to make ready his way we pray. **Amen.**

606. Remember in thy mercy, our Father, all the children of men. Let the whole earth be filled with thy praise and made glad by the knowledge of thy name. Be especially with all missionaries who this day are working in distant lands. Help them to come to know the ways and words of the people with whom they serve. Keep them ever open to the persons around them. Help them to know when they should speak and when they should remain silent. Grant them the grace and humility to learn from those whom they are teaching and to be ready and willing to commit into the hands of those with whom they labor the care and leadership of thy church; through Jesus Christ. **Amen.**

607. Our Father, cause thy churches in faraway lands and at home to come to know that mission and unity are inseparable, that there is but one Lord, one faith, and one baptism. Help all Christians everywhere to join hands and hearts that they may be one even as thou, Father, and thy Son Jesus Christ art one; in whose name we pray. **Amen.**

WORLD ORDER

SENTENCES

Worship the Lord in holy array; tremble before him, all 608.
the earth!

Let the heavens be glad, and let the earth rejoice, 609.
 and let them say among the nations, "The Lord reigns!"

May God be gracious to us and bless us 610.
 and make his face to shine upon us,
that thy way may be known upon earth,
 thy saving power among all nations.

All the families of the nations shall worship before him. 611.
For dominion belongs to the Lord, and he rules over the
nations.

Who would not fear thee, O King of the nations? 612.
 For this is thy due;
for among all the wise ones of the nations
 and in all their kingdoms
 there is none like thee.

You are the light of the world. Let your light so shine 613.
before men that they may see your good works and give
glory to your Father who is in heaven.

For God so loved the world that he gave his only Son, 614.
that whoever believes in him should not perish but have
eternal life.

SCRIPTURE SELECTIONS

Psalms 2. 8. 9. 24. 33. 46. 67. 96. 98. Isaiah 2:1-5.

11:1-10. Micah 4. Matthew 24:1-14. Acts 17:22-31. Romans 13. Revelation 22:1-5.

PRAYERS

615. O God, who hast made of one blood all nations of men for to dwell on the face of the whole earth, and didst send thy blessed Son to preach peace to them that are far off and to them that are nigh: Grant that all men everywhere may seek after thee and find thee. Bring the nations into thy fold, and add the heathen to thine inheritance. And we pray thee shortly to accomplish the number of thine elect and to hasten thy kingdom; through the same Jesus Christ our Lord. **Amen.**

616. Most gracious God, by whose power the broken are made whole, the estranged made known to one another, and the dead made to live again, make of us a people to thee belonging. Redeem the persistent flaw, reveal the hidden unity, and restore thy shattered image; "That thy way may be known upon earth, thy saving power among all nations." **Amen.**

617. Our Father, Creator of all things and of the power of choice that is in man, we humbly pray that thy will be done on earth as it is in heaven.

   As we understand thee as Creator, help us to understand thee also as Lover of the world.

   May we know ourselves as citizens of the world, having the requirements of all flesh and the common, though frequently unrecognized, spiritual needs of all men;

   And we pray that men everywhere may be privileged to be partakers of the fruits of the earth and of thy saving grace.

   Grant to us, O Lord, the vision to see the possibilities of

216

the world as thou dost see them. Purge thy children of all hatred, enmity, vainglory, and greed for power.

Renew us with love, forbearance, humility, and generosity. Help us to understand that, as thy love is extended to all men, so must ours be also.

Grant that those who govern the nations may lead in compassion, economic wisdom, and just laws.

May truth, righteousness, and justice prevail in every nation, and in the relations between nations; and may the fruit of these be peace. As thy Fatherhood implies brotherhood, give thy servants a share in helping to bring about a world in which order abides and the knowledge of thy love brings lasting peace. Amen.

THANKSGIVING AND HARVEST HOME

Sentences

In the beginning God created the heavens and the earth. 618.

The point is this: he who sows sparingly will also reap sparingly, and he who sows bountifully will also reap bountifully. 619.

Thanks be to God for his inexpressible gift! 620.

If you then, who are evil, know how to give good gifts to your children, how much more will your Father who is in heaven give good things to those who ask him? 621.

The earth has yielded its increase; God, our God, has blessed us. 622.

Let us thank the Lord for his steadfast love, for his wonderful works to the sons of men! 623.

624. Know that the Lord is God! It is he that made us, and we are his; we are his people, and the sheep of his pasture.

625. O give thanks to the Lord, for he is good; for his steadfast love endures for ever!

Scripture Selections

Deuteronomy 8. 16:9-17. 26:1-11. 28:1-14. Psalms 65. 67. 103. 104. 126. 145. 147. 150. Matthew 13:1-43. Mark 4:1-34. Luke 12:15-34. 17:5-21. 2 Corinthians 8. 9. Galatians 5:16-6:10. Revelation 14:13-20.

Prayers

626. Father God, we humbly ask forgiveness, for we have squandered that which thou hast so graciously given to the sons of men. We spread the gift of fertile soil to the winds and cause it to be washed into the sea. In our greed we pollute the pure water and lakes and streams. We take the ore from under the earth and cause it to serve mammon. If only, Father, this were the end of it! But even more, we abuse, twist, and manipulate thy gift of our brothers for our private ends. Even this is not the end, for we take the gift of thy Son, and his body the Church, and his Word, and bend them to our desires. Have mercy, most merciful Father. **Amen.**

627. O Father, giver of such bounty as is so fully manifest in this harvest time, we know that we are not worthy to gather up the crumbs from under thy table; yet, out of thy great love and mercy, thou hast not only bestowed this material abundance but beyond all our deserving hast given to us a Savior, Jesus Christ. Help us to believe; and believing, help us to accept; and accepting, help us to act. Thy will, not ours be done. **Amen.**

Unto thee, O God, do we give our thanks: for thy great 628.
mercy toward us; for our creation, preservation, and redemption; for the pardon of sin; for the manifold gifts of
thy love; and for the promise of eternal life in Jesus Christ
our Savior. These are thy great mercies, but as we rejoice
in them we would not forget that thou hast given us yet
more. In the ripening of the grain, in the coming to maturity of the fruit, in the abundance which the land so
freely yields, we see thy hand and we give to thee our
thanks. Cause our spirit of thankfulness to be so enlarged
that we may with full willingness and in thy spirit of
giving share our abundance with all who are in need, that
they too may praise thee; through Jesus Christ. **Amen.**

Eternal Spirit, the source of all being, the ground of every 629.
hope, we gather on this day which is dedicated to gratitude, to offer our thanks to thee.

For lives that have been given opportunity to accomplish
spiritual tasks in a material world; for tools to labor at
these tasks; for abilities and interests; for courage and
patience; and for the will to pursue as well as the con-
crete endowments that make life more challenging, more
exciting, more comely and more pleasant

> **We give thee thanks, O God.**

For inward shepherding; for peace gained in high com-
panionship with thee; for all the spirit can do with its own
solitariness when left alone in a quiet hour of tranquility
with thee

> **We give thee thanks, O God.**

For the fellowship and remembrance of friends; for their
faces and names, and the recall of the joy and light they
have brought to our lives as they with us have surmounted
discouragement, confusion, bewilderment, and loneliness

We give thee thanks, O God.

For the inner fellowship of great souls through whom thou hast blest the world: prophets, martyrs, apostles, producers of beauty, manifesters of goodness and truth, who have become our friends as we have lived through the lives they lived and the works they have produced

We give thee thanks, O God.

For the call to join the family of man in building a world where Christ's will rules and where thou art called Father, and all men are brothers

We give thee thanks, O God.   Amen.

PART 6

SPECIAL SERVICES

Although the basic principles of Christian worship are embodied in *The Service for the Lord's Day* (Part 2), there are occasions in the life of the congregation and for the members of the congregation that require special kinds of Christian observance. Most of the special services find their places in *The Service for the Lord's Day* and are a part of the act of dedication. In some instances appropriate Scripture passages have been suggested. In others the Scriptures have been included in full, for it is helpful to the minister to have these in hand in some cases as he is conducting the worship.

A service of the Laying on of Hands of those baptized has been included. This service was practiced in ancient times as well as by the early General Baptists of Great Britain. Its basic intent is confirmation of the faith that has been expressed in baptism and the commissioning or ordination of those baptized to their lay ministry in the church and world. Included also is a service for the commissioning (or ordination) of deacons. In this service those who have been elected by the church to be deacons are set apart for their special ministry as servants in the church and world.

630. BAPTISM OF BELIEVERS

Baptism* should be a part of the Service for the Lord's Day and administered in the presence of the whole congregation.

Since baptism is an act of dedication, it should rightly come in response to the Word and be placed after the prayers of dedication as a part of the offertory. If possible, baptism should be followed by the laying on of hands, the reception of those baptized into church membership, and the Lord's Supper. Or the act of baptism may come at the beginning of the service, after which those baptized will return for participation in the whole service, the laying on of hands coming as a part of the offertory, followed by the reception into church membership and the Lord's Supper. If the Lord's Supper comes at another service, the laying on of hands and reception into church membership should come at that time.

The minister enters the water and says:

Jesus came and said to them, "All authority in heaven and on earth has been given to me. Go therefore and make disciples of all nations, baptizing them in the name of the Father and of the Son and of the Holy Spirit, teaching them to observe all that I have commanded you; and lo, I am with you always, to the close of the age."

*Scriptures and Prayers suitable for baptism are in Part 5, selections 513-529.

The minister, using his own words or the following, addresses the congregation:

Brethren, you have heard the command of Christ to his Church to make disciples, baptizing them into the name of the Father, the Son and the Holy Spirit. In baptism we are made one with Christ through faith. We are buried with him into death and with him raised from the dead by the glory of the Father to walk in newness of life. This washing of our bodies with water is the outward and visible sign of the cleansing of our inner being through the grace of our Savior Jesus Christ. Not only are we baptized with water but also with the Holy Spirit, for we know that unless one is born of the water and the Spirit, he cannot enter the kingdom of God. By this same Holy Spirit, we are baptized into one body and made members of the whole people of God. Let us therefore in obedience to Christ's command baptize these who have professed their faith in him.

Then the person to be baptized enters the water and the minister says to him:

J———— D————, do you believe in God as your eternal Father, in Jesus Christ as your Savior and Lord, and in the Holy Spirit as your Comforter?

The candidate answers:

I do.

The minister says:

Let us pray:
Almighty Father, receive this the confession of thy servant. Cause him now to know the newness of life which thou

223

hast promised to all who believe and are baptized. May thy Spirit so dwell in him that all the days of his life will be spent in faithful discipleship to thy Son Jesus Christ, our Lord; in whose name we pray. **Amen.**

Then the minister says:

Upon the profession of your faith, on behalf of this congregation, and in obedience to the command of our Lord Jesus Christ, I baptize you, in the name of the Father and of the Son and of the Holy Spirit. **Amen.**

Then the minister baptizes the candidate by immersing him in water.

After all the candidates have been baptized, the minister says:

We have done as our Lord has commanded. Even as these who have been baptized have confessed their faith and committed themselves to discipleship, let us all now renew our baptismal vows. Let us pray:

Our Father, as we have witnessed this act of obedience, we have remembered that day when we too gave witness to our faith in baptism. Make alive that memory by baptizing us afresh with thy Spirit. May we know once again the newness of life which has been so abundantly evidenced by these thy servants who have this day been baptized. Open our hearts to them that as members of this congregation we may receive them into our midst and that they may know amongst us the same spirit of love that was in Christ, who loved us and gave himself for us. **Amen.**

631. COMMISSIONING OF THOSE WHO HAVE BEEN BAPTIZED BY THE LAYING ON OF HANDS AND PRAYER

This act is directly related to Christian baptism and should follow as soon afterwards as is convenient. As soon as the candidates have returned to the service, and before the Lord's Supper, the minister shall address the congregation saying:

We are now to commission those who have been baptized for their ministry as priests and servants of Jesus Christ by the laying on of hands and prayer. As we set them apart for their vocation as Christians, may we once again renew our commitment to the servant ministry of Christ in the world. Let us now, together with them, hear the words of Scripture.

The minister then reads one or more of the following Scripture passages:

You are a chosen race, a royal priesthood, a holy nation, God's own people, that you may declare the wonderful deeds of him who called you out of darkness into his marvelous light.

As each has received a gift, employ it for one another, as good stewards of God's varied grace: whoever speaks, as one who utters oracles of God; whoever renders service, as one who renders it by the strength which God supplies; in order that in everything God may be glorified through Jesus Christ.

Never flag in zeal, be aglow with the Spirit, serve the Lord. Rejoice in your hope, be patient in tribulation, be constant in prayer.

You are the light of the world. Let your light so shine before men that they may see your good works and give glory to your Father who is in heaven.

A new commandment I give to you, that you love one another; even as I have loved you. By this all men will know that you are my disciples, if you have love for one another.

Those who have been baptized kneel now before the Lord's Table and the minister prays extempore or as follows:

Eternal Father, cause thy Spirit to come upon these thy servants to empower them for thy ministry in the world. Enable them as faithful priests of Jesus Christ to bring others to thee in prayer. Help them to speak as thy witnesses to all sorts and conditions of men. Cause them to be so filled with thy love that, as they live in the world, the world may come to know the love which sent thy Son into the world. In all their ministry may they truly serve thee; through Jesus Christ. **Amen.**

Then the minister and one or two lay representatives shall lay their hands in turn on the head of each one who has been baptized and the minister shall pray:

Bless, O Lord, this thy servant and empower him by thy Holy Spirit for the service and ministry of Jesus Christ our Lord. **Amen.**

The newly commissioned ones now stand and the minister extends to them the right hand of fellowship, saying:

So then you are no longer strangers and sojourners, but you are fellow citizens with the saints and members of the household of God, built upon the foundation of the apostles and prophets, Christ Jesus himself being the chief cornerstone. In the name of Jesus Christ and as the representative of this congregation I welcome you. The God of all grace, who has called you to his eternal glory in Christ, will himself restore, establish, and strengthen you. To him be the dominion for ever and ever. **Amen.**

Then the new members, where it is the custom, may sign the Church Covenant and Membership Roll.

The minister and deacons shall then proceed with the administration of the Lord's Supper.

RECEPTION OF CHURCH MEMBERS

The reception of new church members should take place in the Service for the Lord's Day at the time of the offertory. As the gifts are brought to the Table the new members come forward. After the dedication of the gifts, the minister, addressing the congregation, shall say:

Members of this congregation, we welcome in the name of Jesus Christ these new members. They have fulfilled the requirements for membership and are now ready to be received into our church.

Do you so receive them? Do you promise before God and in their presence to give them your love and encouragement that they may grow in their Christian life and commitment?

The congregation shall answer:

We do.

Then the minister may read one or more of the following Scripture passages:

If any man would come after me, let him deny himself and take up his cross and follow me. For whoever would save his life will lose it and whoever loses his life for my sake and the gospel's will save it.

A new commandment I give to you, that you love one another; even as I have loved you, that you also love one another. By this all men will know that you are my disciples, if you have love for one another.

And they devoted themselves to the apostles' teaching and fellowship, to the breaking of bread and the prayers.

For as in one body we have many members, and all the members do not have the same function, so we, though many, are one body in Christ, and individually members one of another. Having gifts that differ according to the grace given to us, let us use them.

Let love be genuine; hate what is evil, hold fast to what is good; love one another with brotherly affection; outdo one another in showing honor. Never flag in zeal, be aglow with the Spirit, serve the Lord. Rejoice in your hope, be patient in tribulation, be constant in prayer. Contribute to the needs of the saints; practice hospitality.

The fruit of the Spirit is love, joy, peace, patience, kindness, goodness, faithfulness, gentleness, self-control. If we live by the Spirit, let us also walk by the Spirit. Bear one another's burdens, and so fulfill the law of Christ. Let him who is taught the word share all good things with him who teaches. And let us not grow weary in well-doing, for in due season we shall reap, if we do not lose heart. So then, as we have opportunity, let us do good to all men, and especially to those who are of the household of faith.

Let us hold fast the confession of our hope without wavering, for he who promised is faithful; and let us consider how to stir up one another to love and good works, not neglecting to meet together, as is the habit of some, but encouraging one another, and all the more as you see the Day drawing near.

The minister then addresses each new member by name:

J................ D................, do you promise before God and this congregation to be a faithful follower of Jesus Christ and to serve him gladly in the fellowship of this church?

Each person as addressed, answers:

I do.

Then the minister says:

Let us pray:
We thank thee, our Father, for these who have come to make their church home with us. May they find in our midst love and concern for them and their well-being. Give to them thy Spirit that they may freely give of themselves in thy service amongst us. Enable them to be faithful members of this congregation, continuing stead-fastly in the apostles' teaching and fellowship, in the breaking of bread and the prayers. May they not only see their role as Christians within the walls of this church building, but also in the world where thou dost seek to make thy will known and where they are called to minister. Grant that they may grow up in every way into him who is the Head of the Church, even Jesus Christ thy Son and our Lord. **Amen.**

The minister, extending his hand to each new member, says:

In the name of the Lord Jesus Christ and on behalf of this congregation I welcome you into the membership of this church and extend to you its Right Hand of Fellowship.

After this, the minister shall say to all of the new members together:

So then you are no longer strangers and sojourners, but you are fellow citizens with the saints and members of the household of God, built upon the foundation of the apostles and prophets, Christ Jesus himself being the chief cornerstone.

Then the new members, where it is the custom, may sign the Church Covenant and Membership Roll. They then take their places in the congregation.

The minister and deacons then proceed with the administration of the Lord's Supper.

633. MARRIAGE

The Christian marriage service should take place within the Service for the Lord's Day. At the time of the Offertory and after the gifts have been presented, a hymn is sung and the bride and groom and their company shall come from the congregation and take their places before the Table. If the marriage service is at another time, it ought to be in the setting of worship with suitable hymns, prayers, and Scripture readings.

The minister says:

Dear friends, M................ and W................ have come to offer themselves to God and each other in the holy bond of marriage.

God has established marriage for our welfare and enjoyment. Marriage makes sacred the union between man and woman and offers to each the opportunity to grow together in more complete manhood and womanhood.

Our Lord has declared that a man shall leave his parents and shall unite with his wife. He has commanded through his apostles that husbands and wives love and cherish each other throughout their lives and that they shall give each other strength and compassionate understanding and together share their joys and pains. The Creator offers to them the privilege and responsibility of parenthood and enjoins them that they support each other in this sacred opportunity with all affection and concern that their children might see in their marriage bond the love which comes from God and which offers hope to all men.

These two who have heretofore traveled separate ways come now to be made one. If any here gathered can show any just cause why they may not lawfully be joined together in marriage, let him now declare it, or else forever hold his peace.

The minister addresses the two persons and says:

If either of you know any reason why you should not be joined in marriage, you must now confess it.

If no impediment appears, the minister says:

Let us pray:

Father of love, who hast brought these two together to be made one in holy marriage, all thy servants here assembled now pray thee to bless them with every good and perfect blessing. May their love never cease to grow in character and fullness; may they have the strength to share each other's joys and sorrows, continually bearing one another's burdens. May their temptations be few and may they always be ready to forgive each other, even as thou through Christ dost forgive them. We ask in the name of Jesus Christ, who has taught us to pray, saying:

Our Father . . .

Then the minister says to the man:

M................., will you have this woman to be your wedded wife, to live together in the holy estate of marriage? Will you love her, comfort her, honor and keep her, in sickness and in health; and forsaking all others keep you only to her, so long as you both shall live?

The man answers:

I will.

Then the minister says to the woman:

W................., will you have this man to be your wedded husband, to live together in the holy estate of marriage? Will you love him, comfort him, honor and keep him, in sickness and in health; and forsaking all others keep you only to him so long as you both shall live?

The woman answers:

I will.

Then the minister may say:

Who gives this woman to be married to this man?

The woman's father says:

I do.

The minister then joins the right hands of the man and the woman. The man, instructed by the minister, says to the woman:

I, M................., take you, W................., to be my wife. I promise before God and these friends to be your loving and faithful husband, to share with you in plenty and in want, in joy and in sorrow, in sickness and in health, and to join with you so that together we may serve God and others, as long as we both shall live. God be my help.

While their hands are still joined, the woman, instructed by the minister, says to the man:

I, W................., take you, M................., to be my husband. I promise before God and these friends to be your loving and faithful wife, to share with you in plenty and in want, in joy and in sorrow, in sickness and in health, and to join with you so that together we may serve God and others, as long as we both shall live. God be my help.

They loose their hands and the minister asks for the ring(s) with these words:

What token have you to symbolize your pledge of the faithful fulfillment of your marriage vows?

Then the minister is given the ring(s) and says:

This ring (these rings) is (are) the outward and visible sign of the inward and spiritual bond which unites this man and woman in endless love.

The minister gives the ring to the man who places it upon the fourth finger of the woman's left hand. In the same way the woman may give a ring to the man. Then the man (followed by the woman, if there are two rings) repeats after the minister:

I give this ring to you as a token of the covenant made between us this day and as a pledge of our mutual love: in the name of the Father, and of the Son, and of the Holy Spirit. Amen.

Then the minister says to the congregation:

Since M................ and W................ have consented to join together in marriage, and have witnessed the same before God and this company, and have pledged their mutual love to each other, and have declared the same by the giving and receiving of a ring (rings), and by joining hands, I declare that they are husband and wife, in the name of the Father, and of the Son, and of the Holy Spirit. Amen.

The God of all love has joined you as man and wife. Go now in peace, trusting that the love which you now know will forever make you one.

The couple may then kneel, as the minister says:

Let us pray:

Father of love and mercy, show thy compassion on this couple who have come before thee in the presence of their friends to pledge themselves to live together in the holy estate of marriage. Grant them the strength and patience, the affection and understanding, the courage and love to abide together in peace and mutual growth according to thy will for them both; through Jesus Christ our Lord. **Amen.**

The minister may add this blessing:

The Lord bless you and keep you: The Lord make his face to shine upon you, and be gracious to you: The Lord lift up his countenance upon you, and give you peace. **Amen.**

The man and woman and their company then take their places in the congregation, and the Lord's Supper is observed according to the Service for the Lord's Day.

At the conclusion of the service the man and woman may be greeted by the members of the congregation.

In this service in which the child is being dedicated to God, the parents and the congregation publicly express their acceptance of the responsibility to offer every help and encouragement to the child, seeking to lead him to Christian discipleship in later life. Since the dedication service involves an acknowledgment of responsibility by parents, it should be held only if at least one of the parents is known to be living a responsible Christian life. Not to take into consideration the faith and life of the parent would be to make a mockery out of the service. The service should be preceded by pastoral instruction on the meaning of Christian parenthood.

The following service should be included within the context of the worship service. It may be inserted as part of the Offertory, an act signifying the offering to God of the child. As the gifts and elements for the Lord's Supper are presented, the deacons, representing the Church, escort the parents and child to the front.

After the dedication of the gifts the minister says:

We welcome in the Lord's name R———— and M————
S————, who have brought their child W————
to be dedicated to God, the maker of all things and giver of all life. In this act of dedication we follow our Lord Jesus Christ, who took little children in his arms and blessed them. Let us now hear the Word of God.

The minister may read an appropriate passage from Scripture, such as:

Deuteronomy 6:4-7. Psalms 103:17, 18. 127:1, 3. Matthew

18:1-5. 19:13-15. Mark 8:36, 37. 10:13-16. Luke 9:46-48. 18:15-17. Colossians 3:20, 21. Ephesians 6:1-4.

Then the minister, parents, and congregation pray responsively the prayer of thanksgiving:

O God our heavenly Father, maker of all things, creator of all life, we praise thy name for thy marvelous works in all the world.

For blessing these thy servants with the gift of this child:

We thank thee, O Father.

For the wonder of creation which is manifested at birth:

We thank thee, O Lord.

For the opportunity of service and of love which is given to each of us to manifest toward this child:

We thank thee, O Lord God our Father. Amen.

Then the minister addresses the parents, saying:

In presenting this child to the Lord, do you promise that through the grace given you and in partnership with the Church, you both will teach him (her) the truths and duties of the Christian faith; and by prayer, precept, and example will bring him (her) up in the discipline and instruction of the Lord?

The parents reply:

We do.

Addressing the congregation, the minister says:

Do you, as members of this congregation, acknowledge and accept the responsibility, together with the parents, of teaching and training this child, that he (she), being brought up in the discipline and instruction of the Lord, may be led in due time to trust Christ as Savior, and confessing him as Lord in baptism, be made a member of his Church? If so, will you signify your acceptance of this responsibility by standing?

The congregation stands. Then the minister takes the child into his arms and pronounces the child's name and an appropriate blessing, such as:

The Lord bless you and keep you: The Lord make his face to shine upon you, and be gracious to you: The Lord lift up his countenance upon you, and give you peace. Amen.

Returning the child to the parents, the minister says:

Let us pray:

Even as Mary and Joseph brought the child Jesus to thy house that he might be consecrated to thy service, so these parents have brought this little one to this place that amidst thy people they might present him (her) unto thee. Give to these parents thy special graces of insight and love that this child under their guidance may grow in wisdom and stature and in favor with thee and man. Grant that we thy people may truly be a household of faith unto this child, providing him (her) with food for the spirit to nourish him (her) through the years of his (her) growth into maturity. With deep gratitude unto thee for this child we dedicate him (her), these his (her) parents, and ourselves to the end that his life may be a blessing unto thee and a service unto man; through Jesus Christ our Lord. **Amen.**

Here the minister may present the parents with a Bible or a New Testament or a certificate for the child, symbolizing the responsibility and the faith entailed in this dedication. The service of worship then continues.

If possible the memorial service should take place in the church sanctuary or chapel at some time after the disposal of the body. The same gathering place from which have pealed forth the joys of baptism, marriage, worship, and the celebration of the victory of Easter is the fitting place to hold a service of memory for one who has gained the final victory over death.

The memorial can be a part of the Lord's Day Service and incorporated as an act of thanksgiving and remembrance for "the saints who from their labors rest." Such a service might be held once a month, or as needed, to include all who have died during the preceding weeks. A family memorial also might be held at the time of the death.

(If the service is a funeral in which the body is present, the casket should be kept closed, in keeping with the Christian view of death: "Why do you seek the living among the dead? He is not here." For such a service the organ may play music which emphasizes majesty rather than sentiment.)

The minister says one or more of the following:

Our help is in the name of the Lord, who made heaven and earth. Lord, thou hast been our dwelling place in all generations. Before the mountains were brought forth, or ever thou hadst formed the earth and the world, from everlasting to everlasting thou art God.

Blessed are those who mourn, for they shall be comforted.

Jesus said, "I am the resurrection and the life; he who believes in me, though he die, yet shall he live, and whoever lives and believes in me shall never die."

If we live, we live to the Lord, and if we die, we die to the Lord; so then, whether we live or whether we die, we are the Lord's. For to this end Christ died and lived again, that he might be Lord both of the dead and of the living.

Blessed be the God and Father of our Lord Jesus Christ! By his great mercy we have been born anew to a living hope through the resurrection of Jesus Christ from the dead, and to an inheritance which is imperishable, undefiled, and unfading, kept in heaven for you.

Weeping may tarry for the night, but joy comes with the morning.

The eternal God is your dwelling place, and underneath are the everlasting arms.

God is our refuge and strength, a very present help in trouble.

Here may be sung a hymn, after which the minister says:

Lift up your hearts.
   We lift them up unto the Lord.

O Lord, open thou our lips,
   And our mouths shall show forth thy praise.

Let us pray:

Eternal Spirit, before whom the generations rise and pass away, even in the presence of death our first words to thee are in praise of thine unnumbered mercies. For the memory of loved ones now departed, in whom we have seen the light of thy presence, we praise thee. For victories of character over trial, of courage over difficulty, of faith over sorrow, and for all souls who have done justly and loved mercy and walked humbly with their God, we sing joyfully unto thee. Grant us now such spiritual triumph in the memory of our friend, that in our hearts death may be swallowed up in the knowledge of thy great victory; through Jesus Christ our Lord. **Amen.**

or

Eternal Father, in whom we live and move and have our being, who by thy mighty power didst raise up our Lord Jesus Christ from the dead, give us strength by thy Holy Spirit, the Comforter. Help us as we worship thee to put our whole trust in thy wisdom and give ourselves to the ministry of thy love. Open our hearts that we may truly hear the words of eternal life as they come to us from the Scriptures that by their encouragement we may be lifted out of our sorrow into thy presence; through Jesus Christ, whom to know is life eternal. **Amen.**

Then a Psalm such as Psalm 16, 23, 39, 116, 121, or 130 may be read or sung.

Then may be read selections from the following, or other suitable passages of Scripture:

"Let not your hearts be troubled; believe in God, believe also in me. In my Father's house are many rooms; if it were not so, would I have told you that I go to prepare a place for you? And when I go and prepare a place for you, I will come again and will take you to myself, that where I am you may be also. And you know the way where I am going." Thomas said to him, "Lord, we do not know where you are going; how can we know the way?" Jesus said to him, "I am the way, and the truth, and the life; no one comes to the Father, but by me."

"Peace I leave with you; my peace I give to you; not as

the world gives do I give to you. Let not your hearts be troubled, neither let them be afraid."

I consider that the sufferings of this present time are not worth comparing with the glory that is to be revealed to us.

We know that in everything God works for good with those who love him, who are called according to his purpose.

Who shall separate us from the love of Christ? Shall tribulation, or distress, or persecution, or famine, or nakedness, or peril, or sword?

No, in all these things we are more than conquerors through him who loved us. For I am sure that neither death, nor life, nor angels, nor principalities, nor things present, nor things to come, nor powers, nor height, nor depth, nor anything else in all creation, will be able to separate us from the love of God in Christ Jesus our Lord.

Christ has been raised from the dead, the first fruits of those who have fallen asleep. For as by a man came death, by a man has come also the resurrection of the dead. For as in Adam all die, so also in Christ shall all be made alive. But each in his own order: Christ the first fruits, then at his coming those who belong to Christ.

But some one will ask, "How are the dead raised? With what kind of body do they come?" You foolish man! What you sow does not come to life unless it dies. And what you sow is not the body which is to be, but a bare kernel, perhaps of wheat or of some other grain. But God gives it a body as he has chosen, and to each kind of seed its own body.

So is it with the resurrection of the dead. What is sown is

perishable, what is raised is imperishable. It is sown in dishonor, it is raised in glory. It is sown in weakness, it is raised in power. It is sown a physical body, it is raised a spiritual body. If there is a physical body, there is also a spiritual body.

I tell you this, brethren: flesh and blood cannot inherit the kingdom of God, nor does the perishable inherit the imperishable.

Lo! I tell you a mystery. We shall not all sleep, but we shall all be changed, in a moment, in the twinkling of an eye, at the last trumpet. For the trumpet will sound, and the dead will be raised imperishable, and we shall be changed.

For this perishable nature must put on the imperishable, and this mortal nature must put on immortality. When the perishable puts on the imperishable, and the mortal puts on immortality, then shall come to pass the saying that is written:

> "Death is swallowed up in victory."
> "O death, where is thy victory?
> O death, where is thy sting?"

The sting of death is sin, and the power of sin is the law. But thanks be to God, who gives us the victory through our Lord Jesus Christ.

So we do not lose heart. Though our outer nature is wasting away, our inner nature is being renewed every day. For this slight momentary affliction is preparing for us an eternal weight of glory beyond all comparison, because we look not to the things that are seen but to the things that are unseen; for the things that are seen are transient, but the things that are unseen are eternal. For we know that if the earthly tent we live in is destroyed, we have a building from God, a house not made

242

with hands, eternal in the heavens. Here indeed we groan, and long to put on our heavenly dwelling, so that by putting it on we may not be found naked. For while we are still in this tent, we sigh with anxiety; not that we would be unclothed, but that we would be further clothed, so that what is mortal may be swallowed up by life. He who has prepared us for this very thing is God, who has given us the Spirit as a guarantee.

So we are always of good courage; we know that while we are at home in the body we are away from the Lord, for we walk by faith, not by sight. We are of good courage, and we would rather be away from the body and at home with the Lord. So whether we are at home or away, we make it our aim to please him. For we must all appear before the judgment seat of Christ, so that each one may receive good or evil, according to what he has done in the body.

Blessed be the God and Father of our Lord Jesus Christ! By his great mercy we have been born anew to a living hope through the resurrection of Jesus Christ from the dead, and to an inheritance which is imperishable, undefiled, and unfading, kept in heaven for you, who by God's power are guarded through faith for a salvation ready to be revealed in the last time. In this you rejoice, though now for a little while you may have to suffer various trials, so that the genuineness of your faith, more precious than gold which though perishable is tested by fire, may redound to praise and glory and honor at the revelation of Jesus Christ. Without having seen him you love him; though you do not now see him you believe in him and rejoice with unutterable and exalted joy. As the outcome of your faith you obtain the salvation of your souls.

I looked, and behold, a great multitude which no man could number, from every nation, from all tribes and peoples and tongues, standing before the throne and before the Lamb, clothed in white robes, with palm branches in their hands, and crying out with a loud voice, "Salvation belongs to our God who sits upon the throne, and to the Lamb!"

Then one of the elders addressed me, saying, "Who are these, clothed in white robes, and whence have they come?" I said to him, "Sir, you know." And he said to me, "These are they who have come out of the great tribulation; they have washed their robes and made them white in the blood of the Lamb."

Then I saw a new heaven and a new earth; for the first heaven and the first earth had passed away, and the sea was no more. And I saw the holy city, new Jerusalem, coming down out of heaven from God, prepared as a bride adorned for her husband; and I heard a great voice from the throne saying, "Behold, the dwelling of God is with men. He will dwell with them, and they shall be his people, and God himself will be with them; he will wipe away every tear from their eyes, and death shall be no more, neither shall there be mourning nor crying nor pain any more, for the former things have passed away."

Here may follow the Gloria, the Doxology, or a suitable hymn of affirmation.

If desired the minister may interpret a Scripture passage dealing with the victory of Christ over death.

One of the following prayers, or extempore prayer, may then be offered.

God of all grace, who didst send thy Son our Savior Jesus

Christ to bring life and immortality to light; most humbly and heartily we give thee thanks, that by his death he destroyed the power of death, and by his glorious resurrection opened the kingdom of heaven to all believers. We bless thee for the assurance that because he lives we shall live also, and that neither death nor life, nor things present nor things to come, shall be able to separate us from thy love, which is in Christ Jesus our Lord. **Amen.**

Our Father, comfort us as we face the valley of the shadow of death. Lift our eyes from the dark depths unto the hills from whence our help comes. Help us to see thy light. Guide us by that light until we come into the fullness of thy presence in which there is no shadow or hiding; through Jesus Christ, our Lord. **Amen.**

Eternal God, let thy mercy rest upon us as we with grateful affection remember our friend who has departed this life. We thank thee for the days upon this earth which thou didst give to him. Cause his memory to live long amongst us and be to us a source of strength. Give, to those who most deeply miss his going, deep wells of consolation from which to draw their comfort, and enable each of us to be thy minister of mercy to these who mourn; through Jesus Christ, our Lord. **Amen.**

Thou art the God of the living. With thee there is no death. Our departed who have passed out of our sight are at home with thee for evermore. As thou didst not lose them in giving them to us, so we have not lost them by their return to thee. Deepen in us this faith in life eternal, and enable us so to live in this life that we shall be the servants of thy will, and in that service come to know thee whom to know is life eternal. **Amen.**

*Then shall be said the Lord's Prayer, after which the
minister shall say:*

Now may the God of peace who brought again from the
dead our Lord Jesus, the great shepherd of the sheep, by
the blood of the eternal covenant, equip you with everything good that you may do his will, working in you that
which is pleasing in his sight; through Jesus Christ, to
whom be glory for ever and ever. **Amen.**

or

May the peace which passes all understanding keep your
hearts and minds in the knowledge and love of God and
of his Son Jesus Christ; and may the blessing of God, the
Father, the Son, and the Holy Spirit, rest upon you and
abide with you now and for evermore. **Amen.**

636.   COMMITTAL

*If a service of committal is held at the grave or crema-
torium, the minister may begin by reading one or more of
the following Scripture sentences:*

The Lord gave, and the Lord has taken away; blessed be
the name of the Lord.

Jesus said, "I am the resurrection and the life; he who
believes in me, though he die, yet shall he live, and whoever lives and believes in me shall never die."

Death is swallowed up in victory. O death, where is thy
victory? O death, where is thy sting? Thanks be to God,
who gives us the victory through our Lord Jesus Christ.

Christ has been raised from the dead, the first fruits of
those who have fallen asleep. For as by a man came
death, by a man has come also the resurrection of the

dead. For as in Adam all die, so also in Christ shall all be made alive.

I know that my Redeemer lives, and at last he will stand upon the earth; and I shall see God.

Then shall be said the words of committal:

Forasmuch as it has pleased Almighty God in his great mercy to receive to himself the spirit of our brother (sister) departed, we therefore commit his (her) body to be consumed by fire, ashes to ashes, dust to dust; in the hope of the resurrection to eternal life; through Jesus Christ our Lord. **Amen.**

Or at a crematorium service, the minister says:

Forasmuch as it has pleased Almighty God in his great mercy to receive to himself the spirit of our brother (sister) departed, we therefore commit his (her) body to be consumed by fire, ashes to ashes, dust to dust; in the hope of the resurrection to eternal life; through Jesus Christ our Lord. **Amen.**

Then shall be said:

And I heard a voice from heaven saying, "Write this: Blessed are the dead who die in the Lord henceforth." "Blessed indeed," says the Spirit, "that they may rest from their labors, for their deeds follow them!"

Let us pray:
Almighty God, who by the death and resurrection of thy Son Jesus Christ didst reveal thy victory over sin and death, grant that we may live in the power of that triumph and that we shall give witness throughout our whole lives to him who is the resurrection and the life,

who liveth and reigneth with thee and the Holy Spirit, ever one God, world without end. **Amen.**

The Lord bless you and keep you: The Lord make his face to shine upon you, and be gracious to you: The Lord lift up his countenance upon you, and give you peace. **Amen.**

637.   MEMORIAL FOR A CHILD
The minister may say one or more of the following:

Blessed are those who mourn, for they shall be comforted.

He will feed his flock like a shepherd, he will gather the lambs in his arms, he will carry them in his bosom.

Thus says the Lord, "As one whom his mother comforts, so I will comfort you."

Jesus said, "Let the children come to me, do not hinder them; for to such belongs the kingdom of God."

A hymn of trust in God may be sung.

The minister then says:

Let us pray:
Eternal God, our Father, thou who lovest us and hast promised that where thy children gather in thy name, there thou art: come into our midst and speak to our condition that we may receive understanding and encouragement. Cause thy Word which is read to become for us the Word of eternal life that there may be renewed within us a living faith and we may come to know the peace which passes all understanding; through Jesus Christ. Amen.

Psalm 23 may then be read or sung:

The Lord is my shepherd, I shall not want; he makes me lie down in green pastures. He leads me beside still waters; he restores my soul. He leads me in paths of righteousness for his name's sake.

Even though I walk through the valley of the shadow of death, I fear no evil; for thou art with me; thy rod and thy staff, they comfort me.

Thou preparest a table before me in the presence of my enemies; thou anointest my head with oil, my cup overflows. Surely goodness and mercy shall follow me all the days of my life; and I shall dwell in the house of the Lord for ever.

Then a selection of the following or other suitable Scriptures may be read:

At that time the disciples came to Jesus, saying, "Who is the greatest in the kingdom of heaven?" And calling to him a child, he put him in the midst of them, and said, "Truly, I say to you, unless you turn and become like children, you will never enter the kingdom of heaven. Whoever humbles himself like this child, he is the greatest in the kingdom of heaven. Whoever receives one such child in my name receives me."

"See that you do not despise one of these little ones; for I tell you that in heaven their angels always behold the face of my Father who is in heaven. What do you think? If a man has a hundred sheep, and one of them has gone astray, does he not leave the ninety-nine on the hills and go in search of the one that went astray? And if he finds it, truly, I say to you, he rejoices over it more than over the ninety-nine that never went astray. So it is not the will of my Father who is in heaven that one of these little ones should perish."

And they were bringing children to him, that he might touch them; and the disciples rebuked them. But when Jesus saw it he was indignant, and said to them, "Let the children come to me, do not hinder them; for to such belongs the kingdom of God. Truly, I say to you, whoever does not receive the kingdom of God like a child shall not enter it." And he took them in his arms and blessed them, laying his hands upon them.

The streets of the city shall be full of boys and girls playing in its streets. God himself will be with them; he will wipe away every tear from their eyes, and death shall be no more, neither shall there be mourning nor crying nor pain any more, for the former things have passed away.

An address based upon one of the passages read may then be given.

The minister then offers prayer, extempore or as follows:

Let us pray:

Eternal Father, we thank thee for this little child who has been amongst us and by his presence has brought blessing to those who have cared for him. We thank thee for the love which he has called forth and for the memories of his presence that will continue to bless his home. Grant that those who have been responsible for his life and who have poured out upon him their affection and love may be deepened in their faith and that even in their sorrow their spirits will be renewed; through Jesus Christ. **Amen.**

O God, who in thy Son didst promise comfort to those who mourn, be with these parents who have suffered the loss of their child. Grant that in their sorrow they may be brought closer to thee and to each other and that their hearts may be filled with thy presence and peace; through Jesus Christ our Lord. **Amen.**

O thou who in thy Son didst take a child into his arms and say "to such belongs the kingdom of God," we rest in the assurance that this little one is with thee. Strengthen our faith that we too may believe that all who become like little children will in the end be with thee. Until that day give to us thy Comforter, the Holy Spirit, that we may know thee whom to know is life eternal; through Jesus Christ. **Amen.**

Then may be said the Lord's Prayer, followed by a hymn and the blessing.

The minister shall say:

Go in peace; and the blessing of God Almighty, the Father, the Son, and Holy Spirit be upon you, and remain with you always. **Amen.**

COMMITTAL FOR A CHILD   638.

At the graveside or crematorium the minister may read one or more of the following Scriptures:

Jesus said, "Let the children come to me; for to such belongs the kingdom of God."

Our Savior Christ Jesus has abolished death and brought life and immortality to light through the gospel.

Jesus said, "Peace I leave with you. Let not your hearts be troubled, neither let them be afraid."

Is it well with the child? It is well.

Then shall the minister say:

Forasmuch as it has pleased Almighty God in his great

251

mercy to receive unto himself this child, we therefore commit his (her) body to the ground, earth to earth, ashes to ashes, dust to dust, in the hope of eternal life; through our Lord Jesus Christ. **Amen.**

Or at a crematorium service, the minister says:

Forasmuch as it has pleased Almighty God in his great mercy to receive unto himself this child, we therefore commit his (her) body to be burned, ashes to ashes, dust to dust, in the hope of eternal life; through our Lord Jesus Christ. **Amen.**

Then may be said:

The Lamb in the midst of the throne will be their shepherd, and he will guide them to springs of living water; and God will wipe away every tear from their eyes.

Let us pray:

Eternal Father, from whom all fatherhoods on earth are named, into thy tender care do we entrust this child, and unto thee do we commit ourselves. Be thou our guide and comfort and give unto us a sure sense of thy never-failing love that we may in that same love and in loving memory of this child minister to all thy children whom we meet on life's way; through Jesus Christ, who himself loved little children. **Amen.**

The Lord bless you and keep you: The Lord make his face to shine upon you, and be gracious to you: The Lord lift up his countenance upon you, and give you peace. **Amen.**

639.   LICENSING OF A MINISTER

This service is a recognition of those preparing for the pastoral ministry. Generally it will take place in the stu-

dent's home church as he enters a theological seminary, but it may be adapted for use by a church to which he may be called as a minister while a student.

The licensing should be set within a full worship service and the act of licensing should take place as part of the offertory. At that time the candidate offers himself to be licensed to preach the gospel.

After the reading and preaching of the Word, the minister says an offertory sentence. In response, the gifts and the bread and wine are brought to the Table. The one to be licensed is escorted to the Table by the chairman of the board of deacons and the minister says:

Let us pray:
Our Father, we offer to thee this bread and wine to be set apart for the remembrance of the passion and coming of thy Son, our Lord; we present to thee these gifts in grateful remembrance of thy mercies to us; and we bring before thee our brother, who is offering himself for the service of the pastoral ministry. With these we offer ourselves that our lives may be spent in the several ministries to which thou hast called us; through Jesus Christ our Lord. **Amen.**

Then the minister says:

The Church is composed of many members with diversities of gifts, and not all members have the same office. Though every member of Christ's Church is a minister, we recognize that there is need for men and women with special training for specific vocations within the Church. It has, therefore, become customary for a congregation sponsoring one making such a vocational decision to offer him (her) a License to Preach. This license expresses the confidence

of the congregation in one of its members who is preparing himself (herself) for a specialized Christian ministry through theological study. J...................... D......................
has offered himself (herself) for the Christian ministry and now comes before this congregation to receive the License to Preach.

The chairman of the board of deacons escorts the candidate to a place before the Table and says:

Upon recommendation of the board of deacons and by vote of this congregation I present to you, J...................... D...................., this License to Preach.*

The chairman of the board of deacons presents the license to the candidate and says:

J................, this License represents not only our endorsement of you for seminary study, but it is also our declaration of confidence in you and our way of assuring you

---

*A "Certificate of License" can be obtained from your religious bookstore or denominational publishing house. One such certificate reads as follows:

"This is to certify that at a meeting of the ....
Baptist Church ...., on the .... day of
.... 19 ...., J.............. D............................,
having given evidence that he possesses gifts for the work of the gospel ministry, was licensed to preach the gospel as he may have opportunity, and to exercise his gifts in the work of the ministry for the period from this date to ....,
19 ...., when his status will be reviewed by the Church (in cooperation with the Associational Committee on Ordinations). When acting as Pastor of a Baptist Church and authorized by that Church so to do, he shall be considered eligible to administer the Ordinances of Baptism and the Lord's Supper; and to officiate at Funerals and Weddings, when compatible with the laws of the state."

that in your vocational preparation you have our continuing blessing and prayers.

The chairman of the board of deacons then presents the certificate to the candidate, after which the minister charges the candidate as follows:

J................., do you, in accepting this License to Preach, promise faithfully to further the interests of the Church of Jesus Christ both in your study and service?

The candidate says:

I do, trusting in the grace of God for help.

The minister says to the congregation:

Do you, the members of this congregation acknowledge and receive J................. D................. as a fully licensed preacher of the gospel, and promise to yield him (her) that esteem, encouragement, and cooperation to which this office entitles him (her)? If so, will you signify your assent by standing and uniting with me in the prayer of consecration?

The congregation stands and joins in the unison prayer:

O God, Father of our Lord Jesus Christ, who sent thy son not to be ministered unto but to minister, and who made him the great Head of the Church, set apart and consecrate this thy servant for the work of the ministry. Give him thy wisdom, and in counsel may he deal wisely as one who has the mind of Christ. Grant him thy spirit of compassion for human needs and fill him with love that he may tenderly care for every soul whom thou dost so graciously love. Strengthen and nourish his faith in thee and in the values of thy Church, that he may increase the faith of his fellow Christians. Cause his study

to be meaningful and his work in thy Church fruitful. And give grace unto us all that working together, seeking to know thy will, we may advance thy cause in this place and throughout the world; to the glory of him who preached good news to the captives, even Christ our Lord. Amen.

After the prayer the minister and deacons may extend to the newly licensed minister the right hand of fellowship, after which the Lord's Supper will be observed. The newly licensed minister may share with the minister in the administration of the Supper.

OUTLINE OF
ORDINATION OF A MINISTER

A WORSHIP SERVICE BASED UPON THE SERVICE FOR THE LORD'S DAY

ACT OF PREPARATION
    Bidding to worship
    Organ prelude and bringing of Bible
    Sentences of worship
    Hymn of adoration
    Confession
      Call to confession
      Prayer of confession
      Silent prayer of confession
      Assurance of forgiveness
      Praise: *Gloria Patri, Gloria in Excelsis,* or hymn
    Occasion of this service
    Announcements

MINISTRY OF THE WORD
    Scripture lessons

Prayer for illumination
Sermon

ACT OF RESPONSE
   Offertory
      Offertory sentences
      Presentation of offering
        (Elements, gifts, and ordinand)
      Doxology
      Offertory prayer
   Ordination
      Presentation of the ordinand
      Ordination vow
      Laying on of hands and the ordination prayer
      Charge to the ordinand
      Charge to the Church
      Presentation of the Bible

MINISTRY OF THE TABLE
  Offertory: gifts, bread and wine, and self
  Prayer of dedication
  Invitation to communion and response
  Affirmation of unity and peace
    Scripture sentences
    Right hand of fellowship (peace)
  Institution of the Lord's Supper
  Prayer of thanksgiving
  Prayer for the presence of the Holy Spirit
  Lord's Prayer
  Breaking and distribution of the bread
  Eating the bread
  Pouring and distribution of the wine
  Drinking the wine
  Sanctus

Prayer of petition
Prayer of intercession

INTO THE WORLD
Hymn or *Nunc Dimittis* and recessional of Scriptures
and bread and wine
Dismissal

640.   ORDINATION OF A MINISTER

Ordination should be set within a full worship service
which includes the Lord's Supper. The act of ordination
takes place as part of the offertory, at which time the
ordinand offers himself to be set apart for the gospel
ministry.

While the service is primarily that of the local church, it
is customary to invite representatives from the association
of churches to participate.

The service will proceed according to the Service for the
Lord's Day until after the singing of the Gloria Patri, the
Gloria in Excelsis or a hymn of praise, at which time the
presiding minister says:

As servants of Christ we are all called to be ministers, but
in addition to this general calling some are called to the
work of the special ministries. We are gathered here to
acknowledge the call of J.................. D.................. to the
pastoral ministry and to set him apart for this service
through prayer and the laying on of hands on behalf of
the whole people of God.

Here participants of the service may be introduced and
any necessary announcements may be made. The reading
and preaching of the Word follows.

258

After this, the minister says an offertory sentence. In response, the gifts and the bread and the wine are brought by the deacons to the Table as the Doxology is sung. The ordinand offering himself is escorted to the Table by the chairman of the board of deacons. The deacons take their places about the Table for the serving of the Lord's Supper. After receiving the gifts the minister says:

Let us pray:

Our Father, we offer to thee this bread and wine to be set apart for the remembrance of the passion and coming of thy Son, our Lord; we present to thee these gifts, blessing thee for the strength and skill to do our daily work; we present to thee also our brother, who is offering himself for the life work of the Christian ministry; and together with these we offer ourselves, asking that thou wilt strengthen us that all our work may be thy service, all our meals a thankful remembrance of thy bounty to us, and that we ourselves may be living sacrifices, holy and acceptable to thee, through Jesus Christ our Lord. **Amen.**

Then the chairman of the board of deacons presents the ordinand to the congregation, saying:

Ordination into the ministry of the Church rests upon the call of God, acknowledged and confirmed by the Church. Upon recommendation of the Ordination Council of ...., I present J.................... D....................
to this church for ordination to the gospel ministry.

The ordinand, standing, is asked by the presiding minister:

In the presence of God and of this congregation, you are called upon to answer, in all sincerity of heart, the questions I now ask of you.

Do you believe in one God, the Father, the Son, and the Holy Spirit; and do you affirm anew Jesus Christ as your Lord; and acknowledge him over all things as Lord of the Church, which is his Body?

The ordinand answers:

I do.

Do you believe that you are truly called of God into this ministry and to pastoral responsibility in Christ's Church?

I do.

Do you promise to lead the congregation faithfully in the public worship of God, to instruct it in Christian truth, to watch over its members in Christian love, and to guide the congregation in all its corporate life?

I will endeavor so to do, the Lord being my helper.

Do you promise to be faithful in prayer and in the reading and study of the Holy Scriptures, and to lead a life worthy of the calling to which you have been called?

I will endeavor so to do, the Lord being my helper.

Do you promise to lead others into an acceptance of the cost and joy of discipleship, and will you thus live in the spirit of Christ by the power of the Holy Spirit?

I will endeavor so to do, the Lord being my helper.

Do you promise to uphold the integrity of the Christian Church, yet never exalt yourself over those who serve Christ in other vocations in the world; will you seek to prepare them for their life in the secular structures, and will you learn from them that you might know where God is acting in our world?

I will endeavor so to do, the Lord being my helper.

Do you offer your loyalty to your denomination as it is

guided by the Holy Spirit and do you give yourself to seek that unity in which all churches will manifest the one faith, one Lord, and one baptism?

I do.

The minister then says:

Since J.................... D.................... has been duly examined by the Council of ...., and since he has now publicly confirmed his call to be ordained to the gospel ministry; I therefore declare on behalf of the church that he has responded faithfully to the call of the gospel and is fit through preparation to be ordained at this time. Let us pray:

Almighty Father, who by thy divine providence has appointed several orders of ministry in thy Church, and who dost call some of thy faithful servants to preach the Word, administer the sacraments (ordinances), order the life of the Church, and prepare the people for their Christian witness; behold this thy servant, now called to this office. So fill him with thy truth and give him of thy life that by both word and good example he may faithfully serve thee in this office, to the glory of thy name and the blessing of thy Church; through Jesus Christ. **Amen.**

The ordinand kneels before the Table and the participating officials lay their hands on his head. The presiding minister says:

Since, from the beginning of the Church, some have been called in the ministry of Jesus Christ to serve in the Church's witness and administration, and since this our brother has been thusly called and found worthy to assume this ministry, we therefore, in the tradition of apostles, disciples, martyrs, and faithful people of all times, lay our hands upon him and signify that he is set apart for this ministry. Let us pray God's blessing upon him:

Almighty God, who hast called this our brother into the pastoral ministry of thy Church, confirm that call now by thy Holy Spirit, as with prayer and the laying on of hands we ordain him to the office and work of that same ministry. Grant him wisdom to understand and power to proclaim thy holy Word. Enable him to lead thy people in acceptable worship. Cause him to be a pastor whose love is as thine own, a teacher whose store of truth is gladly opened to thy people's needs, and a priest who knows that he cannot long find welcome in thy presence unless his brother be with him. Keep him faithful to thy high calling, that in thy good time he may hear thy words, "Well done, good and faithful servant." To this ministry we consecrate him and ourselves that to thee may be given the praise and glory, now and forever; through Jesus Christ our Lord. **Amen.**

Then the ordinand rises and the minister gives him a charge, saying:

You have been ordained to the office of the Christian ministry and by the authority of this church and its sister churches you have been commissioned to preach and teach the Word of God from Holy Scripture, to lead the worship of the church and the administration of the sacraments (ordinances) of Baptism and the Lord's Supper, to be a faithful shepherd of the flock of Christ, and to guide the Christian community in all its corporate activities. Remember always, therefore, how great a treasure is committed to your care. The church and congregation which you serve are the sheep of Christ for which he shed his blood and gave his life. Never cease your labor, your care, and your diligence, until you have done all that lies in you to bring all such as are or shall be committed to you to fullness in the faith and knowledge of our God. I charge you in the presence of Jesus Christ: preach the Word, be urgent in season and out of season, convince, rebuke, and exhort, be unfailing in patience and teaching. Always be steady, endure suffering, do the work of an evangelist, fulfill your ministry.

The Lord bless you and keep you: The Lord make his face to shine upon you, and be gracious to you: The Lord lift up his countenance upon you, and give you peace. **Amen.**

Then the minister turns, facing the congregation, and gives the charge to them, saying:

You, the members of this congregation, I charge to support this man in all the duties of his office, and to esteem him highly in love. Be servants of the Lord, and be acceptable before God as his people. For as there are many members in one body, and all members have not the same responsibility; so we, being many, yet being of one body in Christ, every one of us bears differing responsibilities. Having then gifts differing according to the grace that is given to us, I charge you each in his own ministry, to uphold this man and each other, to hold to the faith handed down as a gift to us, to cling to the hope of life in Christ, and to love one another as he has loved us; through Jesus Christ our Lord. **Amen.**

The chairman of the board of deacons may then give a Bible to the newly ordained minister, saying:

Receive this Bible. All Scripture is inspired by God and profitable for teaching, for reproof, for correction, and for training in righteousness, that the man of God may be complete, equipped for every good work.

The presiding minister then leads the newly ordained minister to the Communion Table and, taking his right hand, says:

I welcome you into the pastoral ministry of the Church of Jesus Christ. May you find joy in leading this people in their service of him who is their Lord. Now on behalf of this congregation I invite you to begin your ministry among them as you preside over the Lord's Supper.

The newly ordained minister takes his place at the Table and leads the congregation in the observance of the Lord's Supper as found in the Service for the Lord's Day.

641. ### INSTALLATION OF A PASTOR

The service of installation may be set within the service for the Lord's Day. The act of installation will then come at the time of the offertory as the congregation presents the pastor-elect to be installed. The service then becomes an act of dedication on the part of both pastor and congregation.

It is fitting that the congregation invite a denominational executive to preside in the act of installation, or if such a one is not available, then a neighboring pastor.

The service of installation may be followed by a reception at which time it is fitting to have addresses of welcome by church and civic representatives as well as a response by the newly installed pastor.

After the offerings have been dedicated, the presiding minister says:

Let us continue our act of dedication as we in the name of the Lord Jesus Christ, the Head of the Church, install our brother, J.................... D...................., as pastor of this congregation. We shall first hear the steps that led this people to the call of this our brother to be their pastor. After this, both pastor-elect and people shall declare their mutual covenant to one another and to God that they will together endeavor to be faithful to their divine appointment and in all things seek the welfare of the Church.

Then a representative of the congregation makes a statement concerning the church's call of the pastor-elect. As a hymn is sung, a representative group of deacons escorts the pastor-elect to the front, where he is met by the presiding minister, who says:

We believe that the call to the pastorate is of both God and his people. You, my brother, present yourself in this the place of your future ministry because this congregation under God has seen fit to call you as its pastor and you, under the leading of God's Spirit, have responded to the call.

Do you reaffirm your faith in God the Father Almighty, and in his Son Jesus Christ our Lord, and in the Holy Spirit, the Counselor; do you believe that in Jesus Christ man has been set free from the bondage of sin and death; and that his Church has been called to proclaim in the world this good news?

The pastor-elect answers:

I do.

Do you believe in your heart that you are truly called of God to be the pastor of this congregation?

I do.

Do you promise before God and in the presence of this people to be a faithful teacher and preacher of the Word of God as found in the Holy Scriptures, to lead this congregation in worship that is worthy of the glory of God, to be a faithful pastor to the people in all their needs, and to equip them for their ministry in the world?

I will endeavor so to do, the Lord being my helper.

The presiding minister then says to the congregation:

Do you, the members of this congregation, receive J................ D................ as your pastor, and before God and in the presence of one another promise him your loyalty and support?

We do.

Then prayer is offered, extempore or as follows:

We thank thee, our Father, for this thy servant who has answered thy call and the call of this thy people to be pastor of this church and congregation. Fill him with thy Holy Spirit that he may make ready to do every good work and give a full measure of devotion in thy service. Make him a faithful servant of thy Word that through his preaching and teaching, men may be won to Christ, be strengthened in their faithfulness, and be readied for their servanthood in the world. Cause this pastor to be so filled with thy love that he will care for all thy people, that in their joy and sorrow, their sickness and health, their doubt and faith, he will stand faithfully beside them feeding and tending this flock; in the name of Jesus Christ, that great shepherd of the sheep. **Amen.**

The presiding minister then says:

In the name of the Lord Jesus Christ and on behalf of this church, I declare you J................ D................ to be duly installed as pastor of this church and congregation.

Then the presiding minister, the deacons, and any others appointed so to do, extend on behalf of the congregation the Right Hand of Fellowship, as the presiding minister says:

In the name of our Lord Jesus Christ, we welcome you as pastor of the .... Church.

The Lord bless you and keep you: The Lord make his face to shine upon you, and be gracious to you: The Lord lift up his countenance upon you, and give you peace. **Amen.**

Then shall the newly installed pastor conduct the Lord's Supper or, if the Supper is not observed, the concluding parts of the service.

COMMISSIONING (ORDINATION) OF DEACONS   642.
The commissioning or ordination of deacons should take place in the Service for the Lord's Day at the time of the offertory. As the gifts are brought forward, the deacons-elect, in an act of self-offering, come forward and take their places before the Lord's Table. After the dedication of the gifts, the minister, addressing the congregation, says:

Members of this congregation: in the name and for the service of our Lord Jesus Christ, we are now to commission (ordain) these whom you have elected to be deacons:

The minister then reads the names of those to be commissioned.

They have been called by you to be servants of Christ to join with the minister in the pastoral work and administration of this congregation. Undergird them with your prayers. Support them in their labors. Give to them your confidence and loyalty.

The minister may then read from the following Scriptures:

The Lord Jesus said: "Whoever would be great among you must be your servant, and whoever would be first among you must be slave of all. For the Son of man also came not to be served but to serve, and to give his life as a ransom for many."

Now in these days when the disciples were increasing in number, the Hellenists murmured against the Hebrews because their widows were neglected in the daily distribution. And the twelve summoned the body of the disciples and said, "It is not right that we should give up preaching the word of God to serve tables. Therefore, brethren, pick out from among you seven men of good repute, full of the Spirit and of wisdom, whom we may appoint to this duty. But we will devote ourselves to prayer and to the ministry of the word." And what they said pleased the whole multitude, and they chose Stephen, a man full of faith and of the Holy Spirit, and Philip, and Prochorus, and Nicanor, and Timon, and Parmenas, and Nicolaus, a proselyte of Antioch. These they set before the apostles, and they prayed and laid their hands upon them.

Having gifts that differ according to the grace given to us, let us use them: if service, in our serving. Never flag in zeal, be aglow with the Spirit, serve the Lord.

As each has received a gift, employ it for one another, as good stewards of God's varied grace: whoever speaks, as one who utters oracles of God; whoever renders service, as one who renders it by the strength which God supplies; in order that in everything God may be glorified through Jesus Christ.

Then the minister says to each deacon-elect:

My brother, do you believe that you are called by God through this congregation to the high office of deacon; do you promise as God is your helper to serve him and this congregation with all faithfulness?

Each deacon-elect replies:

I do.

The deacons-elect may then kneel. The minister and the already-commissioned deacons lay their hands upon them, and the minister sets them apart for their office with prayer, extempore or as follows:

O God, to thee we offer these chosen for the high office of deacon. By thy Holy Spirit give them that grace whereby they shall fulfill with all faithfulness the duties of their calling. Grant them wisdom for the administration of the welfare of this congregation. Cause them to give willingly to those who come hungry and homeless to thy people seeking help. Give them a special sensitivity to human need that they may be true guides of thy Spirit to all who come to this place seeking thee. Now in the name of him who came not to be served but to serve we set apart these as servants of thine and of the household of faith. **Amen.**

The new deacons stand and are given the Right Hand of Fellowship by the minister and their fellow deacons. The minister says:

In the name of our Lord Jesus Christ and on behalf of this congregation we welcome you to the service of deacons. Be good stewards of God's varied grace.

The Lord bless you and keep you: The Lord make his face to shine upon you, and be gracious to you: The Lord lift up his countenance upon you, and give you peace. **Amen.**

The new deacons then take their places at the Lord's Table, to serve with the minister and the other deacons in the administration of the Lord's Supper.

643.　　　　DEDICATION OF CHURCH OFFICERS
The act of dedication should take place in the Service for the Lord's Day at the time of the offertory. As the gifts of the people are presented, the new officers come forward and stand before the Table for the act of dedication.

The minister says:

Friends in Christ, we are gathered in the presence of God to dedicate these who have been chosen for his service in this congregation. As they give themselves to the work of their offices, so we give ourselves to their support and encouragement, seeking with them the consecration which is from God that they may be able to discharge their calling with faithfulness and to the glory of God.

The minister then reads the names and offices of those who are to be dedicated.

The officers being installed respond to the charges given by the minister:

As each has received a gift, employ it for one another, as good stewards of God's varied grace: whoever speaks, as one who utters oracles of God; whoever renders service, as one who renders it by the strength which God supplies; in order that in everything God may be glorified through Jesus Christ.

We will seek to use the gifts which God has given us to his glory and for the benefit of those whom we serve.

Whatever you do, in word or deed, do everything in the name of the Lord Jesus, giving thanks to God the Father through him.

We will seek to do everything in the name of the Lord Jesus.

Attend to the public reading of Scripture, to preaching, to teaching. Do your best to present yourself to God as one approved, a workman who has no need to be ashamed, rightly handling the Word of truth.

We will do our best to be workmen approved of God.

I appeal to you therefore, brethren, by the mercies of God, to present your bodies as a living sacrifice, holy and acceptable to God, which is your spiritual worship.

We give ourselves, body, mind, and spirit to God, that we by his grace may fulfill the calling to which he has called us.

You are not your own; you were bought with a price. So glorify God. Be unfailing in patience. Be steady, endure suffering, do the work of an evangelist, fulfill your ministry. If any of you lacks wisdom, let him ask God who gives to all men generously and without reproaching.

Let us pray:

For the call that has come from thee through this thy people, to serve thee in the work of thy Church

We thank thee, O God.

To the responsibilities of our office, to the well-being of this congregation, and to thy service in this special task

We dedicate ourselves, O God.

Give to us loyal and steadfast hearts; to give and not count the cost; to toil and not seek for rest; to labor and ask for no reward; to have the good conscience that we are doing thy will; to be willing at all times and in all places to give thee the glory,

We beseech thee, O God.

Go before these whom thou hast chosen, O Lord, that in all their doing they may hear thy words: "Well done, thou good and faithful servant"; through Jesus Christ our Lord. **Amen.**

The newly dedicated officers take their places in the congregation and the service continues with the Lord's Supper.

644. DEDICATION OF CHURCH SCHOOL TEACHERS AND OFFICERS

This service may be held during the Service for the Lord's Day, or a worship service of the church school. The newly elected teachers and officers come to the Table at the time of the offertory, or to the front of the room, and face the minister, who says:

Let us pray:

For the call that has come from thee through this thy people to serve thee as teachers and officers in the church school

We thank thee, O God.

To those whom we shall serve in our duties as teachers and officers, to the good of this congregation, and to thy service in this special task

We dedicate ourselves, O God.

Give to us open minds that thy truth may not be hindered by our own peculiarities of thought; give us understanding hearts that we may enter into the lives of those whom thou has called us to teach and lead; grant us sensitive spirits that we may truly hear the questions that are asked and that we may be able to seek answers with patience and love; enable us to work cheerfully and as partners in Christ with our fellow teachers and officers.

We beseech thee to hear us, O Lord.

Be with these thy servants, O Lord, that not only their words but more especially their lives may commend their Master to those whom they serve. We beseech thee through this same Master, even our Lord Jesus Christ. **Amen.**

LAYING OF A CHURCH CORNERSTONE   645.

After the people have gathered about the place where the stone is to be laid, the minister shall say:

In the name of the Lord who made heaven and earth we are gathered in this place to lay the cornerstone of our new church building.

Unless the Lord builds the house, those who build it labor in vain. For no other foundation can anyone lay than that which is laid, which is Jesus Christ.

Then shall the Gloria Patri be said or sung, after which the minister says:

Let us pray:

Eternal God, who hast built thy Church upon the foundation of the apostles and prophets, Christ Jesus himself being the chief cornerstone, grant thy blessing upon us as we gather in thy name to lay the cornerstone of this congregation's new meetinghouse. Grant that the devotion here displayed by thy people may continue until the whole structure is built to thy glory and service; through Jesus Christ our Lord. **Amen.**

The lessons from the Scriptures shall be read. The follow-

273

ing passages are appropriate: Genesis 28:10-22. 1 Kings 5:17-6:1, 11-13. 1 Chronicles 29:10-18. Ezra 3:8-13. Matthew 16:13-27. 1 Corinthians 3:10-17. Ephesians 2:13-22. Hebrews 11:1-10. 1 Peter 2:4-10.

After the Scripture reading a sermon may be given.

Here the representative of the congregation, assisted by the builder, lays the stone in place. As the mortar is applied, the minister or the congregation says:

In the name of Almighty God and to his glory and for his worship and service, we lay this cornerstone. May it be for us a constant reminder that Jesus Christ is the true cornerstone of his Temple, the Church of God; and as this church building grows to completion, may we remember that we belong to that holy Temple in the Lord which is being built up to become a dwelling place for God in the Spirit.

The minister then says:

Let us pray:

We thank thee, Our Father, that thou hast led us to build this house to thy glory. Confirm and bless what we have done this day. Let thy favor rest upon us and establish the work of our hands. Keep us faithful to the task of building that in thy good time there may stand here a house fit for thy worship and from which we may go forth to witness and serve in the world; through Jesus Christ our Lord, who has taught us to say when we pray:

Our Father . . .

The service may conclude with a hymn and the benediction.

The service of dedication may be in two parts: The Opening of the Doors and the Dedication. Or the Act of Dedication may be included as a part of the Service for the Lord's Day at the time of the offertory.

OPENING OF THE DOORS

The congregation may form a procession marching from the former place of worship, if nearby, or from a convenient gathering place, or they may assemble before the locked doors of the church. The minister, standing before the doors, shall say:

Lift up your heads, O gates! and be lifted up, O ancient doors! that the King of glory may come in. Who is the King of glory? The Lord of hosts, he is the King of glory!

The keys may here be presented by the builder to a representative of the congregation who shall then unlock the lock, throw open the doors, and say:

In the name of the Father and of the Son and of the Holy Spirit I open the doors of this church building for the use of this congregation and as a house of prayer for all people.

Then the minister shall say:

Let us pray:
Father God, as we open the doors of this house of worship and service, we open our hearts unto thee. Go with us as we cross this threshold, that by thy presence in the midst of this thy people this house may ever be filled with thy fullness. Cause these doors to be ever open to all men. May they be wide enough to welcome all who need love and friendship and thy fatherly care. And may they also be the way through which thy people go into the world

to bear witness to thy redeeming power among men. We go forward through Jesus Christ our Lord. **Amen.**

Then the Doxology may be sung as the people enter the church building.

ACT OF DEDICATION

After the people have been seated, the minister says:

Our help is in the name of the Lord, who made heaven and earth. Unless the Lord builds the house, those who build it labor in vain. Blessed be the name of the Lord from this time forth and for evermore.

A hymn of praise is sung, after which the minister says:

I was glad when they said to me, "Let us go to the house of the Lord!"

The Lord is in his holy temple; Let all the earth keep silence before him.

"Surely the Lord is in this place;

This is none other than the house of God, and this is the gate of heaven."

Let us pray:

With great joy we come before thee, our Father. We praise thee for thy marvelous works among the children of men, and on this day we praise thee especially for this new work which thou hast brought into being through the vision of thy people. Forgive us for any narrowness of pride which looks only to our own achievement, and give to us that spirit wherein we shall with full willingness of mind and heart dedicate this building to thy eternal glory and to the service of all men; through Christ our Lord we ask this. **Amen.**

The Scripture lessons are now read. The following are suitable passages: 1 Kings 8:12-30, 41-43. Ezra 3:10-13. Psalms 24. 84. 121. 122. Matthew 21:1-17. Ephesians 2:13-22. 1 Peter 2:4-10. Revelation 21:15-27.

After the reading of the Scriptures the sermon is preached.

The sermon is followed by the offertory. As a fitting part of the offertory the congregation presents its new building to God as a gift of thanksgiving and for his glory and service. This act may be symbolized by the laying of the blueprints, or some other suitable sign, upon the Table, after which the minister says:

As a people of God we have gathered about this Table to dedicate this house to the glory of Almighty God and the service of men. Let us now join together in the act of dedication.

To the glory of God the Father, Maker of heaven and earth;
To the glory of the Son, the Savior of the world;
To the glory of the Holy Spirit, the Counselor of the people of God:

We dedicate this house.

For the worship of almighty God;
For the reading and preaching of his holy Word;
For the celebration of the sacraments of the gospel:

We dedicate this house.

For the solemnizing of marriage and the strengthening of family life;
For the dedication, teaching and guidance of children;

For the services of memorial and for the comfort of those who mourn;

For the strengthening of all believers and their training as Christ's ministers in the world;

For the bringing of unbelievers to Christ and for the spread of his gospel among all men:

We dedicate this house.

To the memory of all whose life and love have in times past been given to the furtherance of the life and work of this congregation:

We dedicate this house.

In the name of the Father and of the Son and of the Holy Spirit:

We dedicate this house.

Let us pray:

Eternal God, thou who dost not live in houses made with hands, yet hast promised to be with thy people as they gather in thy name, be present in our midst as we dedicate this house to thy glory and service.

We beseech thee to hear us, O Lord.

Grant that all worship that shall be offered in this place may be worthy of thy great love, that the words of our mouths and the meditations of our hearts may be acceptable in thy sight.

We beseech thee to hear us, O Lord.

Grant us faithfulness to thy holy Word as it is read and proclaimed amongst us; may it ever be for us a light unto our path and a lamp upon our way.

We beseech thee to hear us, O Lord.

Grant that all whose eyes of faith are opened through the ministry of thy Word in this place and who here confess

their faith by their baptism may truly find newness of life
and by thy Holy Spirit become living members of thy
Church.

We beseech thee to hear us, O Lord.

Grant that all who gather about this Table to receive the
bread and wine of the Lord's Supper may be brought to a
living remembrance of Jesus Christ, whom to know is life
eternal.

We beseech thee to hear us, O Lord.

Grant that all who come to this place, whether it be in
joy or in sorrow, in life or death, in victory or defeat, in
doubt or faith, in sin or salvation, may find here thy grace
faithfully ministered; and permit each one to know that in
all things thou dost work good for them that believe.

We beseech thee to hear us, O Lord.

Grant that our prayers may find acceptance with thee, O
Lord, through Jesus Christ, who has taught us to say
when we pray:

Our Father . . .

Then shall the congregation stand and say together:

**In the name of the Father, and of the Son, and of the
Holy Spirit, we do now declare this house to be set apart
and consecrated to the worship and service of almighty
God: to whom be glory and majesty, dominion and
power, for ever and ever.   Amen.**

*Here the Lord's Supper may be celebrated, after which
shall be sung the Gloria or a hymn. The minister then
says:*

Go forth from this place into the world, there to minister
in the name of Jesus Christ, that the world might believe.

Return to this place to receive food for life and to give glory to our God.

The grace of our Lord Jesus Christ, the love of God the Father, and the abiding presence of the Holy Spirit go with you. **Amen.**

647. DEDICATION OF A MEMORIAL

The appropriate time for the dedication of a memorial is as part of the offertory in the Lord's Day Service. After the presentation and dedication of the gifts, the person appointed to present the memorial comes forward, and the minister says to him:

We ask our brother, J................. D..................., to present the memorial.

Then the person making the presentation says:

To the memory (or in the name of) M...........................
D........................... I (or we) present this memorial, to be dedicated to the glory and praise of God.

The church official designated to receive the memorial says:

We accept this gift with thanks as a memorial to the devoted life of God's faithful servant M................ D..................

Then the congregation (or minister) says:

In the faith of our Lord Jesus Christ, we dedicate this memorial to the glory of God, and in memory of his servant M . . . . . . D . . . . . ., in the name of the Father, and of the Son, and of the Holy Spirit. Amen.

The minister says:

Let us pray:

Blessed and glorious Lord God Almighty, by whose power,

wisdom, and love all things are sanctified, enlightened, and made perfect, be gracious unto us that what we now do may please thee, and show forth honor unto thy name. May this memorial and the spirit in which it is given be acceptable to thee. Cause it to be a constant reminder of the life and service of him (her) whom we commemorate this day. And let the beauty of the Lord our God be upon us; and establish thou the work of our hands upon us; yea, the work of our hands establish thou it. Through Jesus Christ our Lord we ask this. **Amen.**

PART 7

WORSHIP
IN THE
PASTORAL MINISTRY

"The church in thy house" was a common experience in both the early Church and the early days of the free church movement. It is in recognition of the importance of the home, as well as the need for the linking of the home and the church, that a section on worship in the pastoral ministry has been included. Through its pastor, deacons, and other visitors the church goes into the home both in normal times of the family's life and during those special events and crises which come to the family from time to time. Whether it be a birth, illness, bereavement, or the dedication of a new home, the church should stand beside its members to share in their joy or sorrow. Materials in this section are intended to be of help for those special occasions. They do not seek in any way to limit the freedom of the Spirit or the exercise of free worship. Rather they point to those areas in which worship can be meaningful in the pastoral ministry and provide guidelines to those involved in the exercise of that ministry.

648.   DEDICATION OF A HOME
The dedication of a home can be a part of a house-warming party in which the members of the congregation gather to help celebrate with the family. The minister says:

We are gathered here to share with our friends the joy which they have in their home and with them to dedicate it to God that it may become an instrument of God's love in the world.

Peace be to this house, and to all who shall dwell in it.

Unless the Lord builds the house, those who build it labor in vain.

Behold, how good and pleasant it is when brothers dwell in unity!

A hymn or solo may be sung, such as "Bless This House."

The minister may then read a passage of Scripture, perhaps one of the following: Deuteronomy 6:1-7. Psalm 128. Matthew 5:3-14. 7:24-27. Luke 2:41-52. 19:1-9. John 2:1-12. Ephesians 3:14-21. Philippians 4:4-8. Colossians 3:12-21.

The Scripture reading may be followed by a brief address, after which the minister says:

Let us give thanks:

O thou who hast ordained that men should dwell together in families, we thank thee for this family in whose home we are now gathered. We offer praise for their devotion to thee and to one another, and for the joy that has come to them as they have seen fit to dwell in this house. We thank thee for all who labored to make of it a fitting and useful dwelling place. We look with grateful hearts to the days and years ahead when many shall find within these walls love and affection, joy and hope. Accept our thanksgiving; through Jesus Christ our Lord. **Amen.**

Let us ask God's blessing upon this home:

O thou who art always ready to give far beyond our expectations, cause thy blessing to rest upon this house and household. Grant that Jesus Christ may come to dwell as Master of this home. May his light and love be abundantly present to all who dwell within these walls and in that same light and love may they show forth Christ in the world. Make this home a place with an open door and a warm hearth, ever bidding welcome to all who need hospitality and friendship. Give to every member of this family a sense of being linked to one another and to thee, and in thee to thy people everywhere, that the unity which is here manifest may become a sign of that unity which thou hast given to all men in thy Son Jesus Christ, who hast taught us to say when we pray:

Our Father . . .

The blessing of God Almighty, the Father, the Son, and the Holy Spirit, be among you, and remain with you always. **Amen.**

WORSHIP IN THE HOME

649.

The family being gathered, the minister or one of the family members may read one of the following or other suitable Scripture passages:

Hear, O Israel: The Lord our God is one Lord; and you shall love the Lord your God with all your heart, and with all your soul, and with all your might. And these words which I command you this day shall be upon your heart; and you shall teach them diligently to your children, and shall talk of them when you sit in your house, and when you walk by the way, and when you lie down, and when you rise.

And they were bringing children to him, that he might touch them; and the disciples rebuked them. But when Jesus saw it he was indignant, and said to them, "Let the children come to me, do not hinder them; for to such belongs the kingdom of God. Truly, I say to you, whoever does not receive the kingdom of God like a child shall not enter it." And he took them in his arms and blessed them, laying his hands upon them.

Jesus said:

"I am the bread of life; if any one eats of this bread, he will live for ever."

"I am the light of the world; he who follows me will not walk in darkness, but will have the light of life."

"I am the door of the sheep; if any one enters by me, he will be saved."

"I am the good shepherd. The good shepherd lays down his life for the sheep."

"I am the resurrection and the life; he who believes in me, though he die, yet shall he live, and whoever lives and believes in me shall never die."

"I am the true vine. Abide in me, and I in you. He who abides in me, and I in him, he it is that bears much fruit."

"I am the way, and the truth, and the life; no one comes to the Father, but by me."

Love is patient and kind; love is not jealous or boastful; it is not arrogant or rude. Love does not insist on its own way; it is not irritable or resentful; it does not rejoice at wrong, but rejoices in the right. Love bears all things, believes all things, hopes all things, endures all things. Love never ends.

Conversation over one or more of the Scripture passages is appropriate.

Then prayer, either extempore or as follows, may be offered:

THANKSGIVING

We thank thee for all the blessings which come so freely from thy hand. For this home and the loved ones in it

We thank thee.

For friends and colleagues, for work to do, and leisure to enjoy

We thank thee.

For the firm earth beneath and the glad skies above; for sun, moon, and stars; for winter, springtime, summer, and autumn

We thank thee.

For good books to read, for the ever-deepening knowledge and skill of science, for art to create and enjoy

We thank thee.

For every noble thought that expands life's horizons and for challenges that come from contemporary crises

We thank thee.

For faith and hope and love as known in Jesus Christ our Lord,

We thank thee. Amen.

PETITION

Eternal Father, from whom every family in heaven and on earth is named, remember with thy special care this family in whose home we are now gathered. Take their joys, their sorrows, their concerns, and their commitments and make them thine. Help them to see in thy fatherhood thy desire that all thy children come to know what it means to be one in thee, and may this family in its unity manifest their oneness so clearly that all who come to know this home may give thee the praise. We pray in the name of Jesus Christ. **Amen.**

FOR NEIGHBORS

Our Father, thou hast commanded us that we love our neighbors as ourselves; yet so often in our business, with our own interests and the impersonal nature of our world, we scarcely know those who live and work near us. Open to us ways of becoming friends and brothers to those near at hand, and use our lives as instruments of thy concern and care in our neighborhood. We pray through him who taught us to be neighborly one to another, even Christ our Lord. **Amen.**

FOR THE CHILDREN

We thank thee, O Father, for these little ones who have been given by the miracle of parenthood into our care. Help us to deserve this responsibility and give ourselves without selfish desire to its fulfillment. Cause us to be good teachers of these our young, to be faithful providers, and above all to be an example worthy of their trust in us.

Help us to know when we should stand with them and when we should get out of the way. We ask this in the name of him who took little children into his arms and blessed them. **Amen.**

For Members of the Family Away from Home

We remember, O Lord, the members of this family circle who this day are not present. Care for them; keep them; cause them to be faithful unto thee; and in due time bring them back to us that together we may share the joy of being one family in thee. **Amen.**

The prayers may conclude with the Lord's Prayer. If convenient a hymn may be sung, after which the minister may say:

May the Lord keep your going out and your coming in from this time forth and for evermore. And the blessing of God Almighty, the Father, the Son, and the Holy Spirit be with you and all whom you hold dear. **Amen.**

THANKSGIVING FOR CHILDBIRTH 650.

The order is intended primarily for the father and mother of the child, but may be used with the whole family. The minister, using his own or the words which follow, says:

Let us offer thanks to God, the Father of all, for the birth of this child and welcome him (her) into this his (her) family in the name of our Lord Jesus Christ. Let us hear what the Scriptures say:

Then may be read a Scripture lesson and there may be conversation concerning its meaning. Suitable passages are: Deuteronomy 6:4-7. Psalms 103:17, 18. 127:1, 3. Matthew 18:1-5. Mark 8:36, 37. 10:13-16. Luke 9:46-48. 18:15-17. Colossians 3:20, 21. Ephesians 6:1-4.

Prayer shall then be offered, extempore or in these words:

O Lord, open thou our lips, and our mouth shall show forth thy praise.

For the universe which thou hast created and dost uphold: for its vastness and wonder:

We thank thee, O God.

For thy new creation in this little child:

We thank thee, O God.

For the joy the parents and family which his (her) coming has brought forth:

We thank thee, O God.

For the safety of his (her) birth and the promise which is his (hers) of a life of health and strength:

We thank thee, O God.

For the ministry of doctors and nurses, family and friends:

We thank thee, O God.

For his (her) future with all its hopes and opportunities:

We thank thee, O God.

Grant thy blessing upon him (her) and upon his (her) parents and family that his (her) coming may deepen the bonds of love which have brought him (her) into the world and that through that same love he (she) may come to know thee, whom to know is life eternal, through Jesus Christ our Lord, who taught us to say when we pray:

Our Father . . .

The Lord bless you and keep you: The Lord make his face to shine upon you, and be gracious to you: The Lord lift up his countenance upon you, and give you peace. **Amen.**

The service should be used only after both the congregation and the ill person have been fully prepared. The healing of the body, mind, and spirit is an act of the Creator-Redeemer God. It can be sought only in the spirit of Christ who prayed, "Not my will, but thine be done." If the service is in the home or hospital, deacons should accompany the minister.

The service begins as the minister reads the following, or other suitable Scripture passages:

And Jesus went about all Galilee, teaching in their synagogues and preaching the gospel of the kingdom and healing every disease and every infirmity among the people.

The Lord is my shepherd, I shall not want; he makes me lie down in green pastures. He leads me beside still waters; he restores my soul. He leads me in paths of righteousness for his name's sake. Even though I walk through the valley of the shadow of death, I fear no evil; for thou art with me; thy rod and thy staff, they comfort me. Thou preparest a table before me in the presence of my enemies; thou anointest my head with oil, my cup overflows. Surely goodness and mercy shall follow me all the days of my life; and I shall dwell in the house of the Lord for ever.

Is any one among you suffering? Let him pray. Is any cheerful? Let him sing praise. Is any among you sick? Let him call for the elders of the church, and let them pray over him, anointing him with oil in the name of the Lord; and the prayer of faith will save the sick man, and the Lord will raise him up; and if he has committed sins, he will be forgiven. Therefore confess your sins to one another, and pray for one another, that you may be healed. The prayer of a righteous man has great power in its effects.

Then the minister says to the sick person:

Do you truly believe that healing grace is available to those who are in need of it?

The sick person answers if he so believes:

I do.

Do you acknowledge that God has given skill and wisdom to physicians that they may work with him to bring about healing and do you put your trust in them as his ministers?

I do.

Then the minister says:

Let us pray:

Our Father, thou who hast given life to this thy child and hast been with him (her) thus far on his (her) life's journey, we call upon thee for thy continuing mercies that he (she), if it be in accordance with thy holy will, may be restored to fullness of health and may once again give thanks to thee in the midst of thy people, and be thy servant in the world; through Jesus Christ the Great Physician. **Amen.**

If it is the custom of the congregation, the minister shall anoint the sick person with oil. Then shall the minister lay his hands upon the sick person's head and say:

Let us pray:

Eternal God, who didst send thy Son Jesus Christ into the world to bring health and liberty to all, by that same power wherein he healed the sick, minister now to this thy servant. Grant that he (she) may be delivered from sickness, brought to full health, and from this day forth serve thee in renewed life and devotion. Lord, hear our prayer; and let our cry come unto thee. O Lord, save thy servant; who putteth his (her) trust in thee; through Jesus Christ. **Amen.**

After a time of silence the minister says:

May the God of peace himself sanctify you wholly: And may your spirit and soul and body be kept sound and blameless at the coming of our Lord Jesus Christ.

The Lord bless you and keep you: The Lord make his face to shine upon you, and be gracious to you: The Lord lift up his countenance upon you, and give you peace. Amen.

SCRIPTURE AND PRAYERS
FOR THE SICK AND INFIRM

Scripture Readings

Psalms: 23. 27. 34. 42. 43. 46. 62. 63. 67. 73:23-28. 86:1-12. 90. 91. 95:1-7. 96. 98. 103. 111. 116. 121. 130. 133. 139. 145. 146. 147. 149. Isaiah 12. 26:1-9. 40:1-11. 40:27-31. 43:1-3. 53. 55. 61:1-3. Jeremiah 17:5-8. Matthew 5:1-16. 6:25-34. 7:7-12. 8:1-17. 9:18-31. 9:35-10. 11:25-30. Mark 1:29-45. 3:7-14. 5:21-43. 6:45-56. 10:35-52. 12:28-34. 14:32-42. Luke 4:31-44. 5:12-26. 7:1-17. 9:28-43. 11:1-13. 13:10-17. 17:5-21. 24:13-35. John 1:1-18. 3:1-21. 10:1-18. 13:1-17. 14:1-11. 15:1-17. 20:19-23. Romans 5:1-11. 8:1-17. 8:18-39. 12. 1 Corinthians 1:18-25. 13. 2 Corinthians 1:3-7. 4:5-18. 5:11-21. 12:1-10. Ephesians 2:11-22. 3:13-21. 6:10-20. Philippians 2:1-13. 3:7-14. 4:4-9. Colossians 3:1-17. Hebrews 2:10-18. 4:14—

293

5:10. 11:1-16. 11.32—12:2. 12:1-14. James 5:13-21. 1 Peter 1:3-9. 2:21-25. 4:7-13. 2 John 1. 4:7-21. Revelation 7:9-17. 21:1-7. 21:22—22:4. 22:12—14:17.

PRAYERS

To be used by the sick:

652. Dear Father, as I am here in the hospital my thoughts frequently linger with the members of my family whom thou hast given me. Their welfare and happiness is a matter of great concern to me, and there is so little that I can do for them in my present condition. As they have been in thy care and keeping, do thou continue to watch over them. Guard them from harm and danger. Keep them close unto thee. And if it be thy will, restore me soon to the family circle; for Jesus' sake. Amen.

653. Still my impatience, Lord.
Quiet my fears, lift my waning faith to match my need.
Help me to forget myself and fill my thoughts with others who suffer pain worse than mine.
Relieve my smallness, O Lord, and release my spirit in fullness unto thee:
That I may face what comes and make it mine;
That I may know thy grace and be lifted up. Amen.

654. This is another day.
I know not what it will bring forth, but make me ready, Lord, for whatever it may be.
If I am to stand up, help me to stand bravely.
If I am to sit still, help me to sit quietly.
If I am to lie low, help me to do it patiently.
And if I am to do nothing, let me do it gallantly.
Make these words more than words; through the Spirit granted to us in Jesus Christ our Lord. Amen.

For one who is gravely ill:

O God, as we stand at the bedside of thy servant J............   655.
D..............., we pray thy special blessing upon him (her).
Lay thy healing hand upon this one whose faith has been
in thee. Make him (her) whole, O Lord. Relieve the
suffering and heal the wound. Soothe the pain and renew
the spirit. If it be thy will, restore J............... D...............
to the health of his (her) former days that he (she) may
once again sing thy praise; this we pray in Jesus' name.
Amen.

Before an operation:

O God, pain and suffering are ever with us;   656.
But in thee, peace and relief are also to be known.
Father God, in faith we lift our hearts and minds to thee
and pray that we may hold thee fast. Guide the hand of
the physician. Be with him in this act of healing. Grant
that through his skill and thy grace this one may become
whole once more; in Jesus' name. Amen.

Confession in the midst of illness:

In the midst of pain and healing,   657.
In the midst of suffering and relief
Thou art present, O God, our God, and
the light of redeeming light shines through.
We confess the careless act, the wayward path,
the stubborn heart
that first broke the spirit and now hinders the body
in its desire for health.
By thy forgiveness and healing hand
Open our eyes: to wholeness and peace
                    to love of life and joy of love
                    to care of health and care of soul

Deliver us and reclaim us, O God, from the shadows of mistaken ways.
Bring us again into the light of thy
redeeming grace;
in thy name we pray. Amen.

Thanksgiving after illness:

658. Loving Father, the boon which we sought has been granted.
The cry of our heart has been heard.
As the night fades into day, so the fever subsides, and restlessness gives way to quiet sleep.
O Lord, may our ineffable joy be pleasing to thee.
Smile upon us in this hour of victory.
Find in our trust and our conviction the qualities of mind and heart more acceptable to thee.
The night brought its terror, the dawn its confidence.
For the strength to do battle, for the occasion to be exceeding glad, we offer the love and thanksgiving of grateful hearts. Amen.

659. Our Father, we thank thee for the blessing of restored health.
For the watchful eye and skillful hand of the physician,
For the drugs and medication which have eased the pain as the body heals,
For rest and care,
For the hospital and this bed,
For the tender care of nurses and the concern of careful doctors,
For the support of friends and the prayers of family,
For a new day and another beginning,
For thy love and thy presence,
O Lord, for all of this we give thee heartfelt thanks. Amen.

For one in a nursing home or home for the retired:

Our Lord, who art the companion of those who need 660.
thee, be our companion now.
Be with us when we are lonely and stand with us even
if no friend is by our side.
Help us to find peace and rest in the common things of life
and friendliness in the ordinary word.
Help us to be sensitive not only to our own needs but to
bear the burdens of others.
In the slow, steady pace of empty nights we would remember thee, whose face is written in the beauty of each
returning day.
When others forget us in their business, thy presence is
closest;
For thou wilt never leave us, nor forsake us.
Thy spirit is to us a companion.
As a wife is to her husband,
As a child is to her father,
so art thou ever present;
through thy Son Jesus Christ our Lord. Amen.

For mental illness:

O God our loving heavenly Father, look mercifully upon 661.
thy servant in his (her) weakness and helplessness. Drive
away the clouds which obscure his (her) understanding
and restore fully to him (her) the kindly light of reason.
Deliver him (her) from all troubled and anxious thoughts,
and from all conflicting and distressing emotions. Restore
to him (her) the full power of self-control, and make
perfect thy strength in his (her) weakness. Help him
(her) to trust thee, and to stay his (her) mind on thee,
that he (she) may be kept in perfect peace, now and
evermore. Amen.

For use by those close to one who is sick:

662. Our Father, how difficult it is to see thy will in a time of need.

    The sight of suffering dims our faith and lessens our hope.

    The sounds of pain silence our prayers.

    Forgive us, O God, and help us to believe and to pray that we come to know thy will for those we love in the midst of their sickness and suffering. Amen.

663. We are frightened, O God, at the thought of losing one so close, one in whom we also die.

    Free us, our Father, from the guilt and the shame of seeking to shape thy will.

    Let us know the grace of thy consoling hand.

    Free us, our father, from doubt and fear.

    Let us know thy will and may it be done. Amen.

664. ## AN ORDER FOR THE BRINGING OF THE LORD'S SUPPER TO THE SICK AND INFIRM

    After the regular observance of the Lord's Supper it is appropriate for the minister and deacons to take the bread and wine which are left and share the Supper with those of the congregation who, because of illness or infirmity, are unable to be present at the worship services of the church. After the group has gathered, the minister or one of the deacons says to the shut-in(s):

    We bring to you this bread and wine which have been set apart for thanksgiving and remembrance. Will you join us in remembering Jesus Christ and giving thanks for his life, death, and resurrection?

    Let us pray:

    O Lord Jesus Christ, be present with us now, as thou wast with thy disciples in the upper room. Thou who art the giver of the feast and the feast itself, preside over this thy time of remembrance; give us of thyself, who art the bread of life, that we may be nourished within unto life eternal. **Amen.**

Lessons may then be read from the following or other suitable Scriptures: Psalms 43:3-5. 116:12-17. Isaiah 53:3-6. Mark 14:17, 22-25. Luke 24:13-35. John 6:35, 51, 53-55. 20:19-23. Romans 3:21-26. 5:1-11. 1 Corinthians 1:18-25. 2 Corinthians 5:7, 8, 14-21. 1 Timothy 2:5, 6. The lessons may be followed by conversation concerning their meanings. The minister or deacon concludes the readings with the words of the institution of the Lord's Supper:

For I received from the Lord what I also delivered to you, that the Lord Jesus on the night when he was betrayed took bread, and when he had given thanks, he broke it, and said, "This is my body which is for you. Do this in remembrance of me." In the same way also the cup, after supper, saying, "This cup is the new covenant in my blood. Do this, as often as you drink it, in remembrance of me." For as often as you eat this bread and drink the cup, you proclaim the Lord's death until he comes.

Then the minister or deacon gives thanks, extempore, or using one of the prayers of remembrance and thanksgiving from Part 3.

Following the prayers the minister or deacon says:

In his name I give you this bread *(he hands the bread to the communicant[s]);* eat it in remembrance of Jesus Christ.

After the bread has been eaten and there has been a time of silence, the minister or deacon says:

In the name of Jesus Christ I give you this cup *(he hands the cup to the communicant[s])* drink of it, for it is the new covenant in the blood of Christ which is shed for many.

After the cup has been drunk and there has been a time of silence, the minister or deacon concludes the service with the Lord's Prayer, extempore prayer, or as follows:

We thank thee, our Father, for bringing us to the Table of thy Son Jesus Christ. In our act of remembrance we have not only remembered him whom to know is life eternal but also our fellow church members who have eaten of this bread and drunk of this cup. Be gracious unto them, our Father, even as thou art gracious unto us. Use them and us as witnesses to thy love in every place where we might be, and grant that thy Church throughout the world might be strengthened in faith and be faithful to the proclamation of thy truth. These mercies we ask in the name of him who said, "Go in peace." **Amen.**

Unto God's gracious mercy and protection we commit you. And the blessing of God Almighty, the Father, the Son, and the Holy Spirit, be upon you and remain with you always. **Amen.**

PART 8

LESSONS
FOR THE CHURCH YEAR

By the fourth century the Christian Church observed a series of festivals centering upon the main events in the life of Christ and the beginnings of the Church. The roots of these festivals go deep into the soil of the earliest Christian centuries. Since that time the festivals gradually have been drawn into the yearly calendar. Beginning with Advent, the celebrations continue through Christmas, Epiphany, pre-Lent, Lent, Easter, Pentecost, and Trinity.

Lectionaries, or tables of lessons, were developed to provide Scripture readings suitable not only for the great festival days, but for each Sunday and weekday as well. These tables had their roots in the pre-Reformation Church and therefore the tables used today in the Roman Catholic, Lutheran, Episcopal, and many of the Reformed Churches bear striking similarities.

In the table of lessons for the first year the Episcopal-

Lutheran pattern has been generally followed. There is some variance with the Roman lectionary, due largely to a different dating following Pentecost, but even in this case the same body of scriptural material is covered. In addition to the Epistle and Gospel lessons of the traditional lectionaries, Old Testament and Psalter readings have been added, providing four readings for each Sunday.

The table for the second year offers alternate Scripture passages related to the festivals, Sundays, and weekdays. It also offers four readings for each Sunday.

While the whole of the Bible cannot be covered in such tables, most of the important passages and virtually the entire Psalter have been included. To follow some such pattern will give the congregation a rich variety of Scripture readings and sermon texts. Most of the Psalms have been set to music and can be sung by choir and congregation. With a total of eight Scripture passages suggested for each Sunday, the pastor can preach sermons based upon the lectionary for almost eight years without repeating a text.

At the end of the tables, lessons have been drawn up for a few special days which churches have traditionally observed. Other texts are also suggested in the worship materials which are provided in this book for special days and occasions.

A TABLE OF LESSONS FOR THE CHURCH YEAR

FIRST YEAR

Sunday (or Other Day)	Old Testament	Epistle	Gospel	Psalm
ADVENT				
1st in Advent	Jer. 31:31-34	Rom. 13:11-14	Matt. 21:1-9	96
2nd in Advent	Mal. 4:1-6	Rom. 15:4-13	Luke 21:25-33	95
3rd in Advent	Isa. 40:1-8	1 Cor. 4:1-5	Matt. 11:2-10	86
4th in Advent	Isa. 40:9-11	Phil. 4:4-7	John 1:19-28	145
CHRISTMAS				
Christmas Eve and Day	Isa. 9:2-7	Titus 2:11-14	Luke 2:1-14	19
1st after Christmas	Isa. 45:1-8	Gal. 4:1-7	John 1:1-14	132
2nd after Christmas	Isa. 63:7-16	Heb. 1:1-12	Luke 2:33-40	85
	1 Sam. 2:1-10	Titus 3:4-7	John 1:14-18	103
EPIPHANY				
Epiphany (Jan. 6)	Isa. 60:1-6	Eph. 3:1-12	Matt. 2:1-12	72
1st after Epiphany	Eccles. 12:1-7	Rom. 12:1-5	Luke 2:41-52	27
2nd after Epiphany	Isa. 61:1-6	Rom. 12:6-16a	John 2:1-11	148
3rd after Epiphany	2 Kings 4:1-15	Rom. 12:16b-21	Matt. 8:1-13	102
4th after Epiphany	Exod. 14:21-31	Rom. 13:8-10	Matt. 8:23-27	63
5th after Epiphany	Ezek. 33:10-16	Col. 3:12-17	Matt. 13:24-30	99
6th after Epiphany	Exod. 34:29-35	1 John 3:1-8	Matt. 24:23-31	95

303

Sunday (or Other Day)	Old Testament	Epistle	Gospel	Psalm
	PRE-LENT			
Septuagesima	Jer. 9:23-24	1 Cor. 9:24—10:5	Matt. 20:1-16	104
Sexagesima	Amos 8:11-12	2 Cor. 11:19—12:9	Luke 8:4-15	139
Quinquagesima	Jer. 8:4-9	1 Cor. 13:1-13	Luke 18:31-43	77
	LENT			
Ash Wednesday	Joel 2:12-19	1 John 1:5-9	Matt. 6:16-21	51
1st in Lent	Gen. 22:1-14	2 Cor. 6:1-10	Matt. 4:1-11	91
2nd in Lent	Exod. 33:12-23	1 Thess. 4:1-7	Matt. 15:21-28	32
3rd in Lent	Jer. 26:1-15	Eph. 5:1-9	Luke 11:14-28	42
4th in Lent	Isa. 55:1-7	Gal. 4:21—5:1	John 6:1-15	40
Passion Sunday	Num. 21:4-9	Heb. 9:11-15	John 8:46-59	143
Palm Sunday	Zech. 9:9-12	Phil. 2:5-11	Luke 19:28-44	62
Maundy Thursday	Exod. 12:1-14	1 Cor. 11:23-32	Luke 23:1-49	88
Good Friday	Isa. 53:4-12	Heb. 10:1-25	John 18:1—19:42	22
	EASTERTIDE (THE GREAT FIFTY DAYS)			
Easter Sunday	Isa. 25:6-9	1 Pet. 1:3-9	John 20:1-18	118
1st after Easter	Gen. 32:22-30	1 John 5:4-12	John 20:19-31	61
2nd after Easter	Ezek. 34:11-16	1 Pet. 2:19-25	John 10:11-16	23

Sunday (or Other Day)	Old Testament	Epistle	Gospel	Psalm
3rd after Easter	Isa. 40:25-31	1 Pet. 2:16-20	John 16:16-22	121
4th after Easter	Isa. 29:9-14	Jas. 1:17-21	John 16:4b-15	98
5th after Easter	Isa. 55:6-11	Jas. 1:22-27	John 16:23b-30	136
Ascension Day (40 days after Easter)	2 Kings 2:9-15	Acts 1:1-11	Mark 16:14-20	47
Sunday after Ascension	Isa. 32:14-20	1 Pet. 4:7-11	John 15:26–16:4a	93

PENTECOST OR WHITSUNTIDE

Sunday (or Other Day)	Old Testament	Epistle	Gospel	Psalm
Pentecost or Whitsunday	Joel 2:29-32	Acts 2:1-11	John 14:23-31a	145

KINGDOMTIDE OR THE TRINITY SEASON

Sunday (or Other Day)	Old Testament	Epistle	Gospel	Psalm
Trinity Sunday	Isa. 6:1-8	Rom. 11:33-36	Matt. 28:18-20	29
1st after Trinity	Deut. 6:4-13	1 John 4:7-21	Luke 16:19-31	1
2nd after Trinity	Prov. 9:1-10	1 John 3:13-18	Luke 14:15-24	55
3rd after Trinity	Isa. 12:1-6	1 Pet. 5:6-11	Luke 15:1-10	18
4th after Trinity	Num. 6:22-27	Rom. 8:18-23	Luke 6:36-42	25
5th after Trinity	Lam. 3:22-33	1 Pet. 3:8-15	Luke 5:1-11	31

Sunday (or Other Day)	Old Testament	Epistle	Gospel	Psalm
6th after Trinity	Ruth 1:1-18	Rom. 6:3-11	Matt. 5:20-26	34
7th after Trinity	Isa. 62:6-11	Rom. 6:19-23	Mark 8:1-9	100
8th after Trinity	Jer. 23:16-29	Rom. 8:12-17	Matt. 7:15-21	39
9th after Trinity	Prov. 16:1-9	1 Cor. 10:1-13	Luke 15:11-32	47
10th after Trinity	Jer. 7:1-11	1 Cor. 12:1-11	Luke 19:41-48	95
11th after Trinity	Dan. 9:15-19	1 Cor. 15:1-10	Luke 18:9-14	57
12th after Trinity	Isa. 29:17-21	2 Cor. 3:4-9	Mark 7:31-37	65
13th after Trinity	Zech. 7:4-10	Gal. 3:16-22	Luke 10:23-37	71
14th after Trinity	Prov. 4:10-23	Gal. 5:16-24	Luke 17:11-19	92
15th after Trinity	1 Kings 17:8-16	Gal. 5:25—6:10	Matt. 6:24-34	102
16th after Trinity	Job 5:17-26	Eph. 3:13-21	Luke 7:11-16	86
17th after Trinity	Prov. 25:6-14	Eph. 4:1-6	Luke 14:1-11	86
18th after Trinity	2 Chron. 1:7-12	1 Cor. 1:4-9	Matt. 22:34-46	138
19th after Trinity	Gen. 28:10-17	Eph. 4:17-28	Matt. 9:1-8	112
20th after Trinity	Prov. 2:1-9	Eph. 5:15-21	Matt. 22:1-14	90
21st after Trinity	2 Sam. 18-21	Eph. 6:10-17	John 4:46b-53	116
22nd after Trinity	Prov. 3:11-20	Phil. 1:3-11	Matt. 18:21-35	118
23rd after Trinity	Prov. 8:11-22	Phil. 3:17-21	Matt. 22:15-22	95
24th after Trinity	1 Kings 17:17-24	Col. 1:9-14	Matt. 9:18-26	134
25th after Trinity	Job 14:1-6	1 Thess. 4:13-18	Matt. 14:15-28	85

Sunday (or Other Day)	Old Testament	Epistle	Gospel	Psalm
26th after Trinity	Dan. 7:9-14	1 Thess. 5:1-11	Matt. 25:31-46	24
Next before Advent	Jer. 23:5-8	Rom. 12:16-21	John 6:5-14	136

Special Days

	Old Testament	Epistle	Gospel	Psalm
New Year's Day	Deut. 8:1-10	2 Pet. 3:8-18	Luke 12:13-21	103
Race Relations Sunday	Gen. 11:1-9	Acts 17:22-30	Luke 10:25-37	117
Memorial Day	2 Sam. 1:17-27	Heb. 11:32—12:2	John 11:1-27	145
Harvest Festival	Deut. 26:1-11	2 Cor. 9:1-15	Luke 12:13-34	148
Reformation Day	Neh. 8:1-8	Gal. 2:20—3:15	John 8:31-36	46
All Saints Day	Deut. 33:1-3	Rev. 7:2-17	Matt. 5:1-12	34
Thanksgiving Day	Isa. 61:10-11	1 Tim. 2:1-8	Matt. 6:25-33	100

A TABLE OF LESSONS FOR THE CHURCH YEAR

SECOND YEAR

Sunday (or Other Day)	Old Testament	Epistle	Gospel	Psalm
ADVENT				
1st in Advent	Isa. 1:10-20	Rom. 10:5-13	Mark 13:1-13	46
2nd in Advent	Isa. 5:1-16	Rom. 10:13-20	Matt. 25:1-13	48
3rd in Advent	Isa. 32:1-20	1 Cor. 3:10-17	Matt. 3:1-11	72
4th in Advent	Isa. 54	Gal. 3:23-29	Luke 1:39-56	97
CHRISTMAS				
Christmas Eve and Day	Isa. 11:1-10	1 Tim. 3:14-16	Matt. 1:18-25	85
1st after Christmas	Zech. 2:10-13	2 Tim. 1:8-12	Luke 2:8-20	89
2nd after Christmas	1 Sam. 1:20-28	Heb. 3:1-6	John 1:1-14	93
	Deut. 11:1-2	Phil. 3:7-14	Matt. 6:19-33	91
EPIPHANY				
Epiphany (Jan. 6)	Isa. 60:1-11, 18-20	2 Cor. 4:3-6	Matt. 2:1-12	105
1st after Epiphany	Isa. 49:1-13	Eph. 2:11-22	Luke 2:39-52	84
2nd after Epiphany	Isa. 35	Acts 20:17-38	Mark 1:14-20	66
3rd after Epiphany	Prov. 25:11-22	Rom. 8:1-9	Matt. 9:9-17	33

Sunday (or Other Day)	Old Testament	Epistle	Gospel	Psalm
4th after Epiphany	Hos. 6:1-6	1 Cor. 3:1-15	John 3:22-36	119
5th after Epiphany	Jer. 7:1-7	Gal. 6:1-5	Mark 2:1-17	119
6th after Epiphany	Jer. 18:1-11	1 Cor. 9:24-27	Mark 4:1-20	119

PRE-LENT

Sunday (or Other Day)	Old Testament	Epistle	Gospel	Psalm
Septuagesima	Isa. 551-13	Rev. 21:1-7	Matt. 11:25-30	147
Sexagesima	1 Kings 8:12-21	Rom. 5:1-11	Luke 6:27-36	15
Quinquagesima	Ruth 2:10-17	2 Cor. 8:1-9	Luke 18:18-30	30

LENT

Sunday (or Other Day)	Old Testament	Epistle	Gospel	Psalm
Ash Wednesday	Jer. 17:5-10	2 Cor. 7:2-10	Mark 7:14-23	51
1st in Lent	Isa. 42:1-9	Heb. 2:9-18	Luke 9:14-29	2
2nd in Lent	Lam. 3:27-41	2 Tim. 3:14-4:8	Luke 4:1-13	14
3rd in Lent	Gen. 11:1-9	Acts 12:1-11	Matt. 21:33-46	13
4th in Lent	Jer. 31:1-9	Heb. 12:22-29	John 8:1-11	12
Passion Sunday	Isa. 52:13-53:3	Heb. 5:1-9	John 12:20-33	74
Palm Sunday	Isa. 4:2-6	Heb. 12:1-6	John 12:12-19	24
Maundy Thursday	Exo. 13:3-10	1 Cor. 10:14-22	John 13:1-16	107
Good Friday	Isa. 43:1-11	1 Cor. 1:18-25	Luke 23:33-47	22

Sunday (or Other Day)	Old Testament	Epistle	Gospel	Psalm
	EASTERTIDE (THE GREAT FIFTY DAYS)			
Easter Sunday	Dan. 3:8-25	1 Cor. 15:20-26	Mark 16:1-7	16
1st after Easter	Isa. 51:1-11	1 Cor. 15:12-22	Luke 24:13-35	113
2nd after Easter	1 Kings 19:1-12	Heb. 13:10-21	John 10:1-10	106
3rd after Easter	Job 14:1-15	1 Cor. 15:35-57	John 14:1-13	108
4th after Easter	Deut. 7:6-11	2 Cor. 5:17-21	John 15:1-10	114
5th after Easter	1 Kings 8:54-61	Rom. 8:28-39	John 17:1-15	115
Ascension Day (40 days after Easter) or Sunday after Ascension	Isa. 32:14-20	1 Pet. 4:7b-11	John 15:26-16:4a	93
	PENTECOST OR WHITSUNTIDE			
Pentecost or Whitsunday	Isa. 61:1-11	Rom. 8:9-17	John 14:15-27	67
	KINGDOMTIDE OR THE TRINITY SEASON			
Trinity Sunday	Job 38:1-11, 31-38	1 Pet. 1:1-13	John 3:1-16	150
1st after Trinity	1 Kings 18:17-39	Eph. 4:7-16	Matt. 16:13-19	146
2nd after Trinity	Prov. 16:16-24	James 3:13-18	Matt. 18:1-14	11

310

Sunday (or Other Day)	Old Testament	Epistle	Gospel	Psalm
3rd after Trinity	Jer. 5:1-3, 21-31	Acts 4:1-13	Matt. 5:38-42	12
4th after Trinity	Josh. 1:1-9	2 Pet. 1:3-11	John 1:35-51	52
5th after Trinity	Judges 7:1-22	Acts 9:1-18	Luke 19:1-10	53
6th after Trinity	Neh. 4:1-6	1 Pet. 5:6-11	Luke 12:35-40	80
7th after Trinity	Amos 3	1 Cor. 10:23—11:1	Matt. 11:16-24	73
8th after Trinity	2 Chron. 6:12-21	Acts 13:42-52	John 17:20-26	133
9th after Trinity	Ezek. 1:28—3:3	1 Cor. 9:16-23	Matt. 5:1-12	3
10th after Trinity	Dan. 3:13-30	Rom. 8:31-39	Matt. 10:28-33	5
11th after Trinity	Prov. 9:1-10	Acts 17:16-34	Luke 6:46-49; 15:1-7	111
12th after Trinity	Isa. 45:18-22	Rom. 11:13-24	Luke 15:1-7	8
13th after Trinity	Hos. 11:1-11	Rom. 9:14-26	Matt. 5:43-48	108
14th after Trinity	Jonah 3:1—4:11	Gal. 1:11-24	Matt. 9:10-13	115
15th after Trinity	Exod. 16:1-15	2 Cor. 4:6-12	John 6:22-34	23
16th after Trinity	Eccles. 12:1-7	2 Tim. 1:1-7	Matt. 19:16-22	125
17th after Trinity	Isa. 55:1-13	1 John 2:7-15	Luke 7:36-50	123
18th after Trinity	Ezek. 37:1-14	2 Cor. 4:16—5:5	John 11:1-4,17-27	75
19th after Trinity	Zeph. 3:17-20	1 Thess. 5:1-11	Matt. 25:1-13	144
20th after Trinity	Micah 6:6-8	1 Gal. 5:25—6:10	Matt. 19:23-30	141
21st after Trinity	Hag. 1:1-8; 2:2-5	Heb. 11:32—12:2	John 4:20-24	135

Sunday (or Other Day)	Old Testament	Epistle	Gospel	Psalm
22nd after Trinity	Zeph. 1:1–2:3	2 Thess. 1:5-12	Matt. 23:36-44	68
23rd after Trinity	Hab. 2:1-4, 18-20	1 Tim. 1:12-17	Luke 18:1-14	69
24th after Trinity	1 Chron. 17:16-27	Philemon	Luke 7:18-28	20
25th after Trinity	Ezra 2:10-13	Rev. 21:1-3, 22-27	Matt. 21:12-16	43
26th after Trinity	Lev. 19:11-17, 33-37	3 John	Luke 6:20-26, 37-38	49
Next before Advent	Micah 4:1-4	1 Pet. 2:1-10	Luke 3:1-18	50

GLOSSARY

Advent (Latin *adventus*, coming) Period beginning at the fourth Sunday before Christmas, a time of preparation for the celebration of Christ's coming.

Agnus Dei (Latin, Lamb of God) An antiphonal invocation asking divine mercy.

Ascription A form of prayer giving (ascribing) glory to God, usually following the sermon or at the end of the service.

Benedictus (Latin, from *benedicere*, to bless) Zechariah's praise for the birth of John the Baptist (Luke 1:68-79).

Canticle (Latin *canticulum*, little song) A biblical hymn, such as *Benedictus*, *Magnificat* or *Nunc Dimittis*.

Communicant (Latin, from *communicare*, to receive the communion) One who receives the Lord's Supper, or one who is entitled to receive the Lord's Supper, generally a church member.

Doxology (Greek *doxa*, glory and *logos*, word) A declaration of praise, generally trinitarian.

Epiclesis (Greek *epiklēsis*, invocation) Prayer for the presence of the Holy Spirit in the Lord's Supper and at baptism.

Epiphany (Greek *epiphaneia*, manifestation) Celebration of the coming of the Wise Men, January 6, as the first manifestation of Christ to the Gentiles.

Eucharist (Greek *eucharistein*, to give thanks) A prayer of thanks, but generally associated with the Lord's Supper; term used by some churches to designate the Lord's Supper.

Gloria in Excelsis (Latin, glory in the highest) A 4th Century hymn based upon the angels' song (Luke 2:14).

Gloria Patri (Latin, glory to the Father) A declaration of glory to God.

Introit (Latin *introitus*, entrance) An entrance hymn.

Jubilate Deo (Latin, be joyful to God) A declaration of joy based upon Psalm 100.

Kyrie (Greek *kyrie eleēson*, Lord, have mercy) The people's petition to Christ for mercy.

Lectionary (Latin *lectionarium*, collection of lessons) A book or list of lessons from the Scriptures covering the church year.

Litany (Greek *litaneia*, petition, supplication) A responsive prayer in which a leader offers petitions which are answered by the congregation, often with an unchanging response.

Magnificat (Latin, from *magnificare*, to magnify, extol) Mary's song of praise (Luke 1:46-55).

Nunc Dimittis (Latin, now dismiss) The song of Simeon (Luke 2:29-35).

Ordinand (Latin, from *ordinare*, to ordain) A person about to be ordained into the ministry.

Rubric (Latin, from *ruber*, red) Directions for a service of worship, sometimes printed in red.

Sanctus (Latin, holy) A threefold "Holy, holy, holy" adapted from Isaiah 6:3, said or sung before the prayer of thanksgiving in the communion service.

Sursum Corda (Latin, lift up your hearts) A versicle inviting the congregation to join in thanksgiving to God.

Te Deum Laudamus (Latin, Thee, God we praise) An ancient hymn of praise.

Venite (Latin, O come) A prayer composed of parts of Psalms 95 and 96.

Versicle (Latin *versiculus*, short line or little verse) A short sentence said by the minister, followed by a congregational response, used often to introduce prayer.